Lithuanian Social Democracy

in Perspective

Published with the cooperation

of the Association for the

Advancement of Baltic Studies

Lithuanian

Social Democracy

in Perspective

1893–1914

Leonas Sabaliūnas

Duke Press Policy Studies

Duke University Press

Durham and London 1990

© 1990 Duke University Press
All rights reserved.
Printed in the United States of America
on acid-free paper ∞
Library of Congress Cataloging-in-Publication Data
appear on the last page of this book.

Contents

For Imsré and Medea

Acknowledgments

T he present study was supported at different times by the National Endowment for the Humanities, Washington, D.C.; the Earhart Foundation, Ann Arbor, Michigan; the Association for the Advancement of Baltic Studies, Hackettstown, New Jersey; the Delegation of the Lithuanian Social Democratic Party in Exile, Chicago, Illinois; and, above all, Eastern Michigan University, Ypsilanti, Michigan. I am most grateful for their financial support.

The book draws upon some of my earlier work, namely, "Social Democracy in Tsarist Lithuania, 1893–1904," *Slavic Review*, June 1972, from which I quote with the editor's permission; newspaper articles in *Akiračiai* (Horizons, 1972); and papers presented at the meetings of the following learned societies: Institute of Lithuanian Studies (Chicago, 1971), American Association for the Advancement of Slavic Studies (Dallas, 1972), and Centre for Baltic Studies (Stockholm, 1987).

Much of whatever merit this book possesses it owes to those who furnished access to their collections or otherwise provided me with essential source materials. Three successive directors of the Scientific Library at the State University of Vilnius—Stasė Vaidinauskaitė-Vaškelienė, Jurgis Tornau, and B. Butkevičienė—supplied me with hundreds of copies of rare printed matter. None of my requests has been denied by them. In addition, the university gave me the opportunity to do research work in its library, as did Romas Šarmaitis, the long-term head of the Institute of Party History in Vilnius, in the library of that agency. His successor

Vilnius, in the library of that agency. His successor to that position, Professor Vanda Kašauskienė, furnished me with copies of needed archival holdings.

I am also grateful to the Rev. Jonas Petrauskas, of the Marianapolis Preparatory School, Thompson, Connecticut, and to Dr. J. S. Kriaučiūnas and the Rev. Rapolas Krasauskas, of the American Lithuanian Archive and Museum, Putnam, Connecticut. They have repeatedly placed their holdings at my disposal and, together with the Immaculate Conception Convent in Putnam, have otherwise assisted me in my research. Other institutions whose librarians and staffs have rendered me valuable services include the following: the Graduate Library of the University of Michigan, the Van Pelt Library at the University of Pennsylvania, the University of Chicago Library, the Interlibrary Loan division at Eastern Michigan University, the New York Public Library, the Library of Congress, the Lithuanian Collection at Kent State University, and the Library of the British Museum.

Thanks are due to those who have translated, or otherwise assisted me with, the Polish texts: John Connelly and the late Professor David Welsh, both of Ann Arbor, Michigan, as well as Albertas Misiūnas, Antanas Norus, and Dr. Stasys Juzėnas, all of Detroit, Michigan. Juozas Vilčinskas, a prominent member of the Lithuanian community in London and the Lithuanian representative at numerous European socialist conferences and congresses, has kindly lent me one of the main works produced by Zigmas Angarietis, and has further answered assorted author's queries. In Chicago, Illinois, Česlovas Grincevičius granted admission to the Lithuanian World Archives, while Dr. Jonas Valaitis readily proffered both advice and support. For convenient teaching schedules and partial release from other service obligations I wish to thank James D. Johnson, then head of the department of political science at Eastern Michigan University. I am most grateful for the editorial assistance of the staff at Duke University Press. Finally, I am indebted to my wife, Ona, for bearing the inconveniences and being my most important source of encouragement.

The statements and interpretations in this study, unless indicated otherwise, are the sole responsibility of the author and thus do not necessarily reflect the views of any of the persons listed above. Any errors, of course, are the author's.

Author's Note

Generally, the spelling of the names of people and places in the text is based on nationality or current territorial status. Thus, Andrius Domaševičius, not Andrzej Domaszewicz; Feliks Dzierżyński, not Felix Dzerzhinsky. Or Vilnius, not Vilna; Suwałki, not Suvalki or Suvalkai. The *Encyclopaedia Judaica* was my main reference book on the spelling of Jewish names. Russian words with Cyrillic letters are, of course, transliterated into Latin characters. Departures from a uniform application of these guidelines, however, do occur. Cases of conventional Westernized spelling, the nature of available information, and the pitfalls of individual judgment occasionally conspire against consistency. References to Moscow and St. Petersburg are the obvious examples.

The replacement, in 1918, of the Old Style calendar by the New Style has been a source of great confusion. The Old Style lagged behind the New Style—generally thirteen days in the twentieth century, twelve days in the nineteenth. In the interests of clarity and accuracy, the text frequently provides dates according to both Old and New Style. In the bibliography and the notes, however, the given dates are those found in the sources.

Introduction

Historical Lithuania first appeared on the map of Europe as a grand duchy forged in the early part of the thirteenth century. It was a sprawling multinational state dominated by a highly privileged aristocracy. The country led an independent existence until a series of acts, including those negotiated in 1385, 1413, and 1569, brought it into close association with Poland. This united Polish-Lithuanian Commonwealth continued until 1795 when, due to the increased power of its neighbors and the flaws in its own constitution, it finally came to ruin. The bulk of its land was annexed by Russia, while Austria and Prussia acquired the rest.

The inception of modern Lithuania could be traced to the early years of the nineteenth century. Efforts at nation-building, though tenuous at the beginning, became more intense as the twentieth century neared. They reached fruition in 1918 when the struggle for Lithuania's national liberation climaxed in the reestablishment of that country's independence. Unlike the ethnically diverse Grand Duchy, the new Lithuania possessed a degree of national cohesion deriving from an emergent peasantry. It evolved out of three administrative provinces of imperial Russia, the whole of the Kaunas (Kovno) guberniia, and the several predominantly Lithuanian districts included in the Vilnius (Vilna) and Suwałki guberniias. Although an additional number of ethnic Lithuanians lived in various parts of the Courland and Grodno guberniias, as well as on the northeastern edge of Germany, the Lithuanian districts located in those three provinces could rightly be termed the core of the future Lithuanian state. Close to 2.7 million people inhabited the area at the turn of the century. Approximately 58.3 percent of them were Lithuanians. The Jews accounted for some 13.3 percent, while the totals for the Poles and the Belorussians were 10.3 percent and 9.1 percent respectively. The percentages of Russians and Germans were low.[1] Generally, the ethnic Lithuanians, who used their own language, occupied a commanding position in the countryside. By contrast, the cities and towns were multinational, mainly Jewish or Polish. Here the Jews generally spoke Yiddish and sometimes Russian; the ethnic Poles and polonized segments of the local population communicated in Polish. The city of Klaipėda (Memel), of course, was German.

Ethnic Environment

The juxtaposition of certain shared characteristics with basic asymmetries produced a number of incongruities in the fabric of ethnic relations. For example, the common elements of espousal of the Catholic faith, a legacy of political union spanning hundreds of years, and opposition to Russian hegemony—all injected cohesive elements into the relations between the Lithuanians and the Poles. By contrast, the heightening of national consciousness occurring in the two communities caused a widening of their rivalry. It prejudiced people's personal lives, increased their sensitivities about the proper place of their respective languages, sowed discord in their local church communities, slanted the interpretation of their common historical experience, and punctuated the differences in their political visions.

Basically, this growing divergence of opinion between the Lithuanians and the Poles derived from two types of nationalist aspirations. In the cultural arena, Lithuania's farm-oriented (but not aristocratic) leaders set out to reverse what they saw as an agelong polonization of that country. A widespread use of Polish as the formal or customary means of communication within the church establishment, at the grand ducal court, among the members of the nobility, in schools and at the university, and during joint legislative sessions combined to foster a ubiquitous Polish presence which, they felt, threatened to obliterate the Lithuanian identity. On the political front, the new leadership sought to wrest as extensive a home rule for their country as conditions would permit. At the same time a large majority of Lithuania's landed nobility, like many Poles, hoped to restore the old union of the two states; only a small group of them, but one that included the founding fathers of Lithuania's social democracy, contemplated new alternatives. The country's new leaders, however, were strongly inclined to distance Lithuania from Russia—and Poland. The two peoples were thus nearing a parting of the ways. To be sure, areas of agreement between them could still be found, but accommodation became increasingly elusive.

Conflict and conciliation also dotted the record of Jewish-Lithuanian relations. Some 250,000 Jews lived in the Grand Duchy on the eve of its destruction at the end of the eighteenth century, although only a small portion of that total resided in ethnographic Lithuania. Their influx into Lithuania proper intensified in the course of the nineteenth century, raising the Jewish total there to more than 300,000.[2] Many of these newcomers swarmed the low-income sectors of the population, but others, together with the members of the old Jewish establishment, managed to attain the commanding heights of the local economy. They were strong in the export business, the clothing trade, the crafts industry, and the various wholesale firms, as well as among the liberal professions. Further, they were prominent as shopkeepers, contractors, moneylenders, and innkeepers.[3] Indeed, the Lithuanians were apt to view the Jews as masters of their economy.

The Lithuanian and Jewish communities inhabited the same territorial area but otherwise led their own separate lives—domestic, religious, cultural, and political. The Jewish neighborhoods were Yiddish-speaking oases, although many educated people there used Russian and occasionally even German. In time most Jews learned to speak Lithuanian, but seldom did. Since Lithuania was relatively free of anti-Semitic excesses and its Jews felt more secure there than in many other parts of eastern Europe, they saw no reason to embrace the languages and cultures of the area's peasant populations to whom they generally felt superior. Acculturation here was neither necessary nor attractive.[4] It was only the socialists who made a determined and partially successful effort to bridge the distance between these discrete worlds.

A modicum of ethnic tolerance enveloped the relations between these two peoples. Many ordinary Lithuanians and their leaders harbored sentiments and aspirations that discomfited the Jews, but they refrained from blatant anti-Semitism. This moderate outlook derived from circumstances which included a number of practical considerations. For example, the Lithuanian leadership, which was getting ready to challenge both Russian domination and Polish nationalism, thought it imprudent to strain its relations with the Jews, too. Further, with the exception of individual cases, members of the Jewish community generally shunned participation in the process of Lithuania's reconstitution prior to 1918. However, while the Lithuanians deplored this aloofness, they did not view it as a threat; the Jewish quest for autonomous existence was devoid of territorial claims. Finally, many Lithuanians were displeased by their economic dependence on the Jews. Yet again, the adjustment of what they termed economic imbalance was not considered to be pressing. Rather, the campaign to assist the Lithuanian businessmen was deferred until such time when they were in a position to compete with the Jews on a more even basis.[5]

World War I and its aftermath cut the Lithuanian Jewry in half. Large numbers of them were forcibly evacuated to Russia in 1915, others became Polish subjects when that country occupied Vilnius in 1920. The Jews who stayed in independent Lithuania were granted wide autonomy, although the increasingly assertive nature of Lithuanian nationalism after 1926 was beginning to undermine the foundations of their economic well-being. The effects of the Great Depression, government support of the cooperative movement, and the emergence of a native middle class only exacerbated the Jewish condition. In 1940 the Russians overran Lithuania, as they did the other two Baltic states. A year later, however, they were replaced by the Germans, who turned against their erstwhile Russian partners. The fury of German racial animosities doomed the Lithuanian Jews to extinction.

The small Russian minority of pre-1914 Lithuania comprised some 31,000 Old Believers who took refuge from religious persecutions in seventeenth- and eighteenth-century Russia, members of aristocratic families and high-ranking army officers given landed properties in Lithuania after 1795, the corps of administrative and military personnel, and, most important, the colonists settled on confiscated estates after the Polish-Lithuanian insurrections of 1830 and 1863.[6] Whether as members of the Russian Orthodox community or of the Russian governmental system, these people were alien from the cultural and political aspirations of the local residents. After the outbreak of World War I, most of the colonists headed for Russia. In contrast, more than 30,000 Old Believers remained in the newly independent Lithuania, which granted them both religious freedom and financial support.

The character of Lithuania's economy at the turn of the century was predominantly agricultural. Some 73 percent of the population depended on farming for its livelihood, while 19 percent were employed in industry and trade. The remaining 8 percent were engaged in other types of pursuits.[7] A great majority of farms, some 93 percent of the total, consisted of peasant holdings that cultivated approximately half of the arable land. The number of large estates made up only 4 percent of all of the area farms, but the amount of land they owned was considerable, more than one-third of the total. Although the bulk of the population still lived on farms or in small villages, this traditional society had been far from static; incipient urbanization was beginning to modify its predominantly rural character. As a result, the small cities grew larger. On the eve of World War I, some 24,000 people lived in Šiauliai and 31,000 in Klaipėda, while the Kaunas total was 97,000.

The population of the biggest city, Vilnius, had climbed to over 200,000.[8] Despite its decidedly Jewish and Polish ethnocultural makeup, Vilnius became a wellspring of Lithuania's political renewal, as well as a chief center of its social democratic activity. The city's total labor force numbered approximately 40,000 persons. Most of them, or 41 percent, worked in the service sector. Further, artisans accounted for 34 percent of the total, while factory workers comprised 14 percent. The remaining 11 percent found other types of employment.[9] The industrial laborers usually worked a twelve-hour day. Men earned approximately twenty-one rubles a month, while women were paid only nine. Wages in the small craft shops were generally lower than those in industry. Considering the relatively high monthly cost of living, which was estimated at more than thirty rubles for a family of four, the artisan and working-class groups must have lived at or near a subsistence level. The inability of the urban sector to absorb the influx of rural folk forced large numbers of people, perhaps as many as one-fourth of Lithuania's total, to migrate either to other cities of the empire or to other countries in search of work.

Religious Culture

The church, as a spiritual society or a source of cultural effort, held a pivotal position in Lithuania.[10] A perfunctory attempt to embrace Christianity was made there in the middle of the thirteenth century,

but conversion began in earnest only in 1387, a concomitant of Lithuania's partnership with Poland. The Reformation then led to a century
and a half of conflict between the Catholic and Protestant churches.
Attracted by prospects of greater freedom and additional rights, the
bulk of the upper aristocracy became either Lutherans or Calvinists.
When during the second half of the sixteenth century many other
estate owners followed the lead of the magnates, Catholicism appeared
to be doomed to wane before the rivalry of the new religious movement. But Protestant churches failed to consolidate their early advance. Divisions within the Protestant movement, its inability to
reach the common people, support of Catholicism by the country's
rulers, and especially the counterdrive undertaken by the Jesuits, invited to Lithuania in 1569, combined to restore the Catholic prepon-
derance and relegate the Protestant denominations to a secondary role.
The seventeenth and eighteenth centuries witnessed the flowering of
religion in that country. However, since that was also the time of
aristocratic privilege and Polish cultural expansion, the Lithuanian-
speaking members of the lower strata seldom had the opportunity to
contribute to this renaissance.

Following the collapse of the Polish-Lithuanian state in 1795, the
Russians sought to subject the Catholic ecclesiastical authorities to
their secular control. Pressure upon the church intensified after the
two insurrections of 1830 and 1863. The tsarist authorities set out to
russianize the area and enhance the position of its Orthodox church.
Considering Catholic churches and religious orders enemies of the
Russian government and wellsprings of Polish influence, the St. Petersburg bureaucracy commenced an assault upon the church. Provincial governors barred the construction of new churches and closed
those implicated in the 1863 uprising. They also confiscated church
properties, shut down hundreds of monasteries and convents, hindered
the admission of students to theological seminaries, and otherwise
obstructed the operations of the church. Government repression, however, only hardened the church in its determination to resist alien
rule. Its leaders, such as Bishop Motiejus Valančius (1801–1875), were
among those who inspired that twofold national awakening of Lithuania which challenged the country's domination by the Russians and
asserted its separate identity in relation to the Poles. Religious officials
undertook the publication of newspapers and periodicals. They ad-
monished the people not to speak Russian, not to attend Russian

churches, and especially not to enroll their children in Russian schools. Instead, parents were urged to organize secret schools or teach their children at home. In time, the country's theological seminaries comprised nuclei of national activity where students formed secret clubs, set up private libraries, and engaged in journalistic writing. Finally, as they continued to expand the range of their civic initiatives, the Catholic clergy began to scan the field of party politics.

Lithuania's vigorous religious activity subsumed the function of education. A milepost in the development of that country's learning was the arrival of the Jesuits, who upgraded both the school system and the instructional process. While churches, other religious orders, and noble estates retained full charge of the primary schools, the establishment and operation of both secondary schools (called colleges) and institutions of higher education (academies) was centralized in the Jesuit order. It first established a college in Vilnius, in 1570, and then in other parts of the country. In 1579 it founded the Vilnius Academy (designated as university in 1803). Initially it comprised the schools of theology and philosophy, while later additions included those of law and medicine. The language of instruction in most primary schools was Polish, although some used Lithuanian. With the exception of the Piarists, who employed Polish in the several colleges they managed to operate, the higher schools relied on Latin for their instructional needs.

Dissolution of the Jesuit order by the pope in 1773 led to important changes in the system of formal education. The government established an educational commission to operate the Jesuit-run schools and supervise those maintained by others. Influenced by the ideas of the Enlightenment, the liberal reformers made education a concern of the state. When the Russians annexed Lithuania, they retained the educational commission, but agreed to fund only the University of Vilnius. Religious orders then generally assumed responsibility for the secondary schools, while the primary ones depended on local churches. Lastly, bent on a policy of russification, the government shut down the university in 1832 and then, in 1864, closed all parish schools, too. The purpose of these closings was to enroll the local student population in hundreds of existing or newly created Russian schools. The Lithuanians rallied their energies to frustrate the government in that endeavor.

Besides the Catholics, members of other faiths were concerned with education. Prior to 1795 various monastic orders maintained several Russian Orthodox schools and an entire network of Uniat establishments. Protestant dignitaries like the Radvila family in Kėdainiai, and occasionally townspeople, sponsored a number of high schools and centers of Protestant culture, while counting on parish communities to support the primary instruction.[11] Torah learning, of course, permeated the local Jewish population.[12] During the seventeenth century the Lithuanian Jewry acquired the kind of identity and high religious culture that spread beyond the borders of that state. The spiritual leader who later symbolized the advanced degree of distinction here was Elijah ben Solomon Zalman, the Gaon of Vilnius. Religious and secular books published here in the nineteenth century circulated in the Jewish world, while intellectual leaders, rabbis, and other religious workers trained in Lithuania's yeshivas answered the needs of diaspora communities. Finally, although Jewish scholarship in Lithuania had a traditional bent, it also contributed to the Jewish Enlightenment (Haskalah) ideology and facilitated the rise of the Zionist and socialist movements.

National Awakening

The Lithuanians were a people whose awareness of their own ethnic and national identities heightened considerably in the second half of the nineteenth century. The process of nation-building commenced earlier in the century, but the appearance of such illicit journals as *Aušra* (The Dawn, 1883–1886), *Varpas* (The Bell, 1889–1906), *Apžvalga* (The Review, 1890–1896), and *Tėvynės sargas* (Guardian of the Homeland, 1896–1906), all of which were published in Germany and then smuggled across the border into Lithuania, dramatized both the intensity and the breadth of the effort in later years. Despite two Polish-Lithuanian revolts against the Russian government, in 1830 and 1863, the nature of this national movement was essentially a cultural one. For a long time political aspirations, including the question of the country's independence, elicited no serious consideration. To the realistic pioneers of the Lithuanian awakening, political schemes seemed far-fetched.

The period of cultural activity was started by a group of individuals who would eventually earn places in the pantheon of Lithuanian regeneration. Among them were Simonas Daukantas (1793–1864),

Bishop Motiejus Valančius (1801–1875), Laurynas Ivinskis (1808–1881), Rev. Antanas Tatarė (1805–1889), Mikalojus Akelaitis (1829–1887), Bishop Antanas Baranauskas (1831–1902), and Rev. Antanas Vienažindys (1841–1892). Considered as a whole, their researches into Lithuanian history and language, pastoral letters and religious hymns, collections of poems and mournful songs, and various other works intended for the common people supplied the elements that entered the mind-set of an emergent nation.[13] Seeking to combat the Polish and Russian influence on the Lithuanians, this cultural thrust concentrated on the establishment of hundreds of secret schools, the development of teacher training programs, and the formation of numerous student clubs. Similarly, it spurred interest in Lithuanian affairs among students enrolled in the country's theological seminaries and those attending universities abroad. Further, the movement was concerned with the preservation of Catholic churches and religious orders, where it hoped to extend the use of the Lithuanian language. At home and especially abroad the Lithuanians operated several printing presses which, from 1865 to 1904, published some 3,200 titles; in 1899, they were issuing a total of eighteen different newspapers and periodicals.[14] Finally, what mesmerized the national movement was the struggle for the right to publish books and periodicals in the Latin alphabet. This particular right was lost in 1864 when the authorities imposed the Cyrillic script on the Lithuanians in the wake of their failed uprising against the Russians. The tsarist government hoped that the new alphabet would help them russianize these people. The battle of the alphabet, which they won in 1904, was the chief immediate concern of the Lithuanians.

The 1890s witnessed a fundamental change in the character of the national movement—politization. Its principal cause was the advent of Lithuanian Marxism. Conceived as a means of class emancipation and national liberation, the Social Democratic Party of Lithuania imparted a political purpose to the national renaissance. The first modern political party—with its own goals, leadership, organization, factions, methods of procedure, and body of followers—had come upon the local scene. A subsequent formation of other parties and splinter groups, coupled with an intensification of antigovernment propaganda extending throughout the empire, provided a further stimulus to political action.

No less than three main political groupings sought to articulate and aggregate the interests of the Lithuanian people. Founded between 1905 and 1907, the Lithuanian Christian Democratic Union (Lietuvių krikščionių demokratų sąjunga) constituted the moderate right. The originators of the party and authors of its first platform were three Lithuanian professors affiliated with the Theological Academy in St. Petersburg: Jonas Mačiulis-Maironis (1962–1932), Aleksandras Dambrauskas (1860–1938), and Pranciškus Būčys (1872–1951). The Christian Democrats pictured Lithuania as an autonomous part of the Russian empire. Its democratically elected legislature, sitting in Vilnius, would be placed in charge of local administration, education, courts, and law enforcement agencies. In addition to such political objectives, the party favored progressive labor legislation, aiming particularly for an improvement of economic conditions that would give the marginal farmers new opportunities to better their lot. Although they lagged behind the leftists in party organization, the Christian Democrats and their various affiliates managed to assemble a large political following. During the years immediately following the restoration of Lithuania's independence in 1918, they emerged as the chief arbiters of that country's political life. One of their leaders, Aleksandras Stulginskis (1885–1969), served as president of the republic, although it was the Rev. Mykolas Krupavičius (1885–1970) who remained the dominant figure in the party.

The Democratic Party of Lithuania (Lietuvos demokratų partija), an aggregate of liberally oriented individuals and groups which evolved between 1902 and 1906, represented the middle line of political action. Among its founders were Kazys Grinius (1866–1950) and Antanas Smetona (1874–1944), two prominent personalities who would later serve as presidents of independent Lithuania, as well as such civic leaders as Jonas Bortkevičius (1871–1909), Felicija Bortkevičienė (1873–1945), Jonas Vileišis (1872–1942), and Povilas Višinskis (1875–1906). The framing of this party's objectives started with the publication, in 1902, of a draft program that was subsequently adopted in an amended form. The main propositions set forth in these documents and interpretive statements included, as the ultimate goal, the creation of an independent Lithuanian state; its subsequent federation with others was seen as a possibility. The immediate aim of the Democrats, however, was to wrest a broad autonomy from the Russians, including a legislature set up in Vilnius.

Government by the people, extending from the local church communities to the upper regions of public administration, was an aspiration that permeated the Democratic vision of the country's future. Convinced that such democratization of government operations depended on a prior collapse of the Muscovite police state, the Democrats pledged their cooperation with the revolutionary parties operating in various parts of the empire. Unlike the Marxists, however, the Democrats were ill at ease with the concept of class-based politics. While quite knowledgeable about the process of social stratification and its various effects on party operations, they were reluctant to turn their party into a vehicle of class action. Instead, the Democrats promised to advance those national and political objectives that, in their view, had the support of most groups of people. And yet, even as it stressed the commonality of interests, the Democratic party retained a particular concern with the needs of the underprivileged social strata—urban and rural laborers, petty craftspeople and manufacturers, small farmers, and the landless peasantry. Eventually, the party succeeded in making deep inroads on the Lithuanian countryside. Since a large majority of the civic-minded population was in agriculture, the constituency the Democrats built up there ensured their meaningful participation in the politics of national liberation.

The Democratic party was always lacking in cohesion, a condition that contributed to its internal splits and eventual demise. One of its offshoots was the Peasant Union (Valstiečių sąjunga), which emerged in 1905 as a faction within the parent party but later became a separate political group. It was formed by Danielius Alseika (1881–1936), Juozas Gabrys (1880–1951), and Ernestas Galvanauskas (1882–1967), men who represented a more active and more radical wing of the party. These people hoped to mobilize the poorer section of the peasantry for political action. In 1922 the Peasant Union linked up with other former Democrats to form a new party known as Peasant Populists (Lietuvos valstiečių liaudininkų sąjunga). Espousing a liberal persuasion, the Populists, like their predecessors, located the hard core of their supporters in the rural stratum of the population. The old Democratic party ceased to function.

In addition to the secession which ended in the formation of the Populist movement, in 1907 Smetona abandoned the Democratic fold in order to promote his own brand of a center party. Basically, his were cautiously reformist efforts designed to advance the cause of national unity. They gave birth to two groups, the National Progress (Tautos pažanga) and the Agrarian Union (Žemdirbių sąjunga), which in 1924 coalesced into the Lithuanian Nationalist Union (Lietuvių tautininkų sąjunga). The roster of Smetona's Nationalists included the Rev. Juozas Tumas-Vaižgantas (1869–1933), Augustinas Voldemaras (1883–1942), Juozas Tūbelis (1882–1939), and many others who had distinguished themselves as community leaders or in the struggle for their country's independence; nevertheless, a relatively conservative domestic stance limited their chances at the polls. Nationalist political fortunes changed only in late 1926 when a forceful overthrow of the government raised Smetona to the presidency of the republic, a position which he had briefly held previously. Smetona eventually discarded the democratic form of government in favor of a moderately authoritarian regime, which he headed until 1940, when Lithuania, together with Latvia and Estonia, became a victim of Soviet aggression.

These two prewar political parties, the Democrats and the Christian Democrats, were rightly credited with numerous civic initiatives during the twenty-odd years before the restoration of Lithuania's independence. However, as already indicated, it was the Social Democrats who constituted the first, and in some respects the major, political force of the period. It is their experience that is the subject of the present study. The name of their party changed several times. It was first known as the Lithuanian Social Democratic Group, then as the Lithuanian Social Democratic Party, and finally as the Social Democratic Party of Lithuania (Lietuvos socialdemokratų partija, LSDP). Its widely used abbreviation, LSDP, is retained in this book. In the discussion that follows, we shall seek to sketch the immediate sources of Lithuanian Marxism, review the different stages in the development of the Social Democratic organization, and survey the course of party operations during and after the revolution of 1905. Permeating the chronologically arranged parts of the book will be references to such perennial concerns as images of Lithuania's alternative futures, programs of social reconstruction, internal conflict and conciliation, and the grievous cost of underground activity.

Part I

Arrivals on the Scene

1893–1903

1

The Jewish and Polish Precursors

The Jewish Lead

The inception of Lithuanian social democracy owes much to the problems and the activities of the Jews. By a series of decrees—the last coming in 1835 under Tsar Nicholas I—the Jews were restricted to a belt of territory in western Russia extending from the Baltic Sea to the Black Sea, the so-called Pale of Settlement. Within this territory they could move about, and in the latter half of the nineteenth century there was a significant migration to Lithuania, already a major center of Jewish culture. Barred by the government from settling on farmland, these Jewish newcomers flocked to the towns, straining an economy already troubled with an excessive supply of labor.[1] The lot of the Jewish laborers, like that of other laborers, was not a happy one, and socialist ideas found numerous supporters among them.[2]

A mode of existence conducive to protest eventually combined with another development, the appearance in Lithuania of persons committed to revolutionary causes. There were a number of revolutionaries among those who had to leave the Russian interior. Others converged toward Lithuania for the express purpose of working among the Jewish laborers there.[3] By 1892 Jewish social democracy in Lithuania had acquired a measure of organization. Secret groups appeared first in Vilnius, where some 150 Jewish workers had by that time been enlisted in the Marxist cause, then in Kaunas and other localities.[4]

Julius Martov (1873–1923), an exile who in 1893–1895 had lived and worked in Vilnius, wrote a profile of the Jewish social democratic elite there.[5] Its leader was Arkadi Kremer (1865–1935). Taciturn yet convincing, endowed with a clear mind and conversant with the ways of conspiratorial existence, he was a capable organizer of underground work, though not a good agitator. Kremer was the head of the organization, but according to Martov its soul was Matla Srednicki (1867–1943). Although lacking in physical strength, she was always on the go and in good spirits, and she immersed herself in the organization's everyday concerns. The group's most erudite Marxist theoretician was Isaiah Eisenstadt (1867–1937), whose wife, Lyuba Levinson (1866–1903), an indefatigable and accomplished propagandist, enjoyed a great popularity among the workers. In matters of propaganda and organization Samuel Gozhansky (1867–1943) was the outstanding figure. Unlike most of his collaborators who were under police surveillance, Gozhansky was a "legal" person, a teacher in a Jewish school. Interested in questions of general theory, Gozhansky endeavored to impart a systematic and unified character to the activities of the Jews. Finally, Zemah Kopelson (1869–1933) concentrated on relations with other organizations operating in the towns of Lithuania and Poland.

This array of Jewish leaders, to which many other names could be appended, made notable contributions to Marxism in Russia. Two achievements merit a brief mention: the adoption of a new strategic device to advance class interests, and the attempt to give the Jewish social democratic movement in Russia an organized character. Notwithstanding their success in molding an underground web of mutual-aid societies and strike funds, the Jewish leaders undertook a thorough review of the nature of their work in 1893–1894. Until then their efforts, termed propaganda, had consisted mainly of self-education and the introductory study of Marxism, and had been limited to small workers' circles. What now became a matter of major concern to many leading socialists was their inability to reach the laboring masses and involve them in the socialist cause. The corrective they intended to use to accomplish that purpose was agitation. An adaptation of a technique used by the Union of Polish Workers, agitation would focus for the time being not on the imperatives of Marxism but on workers' everyday needs and demands. The means of communication would be the language that ordinary laborers understood—Yiddish in the case of the Vilnius Jews. The adherents to the new strategy seemed to be convinced that eventually the battle for workers' day-to-day economic needs would mature into a class confrontation on broader political issues.[6]

The new plan required written elaboration. *On Agitation*, a pamphlet prepared by Kremer and edited by Martov, answered the need. The new idea it articulated met initially with strenuous opposition, both in St. Petersburg, where it appeared in 1894–1895, and in Vilnius. When it prevailed, *On Agitation* became a guide to action which "within a few years made socialism the militant faith of a sizable portion of the Russian proletariat."[7]

As early as 1895 the Vilnius leaders recognized the need to equip their extensive activities with greater unity and direction. Martov pointed out that their goal was to form a specifically Jewish organization to lead and educate the Jewish proletariat. The organization's main concern, he said, would be the economic, civic, and political emancipation of the Jewish working class in Russia.[8] A conference of Jewish social democrats representing several cities then met in Vilnius and concurred in the need for such an organization.[9]

The founding of the General Jewish Workers' Union in Lithuania, Poland, and Russia, known as the Bund, occurred on September 25–27/October 7–9, 1897. The thirteen delegates who gathered in Vilnius felt that the possible formation of an all-Russian social democratic party, which would attempt to include all the social democratic groups operating in the empire, necessitated prior creation of an exclusively Jewish organization. Only so united could the Jewish proletariat hope to win for itself a measure of autonomy within the future Russian party, or to play an important part in it.[10]

The coming of the Bund was a momentous development for Russian as well as Jewish social democracy. By 1904 the numerical following of this new party climbed to approximately 23,000, a total which included 6,390 supporters living in the Lithuanian parts of the empire.[11] It is possible that these reported membership figures were higher than the actual count, for in some cases the members of the Bund-directed labor unions were presumed to be members of the Bund itself.[12] However, the questions associated with the definition of membership did not belie the mass character of the movement; it was undoubtedly the largest socialist party in the area. The Bund participated prominently in the affairs of the Russian Social Democratic Labor Party (RSDLP, the initials in English of Rossiiskaia Sotsial-Demokraticheskaia Rabochaia Partiia), which it helped to form in 1898 and in which it enrolled as an autonomous unit. Eventually,

however, Jewish national aspirations ensnared the Bund in a pro-
tracted conflict with many members of the Russian party, and relations between the two became strained.

The Polish Presence

Progress in the development of the Jewish labor movement sharpened
the conflict between employers, who were generally supported by
the government, and the employees. Seeking additional support and
greater effectiveness, the Jewish leaders, as early as 1889–1891, established contacts with the Lithuanians, hoping to prevail upon them to
begin systematic socialist activity among the Christian workers in
Vilnius and elsewhere. This Jewish initiative acted as a stimulant to
Lithuanian social democracy.[13]

The first revolutionary and socialist groups among Christian
workers emerged in the years from 1889 to 1892. Adverse conditions
in agriculture toward the end of the 1880s caused a migration of rural
laborers to the towns, a development which further weakened the
general economy and made the hard-pressed workers more responsive
to socialist ideas than they probably would have been in prosperous
times. Incipient socialism among these workers divided them into
two ethnic camps, the Polish and the Lithuanian. Founded in 1892,
the Polish Socialist Party (Polska Partia Socjalistyczna, PPS) aspired to
extend its activities not only throughout the whole of Poland but
throughout Lithuania as well.[14] The intentions of the PPS reflected the
view then shared by many Poles that Lithuania was but a Polish
province and Lithuanian separatism a heresy. In January 1893 a number of Polish intellectuals in Vilnius met to discuss a report by an
organizer from Warsaw, Stanisław Mendelson (1857–1913), who called
for the formation of a PPS chapter in Vilnius. A majority of those
present agreed with him, although some favored a separate Lithuanian
organization.[15] Thus, a nucleus of Polish socialism under the direction
of Aleksander Sulkiewicz was established in Vilnius.

Subsequent efforts, including two-month talks held between the
Lithuanians and the Poles in 1894, failed to arrest the parting of their
ways. Although the two sides differed on tactics and on other issues,
the crux of the matter was the Lithuanian insistence (and the Polish
objection) that the Social Democratic Party of Lithuania (LSDP) be
treated as a distinct entity. When the LSDP suggested that the two

parties unite in a federation, the PPS said that was unacceptable "separatism." To the Lithuanians, on the other hand, the Polish idea of the LSDP blending into the PPS smacked of that country's "imperialism."[16] Their search for ways of interparty cooperation having been unsuccessful, the two groups descended to active polemics against each other.

Although the PPS attached a good deal of importance to its work in Lithuania, it was not entirely successful there. Concerned mainly with the spread of its literature, the PPS relied on the area's Polish intelligentsia and had little if any support among the workers.[17] Polish-Lithuanian rivalry in Vilnius continued until 1906, when the PPS units in Lithuania yielded to the LSDP.

Lesser Groups

The incursion of the RSDLP into Lithuania dates from the middle of 1901. A nucleus of the Russian party was formed there partly by those who were connected with the smuggling of *Iskra* (The Spark) into Russia. Its most prominent figures were two officers, I. Klopov (1865–1949) and F. Gusarov (1875–1920). The group was small and its activities were confined largely to the Vilnius tanners, although some of its support derived from the Russian residents of Lithuania's smaller towns. The two factions of the RSDLP, the Bolshevik and the Menshevik, coexisted in relative harmony. In 1904 the RSDLP created a committee to coordinate its work in the northwestern region of the empire, including Lithuania. But here, whether before the revolution of 1905 or during it, the RSDLP led a marginal existence. On the eve of that revolution its chapter in Vilnius had 120 organized workers.[18]

The Social Democracy of the Kingdom of Poland and Lithuania (Socjaldemokracja Królestwa Polskiego i Litwy, SDKPiL) also had branches in Lithuania. In 1901–1904 it sponsored several strikes and political demonstrations in Vilnius and Kaunas. Representatives of the party attended, in an advisory capacity, the second congress of the RSDLP in 1903. There they opposed the inclusion of national self-determination in the program of the Russian party, and then left the meeting when their efforts failed. Owing in part to defection of its members to the RSDLP, the influence of the SDKPiL in Lithuania after 1903 was on the wane.[19] When the two parties united in 1906, the 150 members of the SDKPiL in Vilnius switched to the RSDLP.

2

The Inception of Lithuanian Social Democracy

Two Circles Become One

The genealogy of Lithuanian Marxism, which as a political movement eventually evolved into the LSDP, was linked to the activities of two socialist groups—although other groups are known to have led a parallel existence.[1] Evgenii Sponti (1866–1931), a Belorussian graduate of a military school in St. Petersburg, headed the first group. Assigned to military duty in Vilnius, where he relocated in 1887, Sponti joined an informal study group made up of several army officers. Although initially interested in the activities of The People's Will, all of these officers were soon drawn to Marxism. When disrespect for superiors brought about his dismissal from the military service in 1889, Sponti extended his contacts with the Marxist underground; he linked up with local groups of workers, intermittently directing their activities until his departure from Lithuania in 1893.

The beginning of the second group came in the fall of 1892 when two students, Leonas Mikalauskas (1870–1899) and Bronislovas Urbonavičius (1868–1903), succeeded in establishing ties with several craftspeople employed in the small Vilnius shops. An "ardent fanatic" according to some accounts,[2] Urbonavičius felt that revolution in Russia could be accomplished in a relatively short period if the revolutionaries in that country and its borderlands acted in concert. He would pick out the most promising workers, instruct them in the essentials of socialism, and then send them off to distribute socialist literature and promote the further development of class consciousness. Whereas their dissemination of information about socialism was widespread, their interest in attending the group's meetings or contributing to its strike fund was minimal. On the whole, the success of Mikalauskas and Urbonavičius was limited; their work with the Christian laborers in Vilnius was hastily conducted, and the group itself soon fell under the influence of the newly created PPS.[3]

Lack of proper attention to the needs of conspiratorial work on the part of the Mikalauskas-Urbonavičius group, as well as its affinity with the PPS, led the Sponti organization to take an independent course. It trained its future agitators in a more thorough and methodical way, trying to provide them with the tools and qualities essential to underground work.[4] To be sure, the two groups had much in common. Both propagated socialist ideas among the same categories of labor, both relied on Polish publications, and both communicated in Polish. Still, they were independent and even quite different from each other.

On April 19 / May 1, 1893, the two groups uncharacteristically joined to observe May Day, the first such demonstration by the Christian workers in Vilnius. (The city's Jews held their first observance in 1892.) It was on that day that the rank and file affiliated with the two groups became aware of each other's existence. The discovery, however, was of little consequence, as the two organizations kept their distance from each other.

That particular May Day was an unremarkable event. The turnout consisted of some forty demonstrators. The worker participants were not sufficiently class-minded, while their leaders were both cautious and impractical. Around them were the usual number of passersby who distracted the demonstrators and put them in a bad mood. Mikalauskas and one other worker, as the representatives of the two groups, addressed the small gathering. The speakers urged the workers to establish strike funds and seek to improve their economic condition. In addition, they stressed the necessity of struggle for political rights and the cause of socialism. Finally, their acclamations of the incipient labor movement and of "our brothers in the West," who were said to set an example for the Vilnius socialists, brought the two-hour meeting to an end.[5] The demonstration must have disappointed its socialist organizers, for according to one account, the two speeches made no impression on the audience.[6] Nevertheless, it set a precedent for subsequent practice. From this point on the celebrations of May Day, which typically clamored for improved working conditions and basic civil liberties, became regular annual manifestations of Marxist sentiment.[7]

Soon after the May Day rally of 1893 the local police, disturbed by the spread of Polish socialist literature, came upon the Urbonavičius group, and with the aid of persons who viewed socialist agitation with disfavor, government authorities made short shrift of it. The Sponti organization survived. But the fear of police action forced it to interrupt its activities for several months, and it suffered a partial loss of influence and contacts.[8]

Noble Roots

The founders of the LSDP were two descendants of Lithuania's nobility who knew hardly any Lithuanian—Alfonsas Moravskis (1868–1941) and Andrius Domaševičius (1865–1935). In the summer of 1889 Zemah Kopelson visited the city of Panevėžys, where he met these two vacationing students, then still attracted to (but veering away from) the conspiratorial organization of the so-called new *narodniks*. The Jewish leader apprised them of his efforts to involve the workers employed by the craft industries in the economic and political struggle for the advancement of their class interests. According to Domaševičius, this meeting with Kopelson made a "deep impression" upon the two Lithuanians, contributing both to their own eventual espousal of the socialist cause and to the beginnings of Marxian activity among the Lithuanians.[9]

Moravskis, a former student at the universities of Kharkov, Kazan, and Kiev, moved to Vilnius in 1892. Rather gloomy, taciturn, and overly cautious, he spent much of his time establishing contacts with workers, writing numerous socialist tracts, and charting the course of the incipient party. To escape possible arrest, Moravskis, with the consent of Domaševičius, left Lithuania in 1897 for Western Europe, where a year later he formed the Union of Lithuanian Social Democrats Abroad. Through it he tried to communicate with Lithuanian socialists in Western Europe and the United States, and, in collaboration with his Latvian colleagues, to acquaint Western socialists with socialism in his country. After the turn of the century his commitment to revolutionary action ebbed. Moravskis returned to independent

Lithuania after World War I, where he served as a faculty member at the University of Kaunas.[10]

Domaševičius was a physician who had studied at Kiev University and practiced medicine in St. Petersburg. At the behest of Moravskis he settled in Vilnius in 1893. There he became one of the "twelve Lithuanian apostles" who attempted to halt the further polonization of that city. An obstinate man, imbued with initiative and enthusiasm, and "handsome as a doll," Domaševičius was popular and influential with the local leftist intelligentsia. He was briefly arrested in 1897, then rearrested in 1899 and exiled to Siberia. Released in 1904, he returned to Vilnius to become a central figure both in the 1905 revolution in Lithuania and in the struggle for that country's national liberation during World War I.[11]

Moravskis and Domaševičius shared a common political outlook and developed a long-standing friendship. The latter in particular often recalled the closeness of their families in Panevėžys, their bonds of childhood, the strong ties of common purpose, and the nights they spent together making plans for the future.[12] Despite the friendship, however, their collaboration in the 1890s was marked by frequent arguments. Aided by his ties with the Bundists and attracted to the movement toward workers' economic well-being, Moravskis was disposed to seek contacts with socialists of other nationalities, alert to (perhaps even intimidated by) the demands of underground existence, and circumspect in the choice of his associates. By contrast, Domaševičius was impetuous, trusting, daring in new enterprises, but somewhat incautious. These different experiences and traits were probably the reason why the two men generally kept their respective circles separate and why the tsarist police inflicted less damage on the Moravskis groups than it did on those affiliated with Domaševičius.[13]

Moravskis and Domaševičius are rightly considered the builders of the LSDP. But other prominent names were also associated with the party at one time or another during the 1890s. Stanisław Trusiewicz (1870–1918) was one of them. A restless person and one hard to get along with, this former member of the Proletariat Party was better versed in Marxist literature than any of his colleagues. In 1894–1895 Trusiewicz, Moravskis, and Domaševičius worked in unison, but in 1896 their cooperation found a snag in the national question.[14] Feliks Dzierżyński (1877–1926) attended the 1896 congress of the LSDP as a representative of the socialist youth in Vilnius. In 1897 the party ordered him to Kaunas, where he was to form an LSDP chapter. He was arrested there later that year and thus was removed from party work until 1899, when he escaped from his confinement in Viatka guberniia. Like many members of the landowning class from which he descended, Dzierżyński disapproved of Lithuanian separatism. He deserted the LSDP, helped to form the SDKPiL, and then gravitated toward the RSDLP.[15] Vladimir Perazich (1868–1943), an uncommonly sympathetic Serb who had studied at Vienna University and had been friends with Viktor Adler (1852–1918), worked with the LSDP in 1896–1897. This former member of the Austrian Social Democratic Party also opposed the national inclinations of the Lithuanian socialists, and in 1898 joined the RSDLP.[16] Trusiewicz, Dzierżyński, and Perazich ended up as Bolsheviks. Finally, unlike these fellow activists, Aleksandras Birinčikas (1870–1940) was a laborer. One of the party's founders, he is said to have been without peer as a speaker and organizer.[17] According to Moravskis, however, Birinčikas and Trusiewicz were responsible for sowing discord, in the mid-1890s, between the worker members of the party and its educated corps. Their brief "workers' opposition" appeared reluctant to start mass action among the workers, preferring instead to enhance the general education of agitators. In addition, it frowned on the political aspirations articulated by the intelligentsia, which it viewed as too patriotic, and resisted efforts to enlist the workers in secret party organizations.[18] Birinčikas was arrested in 1897, but then resumed party work upon his release in 1904.

In 1893 Sponti, who had to leave Vilnius, needed a successor to continue his work there. Closer to the Lithuanians than to the PPS, Sponti entrusted his following to Moravskis.[19] Initially the Lithuanian effort there was limited to two worker groups.[20] Moravskis, with the aid of Józef Olechnowicz (c. 1862–1905) and Grzegorz Malewski, was responsible for one group, while Domaševičius and Birinčikas led the other. The number of organized workers, however, soon climbed to more than two hundred. They were recruited mostly but not exclusively from among the Vilnius residents, as the rural audience was still untouched by socialist propaganda. This body of followers was led by a secret nucleus of twenty-odd workers and intellectuals.[21] To firm up the sense of group identity, Domaševičius and Moravskis contemplated a party platform that, while modeled on the Communist Manifesto, would be adapted to the needs of Lithuanian workers. In addition, they considered the agrarian problem, their publishing needs,

and the organizational aspects of their work. Ordinarily the two leaders were responsible for the resolution of the main issues, while the
routine problems were settled at their joint meetings with the leading
agitators.[22] Finally, the group's ordinary workers were organized in
different circles, where they discussed both workplace concerns and
questions of general interest to the socialists. Moravskis expected
them to start with the theory of value and then proceed with the Erfurt
Program of the German Social Democratic Party. *Development of the
Monist View of History*, by Georgii Plekhanov, seemed to be their
capstone text.[23] For materials of a practical sort, however, the group
initially relied heavily, if not uncritically, on PPS-supplied literature,
including that party's journal *Przedświt* (Morning Twilight) and various other pamphlets.[24]

Refraining from mass agitation among the workers, the handful
of educated socialist leaders at first concentrated their energies on
small groups of laborers—shoemakers, carpenters, tailors, tanners,
metal workers, and others. By late 1895, however, as the labor movement grew stronger and more students and intellectuals became attracted to socialism, they were confident enough to begin a sustained
effort to penetrate the Vilnius proletariat.[25] Convinced that the assumption of political obligations depended on a prior satisfaction of
basic material needs, the Lithuanians, like their Jewish counterparts,
initially aimed at improving workers' economic well-being and sharpening their sense of class identity. In general, their conception of party
operations bordered on "economism." Soon, however, their activities
acquired a political note, too, because agitation against a repressive
Russian government was difficult to avoid.[26] Conditions of alien rule
helped to politicize Lithuanian social democracy.

The Birth of a Party

The LSDP began to develop into a political party in 1895 with a series
of consultations followed by a preparatory conference. The year was
a time of decision. It witnessed an exchange of views which presaged
divergent roads for the Vilnius social democrats. Conflicting national
objectives first separated the Jews and the Christians and then split
the latter, too. The purposes of the talks between the Lithuanian-
Polish and the Jewish groups were to chart their future relations and
to reach an agreement on matters of agitation. Representing the first

group were Moravskis, Domaševičius, and Trusiewicz. Kopelson and Gozhansky usually spoke for the second. (It appears that members of the PPS took no part in these deliberations.) The Lithuanian-Polish spokesmen advanced the idea of a party designed to unite the Lithuanians and the Jews for work in Lithuania. The Jews found this proposal unacceptable, perhaps for two reasons. They were bent on the formation of a separate party to represent the Jewish proletariat in Russia. Also, the Jews initially considered themselves Russian Marxists, whereas the Lithuanians and the Poles were beginning to develop their own separate identities. The question of agitation presented no undue problems. The two sides agreed to conduct agitation on the basis of workers' everyday needs, and to be in touch with each other.[27] All of which meant that in the future, as in the past, the efforts of the Lithuanians and the Jews would be mutually supportive but separate.

Had it not been for conflicting national allegiances which destroyed the unity between the Trusiewicz and the Domaševičius-Moravskis groups, 1895 would have been an auspicious year for Lithuanian social democracy. Trusiewicz feared that the forging of strong ties between Lithuania's social democrats and liberals, sought by some people, would be detrimental to the former. Domaševičius and Moravskis, on the other hand, had no such foreboding. They thought the sources of liberal support were narrow and the group's objectives rather modest. Even minor government concessions—such as improved protection from police brutality, acceptance of the native languages as the media of instruction in Lithuania's schools, lifting of the ban on books and periodicals printed in the Latin alphabet, or amelioration of the rural economy—would suffice to deprive that group of the reasons for its continued existence. Some of its former members would then adopt a conservative outlook, while others would affiliate with the social democrats. The two founders of the LSDP hoped for such a polarization between right and left, for they aspired to form a broadly based progressive movement consisting of the country's proletarian elements and of those among the intelligentsia and the younger generation who sought the promotion of its national interests.[28] Besides, a tilt of the farm-oriented liberals to the LSDP was bound to facilitate that party's inroads on the village proletariat.[29] Unable to dissuade Domaševičius and Moravskis from cooperation with the liberals, Trusiewicz in 1896 founded his own party, the Union of Workers in Lithuania. The party stipulated the establishment of a democratic government in Russia as one of its goals. It further proposed that the Russia of tomorrow should grant its subject nationalities a number of concessions, including a measure of self-government. Lastly, it stated its readiness to become an autonomous member in a future all-Russian social democratic party.[30] The Union, however, was a failing body; it had some success only in Vilnius. In 1899–1900 Trusiewicz and Dzierżyński, who also fell away from the Domaševičius-Moravskis axis, joined Rosa Luxemburg (1871–1919) in founding the SDKPiL. In 1906 this hybrid party became a part of the RSDLP. An impressive leadership and a purported membership (in 1907) of twenty-five thousand enabled the SDKPiL to play a prominent part in the subsequent development of Russian and Polish social democracy.[31]

The conference of Lithuanian social democrats which laid the basis for the founding of the LSDP occurred in the summer of 1895.[32] It reviewed the tactics of the labor movement, heard a report on the group's activities, and discussed its relations with other revolutionary groups. The conferees then agreed upon a program congruent with the views of Domaševičius and Moravskis, designating the two men, along with Trusiewicz, as the group's corps of officers. This triumvirate of leaders was expected to assume the direction of all of the Marxist groups in the greater Vilnius area save the Jewish one. The Vilnius units and similar groups operating in other cities were then to coalesce in a single social democratic organization. The period of inception ended with the first, or constituent, party congress in Vilnius, on April 19 / May 1, 1896—actually, shortly after the day whose symbolic meaning the LSDP wished to retain.[33] Present at the creation were Domaševičius and Moravskis, members of the organization's central committee. Further, Aleksandras Birinčikas, Andrzej Gulbinowicz (b. 1874), Franciszek Kaczmarczyk, Romualdas Maleckis (1877–1942), Józef Olechnowicz, and Petras Suknelevičius (1871–1940) participated as the leading worker agitators. The socialist youth were represented by Feliks Dzierżyński and Konrad Kasperowicz (b. 1878). Finally, the delegates included Juozas Bagdonas (1866–1956), Kazys Grinius, and Stasys Matulaitis (1866–1956). The PPS mentioned these three to Domaševičius as possible contact persons in the Suwałki region. Thereupon, after an 1895 Easter time meeting with Domaševičius, they formed an allied group to promote the publication of socialist literature.[34] (Of the three, Matulaitis achieved considerable prominence in the world of Marxist politics, while Grinius, who was elected president of Lithuania in 1926, and Bagdonas associated themselves with the Democrats.) The thirteen delegates formally adopted the party program drafted the preceding year. Since Domaševičius spoke only a rudimentary sort of Lithuanian, he wrote the program in Polish and Grinius then translated it into Lithuanian. The program included a call for the formation of a federal state without Russia.[35] A discussion of the national issue appears in the next chapter.

Besides the position on the national question, the program offered an analysis, in Marxist terms, of the local economy, expounding the view that existing social and economic ills could be corrected only if socialism supplanted capitalism. It also referred to the economic and political nature of the class struggle and assigned to the proletariat a key role in the quest for a socialist future. Finally, after specifying an array of desired civil liberties and economic aims, the program ended with statements of party policy on a number of items: matters of tactics, relations with the Jewish proletariat, and attitudes toward the Russians.[36] Various strands of experience were woven into the program. Referring to the proposed solution of the national question, a founder of the LSDP recalled that the example of the multinational Swiss federation was especially popular with the social democrats of similarly diverse Vilnius.[37] Also, after a passing reference to views current among Austrian socialists, he singled out the clearly separatist platform of the PPS, which made a strong impression upon the Lithuanians.[38] Finally, a textual analysis of the LSDP programs made in 1966 has established as their main sources the resolutions of the Second International, the platform of the PPS, and the tactics which the Social Democracy of the Kingdom of Poland adopted at its first congress in 1894. The deepest indebtedness, however, was to the Erfurt Program of the German Social Democratic Party, with which the Lithuanians had fairly close ties.[39] The influences over the LSDP were clearly Western.

The urban following of the Lithuanian party during the first stage of its existence was not large, but the temper of its activity was marked by optimism. Exclusive of the membership in the several labor unions, the adherents of the LSDP ranged from two hundred to four hundred workers concentrated mainly in Vilnius; the search for support in the outlying towns of Kaunas, Panevėžys, Šiauliai, and Vileika had been launched only recently.[40] In factories and shops strike funds were formed. Those most active in them were urged to enroll in the LSDP. Composed of workers and members of the intelligentsia, the Central Group of Agitators directed the work of the funds and of individual party members. In turn, the group was subordinated to the party's central committee elected by the congress.[41] It is possible that this mode of organization was patterned on the one devised by the Jews.[42]

In addition to the regular party organization, groups of high school students leaning toward socialism did the LSDP a valuable service. Kept back from dangerous assignments, they usually helped the party organizers educate the workers, especially in such fields as natural sciences and economics.[43] To intensify its work among the students, the LSDP sponsored a conference of social democratic youth. Held in Vilnius in 1896, the gathering included representatives from various Lithuanian towns, as well as those from Riga and Minsk.[44] Considered as a whole, this coterie of workers, professionals, students, and their sympathizers formed the nucleus of an emergent socialist subculture. Its members disseminated Marxist literature, attempted to arouse public feeling, set up their own study groups and social clubs, intermarried, and augmented the ranks of party activists.[45] Mounting confrontations with the authorities heightened their socialist consciousness and reinforced their determination to persist against government repression.

An assessment of party propaganda directed toward the agricultural sector suffers from a lack of documentary evidence. Presumably, the first steps there were aimed at those working on large landed estates. For example, two agricultural strikes are known to have occurred on such properties in 1894 and another three in 1896.[46] Further, in a leaflet which the tsarist police attached to its 1899 files, the LSDP assured the rural workers that the "light of socialism" was beginning to penetrate to the darkest backwaters of Lithuania, and then urged them to do what their urban brethren had done, namely, to close ranks, form unions, heighten their own labor consciousness, and fight for the amelioration of their "bitter fate."[47] On the other hand, Matulaitis recalls his own efforts, in 1896, to form party cells among the small farmers.[48] In any case, the LSDP incursion into the rural terrain in the latter part of the 1890s was tenuous.[49] When a concerted drive finally came, as it did in 1902, its object in the countryside was not the laborer but the farmer.

The illegal newspapers of the LSDP were published in Lithuanian and Polish. As shown by the list of periodicals reproduced in appendix

A, three issues of *Lietuvos darbininkas* (The Lithuanian Worker; its Polish edition was entitled *Robotnik litewski*), published in Switzerland, France, and East Prussia, appeared in 1896–1899. Their publication was facilitated by Julian Marchlewski (1866–1925) and other members of the Social Democracy of the Kingdom of Poland, whom Domaševičius and Moravskis contacted in Paris in 1896 and 1897. (In 1900 the name of the party was changed to Social Democracy of the Kingdom of Poland and Lithuania.) In 1897–1898 nine issues of *Echo życia robotniczego* (Echo of Workers' Life) were reproduced on a hectograph in Vilnius for the Polish-speaking readers. Two issues of *Aidas Lietuvos darbininkų gyvenimo* (Echo of the Life of Lithuanian Workers) appeared in 1899, the first issue in Polish and Lithuanian, the second only in Lithuanian. Both were published in East Prussia. In addition to these periodicals, the Vilnius organization of the LSDP operated a secret library of socialist materials. Its holdings in Lithuanian, Russian, Polish, Jewish, and German languages totaled eight hundred brochures, appeals, newspapers, and journals.[50]

The Second Coming

A police crackdown on revolutionaries in 1897–1899 terminated the first period in the history of the LSDP. It also modified the nature of that party's activities during the period that followed. As many as 280 members of various social democratic and labor groups were placed in prison. The arrests and subsequent political trials resulted in the banishment of more than forty persons, including Domaševičius, Jokūbas Daumantas (d. 1924), Matulaitis, Trusiewicz, Birinčikas, Olechnowicz, and Dzierżyński. Others, like Moravskis and Suknelevičius, fled the country to avoid a similar fate.[51] This government sweep eliminated the entire leadership of the LSDP, and for a time the party itself virtually ceased to exist.[52]

The resurgence of the LSDP in 1900–1902 was the work of a new breed of men, among whom two Lithuanian students deserve mention. Vladas Sirutavičius (1877–1967), a remnant of Lithuania's aristocracy, was enrolled in the St. Petersburg Technological Institute. He was a well-liked person and a gifted speaker who knew how to handle theoretical matters in a way that ordinary workers understood. In 1899 Sirutavičius went to Vilnius, where, after consultations with several workers, he formed a provisional central committee.[53] A year

later another student from that same institute, Steponas Kairys (1878–
1964), arrived and joined in the work of restoring the party to life.
Kairys was entrusted with the conduct of party propaganda; most of
the main LSDP appeals were credited to him. He served on the central
committee almost without interruption from 1901 to 1944, although
his involvement in party affairs during 1908–1911 was minimal. Until
his death in New York in 1964 Kairys held a pivotal position in
Lithuanian social democracy.[54]

A discussion of the LSDP elite during the 1900–1904 period should
also include several other persons. From 1902 to 1905 Augustinas
Janulaitis (1878–1950) edited *Darbininkų balsas* (The Workers'
Voice), the party's organ published in East Prussia. Impetuous in his
habits and frowning on compromise, Janulaitis did not hesitate to
attack his political opponents, namely, Russian officials and Lithuanian moderates.[55] Kipras Bielinis (1883–1965), the man of forty crypto-
nyms, was responsible for the first anti-Russian demonstration in
Lithuania during the revolution of 1905. The son of a man famous in
Lithuanian history for smuggling illegal books into the country, Bielinis was said to have organized thirty political meetings and demonstrations in 1905. Mykolas Biržiška (1882–1962), a future scholar devoted to the literary and cultural aspects of Lithuanian history,
achieved considerable prominence in the party, particularly during
his service on its central committee in 1907–1912. Also active in the
LSDP was Jonas Biliūnas (1879–1907), a writer who died of consump-
tion at twenty-eight. He formed primary party organizations, wrote
political booklets, and contributed to illegal liberal and socialist
journals.

One might also comment on the role of Vincas Mickevičius-
Kapsukas (1880–1935), the man who in 1919 was chosen as the head
of a Communist government in Lithuania and Belorussia. Constantly
disposed to action, Kapsukas was a highly impressionable person who
traversed the entire spectrum of leftist parties. In the spring of 1903
several Lithuanian socialists, who deplored the LSDP neglect of the
village proletariat, met in Šiauliai to consider the expansion of their
activities among the low-income sectors of the rural population. At
the conclusion of their discussions, they named Juozas Paknys (1883–
1948), Kazys Mažonas (b. 1886), and Vladas Požela (1879–1960) as
members of the group's steering committee charged with procuring
the publication of a planned journal. When the group reconvened in

1904, Kapsukas, who in the meantime had accepted the offer to serve as the managing editor of the journal, suggested that the periodical should be known as *Draugas* (The Friend) and its sponsor as the *Draugas* Organization.[56]

The adherence of Kapsukas to the *Draugas* Organization, which was later retitled the Lithuanian Social Democratic Labor Party (Lietuvių socialdemokratų darbininkų partija), attested to a complex pattern of that man's political affiliations. Briefly enrolled in Bern University, where he studied sociology and political economy, Kapsukas began his political career in liberal quarters, contributing to some of their periodicals and assisting in the editing of others. Then came a period of transition. In 1903–1905, while he was still leaning toward Russia's Socialist Revolutionaries, Kapsukas first gravitated toward the LSDP, then severed his ties with it and formed the ephemeral Lithuanian Social Democratic Labor Party, and finally again coalesced with the LSDP. Communist writers emphasize that this particular quarrel between Kapsukas and the LSDP was due primarily to policy differences.[57] It is true that a variation in party tactics was apparent, but other causes were equally important.[58] It seems that there were a number of persons, presumably including Kapsukas, who were disenchanted with the liberals but not yet affiliated with the social democrats. Experiencing inner struggle, doubt, and vacillation, they were going to publish a journal in which they planned to discuss problems of policy and purpose. However, they put off publication in the hope that the LSDP would agree to sponsor it. Kapsukas joined that party in 1903.[59]

Meanwhile another, perhaps decisive, matter arose. A personality conflict developed between Kapsukas and Janulaitis, the man who was both the editor of the main LSDP publication and the party's representative abroad. Kapsukas asked the party's central committee to intervene and settle the dispute, but the central committee hedged. Unable or unwilling to air his views in existing periodicals and eager for action, Kapsukas began to publish *Draugas* in 1904. Initially he had no plans for any kind of separate social democratic organization, and was still hoping for a reconciliation with the LSDP. But when it became obvious that the party stood by its editor, Kapsukas broke away from the LSDP and joined the *Draugas* group.[60] The rupture, however, was short-lived. In 1905 Kapsukas resubmitted to the LSDP and was elected to its central committee. The Lithuanian Social Democratic Labor Party ceased to exist.

For Kapsukas the LSDP was but a way-stop on the course of his political transformation. In 1910–1911, while serving time in the Warsaw prison, Kapsukas became favorably impressed with the SDK-PiL. These Polish influences began to wane, however, when his place of detention shifted to Vladimir and then, in 1913, to Krasnoiarsk. It was here that Kapsukas met Iakov Sverdlov (1885–1919), a prominent member of Lenin's party apparatus. The two men developed a close personal relationship, spent long hours in political conversation, and later corresponded with each other.[61] Kapsukas was on his way to becoming a Bolshevik.

A majority of party leaders who rallied to revive the LSDP were sons of farmers with medium holdings. Professionally they belonged to the middle class, and were studying to be lawyers, engineers, writers, and professors. At the time of the party's reconstruction most of them were under twenty-five. Together with the rank and file they discussed problems of special interest to socialists, such as the history of the labor movement in the West and in Lithuania, the nature of the capitalist economy, and the respective roles of employers and employees. Kairys recalls that ordinary workers and their educated leaders developed relations of mutual trust.[62]

From 1901 through 1906 the party produced thirty-six issues of *Darbininkų balsas*. To its Polish supporters the LSDP offered *Echo życia robotniczego na Litwie* (Echo of Workers' Life in Lithuania); its nine issues came out between 1902 and 1906. *Darbininkų balsas* served mainly as a propaganda and a communications device, concentrating on current political events. Its emphases given to theory and tactics were somewhat lower. In addition to periodicals, the party resorted to pamphlets and appeals. The number of pamphlets listed in *Darbininkų balsas* in 1904 was close to forty. LSDP appeals were issued both by the central committee and the local organizations, sometimes in editions of as many as fifty thousand copies.[63]

A Changed Complexion

The new LSDP differed from the old one in a number of ways. For one, it acquired a degree of ethnic unity that it did not have previously, a change applicable to both leaders and ordinary members. Arrests tended to limit the range of LSDP operations to Lithuania proper. Further, an economically inspired migration from the rural to the urban areas increased the proportion of ethnic Lithuanians among the city residents. Lastly, as the party enlarged its activities beyond the environs of the multinational Vilnius area, spreading into provincial towns and rural communities, it enlisted a body of supporters who were predominantly Lithuanian. The Polish language, too, gradually receded and was replaced by Lithuanian.[64]

The rebuilt party differed from its former self in yet another respect, its socioeconomic base—a subject discussed in chapter 12. Earlier the social democrats had concentrated their efforts on city workers, especially on those in small craft industries.[65] Like socialists in many other countries, they held the peasantry in low regard.[66] But after the turn of the century they redirected their search for support to include the amorphous category of the underprivileged: farm labor, landless peasants, and especially the small landholders. This strategy brought the party to a point where its sources of support were predominantly rural.[67] Moreover, as unrest in the Russian empire mounted, most of Lithuania's rural youth who tended toward the LSDP were probably attracted by that party's activism, not by its class nature.[68]

Finally, the revival of the LSDP witnessed, and aided, a progressive divergence between liberals and socialists. The preoccupation of a portion of Lithuania's intelligentsia with that country's national awakening had produced, in the 1890s, a symbiosis between nationally minded socialists and radically inclined liberals. The socialists sought the help of the liberals in translating, publishing, and transporting needed materials. The liberals expected their partners to arrest further polonization of Lithuania's outlying areas. The efforts of the liberals were designed to counter the PPS with the LSDP, to set off Piłsudski against Domaševičius. Liberal support of the socialists had little or no ideological tinge; it was prompted by national motives.[69] After 1901–1902, however, their collaboration seemed to ebb. The liberals began to evolve into a political movement, which they were not before. The LSDP discomfited the liberals by its influence on certain segments of the rural society, because the liberals themselves were dependent on these social strata.[70] The two parties thus punctuated their individuality, although the bridges which they built in the past had not been burned.

3

National Objectives

The Motives of the Framers

The policymakers of the LSDP had two main objectives—to heighten workers' class awareness and to further Lithuania's national renaissance. These goals determined the basic qualities of Lithuanian social democracy during the years under review. Eventually, for a number of reasons, the party's stand on the national question overshadowed its service in the cause of labor. Perhaps this was the right course, because the national question was essentially one of Lithuania's future existence. At party conferences and congresses, or in party publications, the matter of the country's future existence was subsumed into such operational concepts as independence, federalism, autonomy, and separatism. The separatism of the LSDP, as noted above, initially meant the abandonment of the Russian fold. Parenthetically, it also meant the establishment of a distinctly Lithuanian identity with respect to the Poles. Although the leading social democrats never elaborated the reasons for their demand of independence for Lithuania, especially in Marxist terms, some interpretation of their motives is possible.

First, to the Lithuanians, as to the Poles and other nationalities, the tsarist regime was an alien and oppressive reality whose unpopularity was deepened by its policy of Russianization. The tsarist government and its policies generated enmity toward Russia, and there were many who doubted that Great Russian nationalism in a democratic Russia of the future would be any more tolerant of minority aspirations.[1]

Second, socialist literature in Lithuania, and elsewhere, was rich in references to Russia as a backward country that retarded progress.

Backwardness was alleged in Russia's general economic development as well as in the development of its revolutionary movement. The LSDP maintained that it ought to support the revolutionary movement in Russia but not count on it. In general, the argument about Russia's social and political lag tended to impart a pro-Western direction to the LSDP.[2] Later, this Western motif yielded two corollary propositions. Causally, the LSDP began to allude to the principle of national self-determination as a motive of its efforts at Lithuanian emancipation. As for the purpose of these efforts, Lithuania was meant to federate with those neighboring countries whose level of social and political development resembled its own, a qualification hindering Russia's inclusion in the contemplated union of states.[3]

Third, evidence shows that the LSDP attempted to justify its separatism by adducing an ideological coloration. The party averred that the interests of the proletariat were paramount. On the other hand, it also supported (but did not consider as "sacred") the furtherance of the Lithuanian language, traditions, and national identity.[4] The workers' movement was an international one, so ran the argument,[5] because its ultimate goals were the same throughout the world. However, each nation possessed a set of distinctive traits which the proletariat valued and to which it adjusted. Opposed to oppression in any form, the proletariat was also opposed to the oppression of one nation by another. Lithuania endured such an oppression. Not only did the Lithuanian workers suffer as workers, but they also suffered as Lithuanians.[6] Since the LSDP struggled for the freedom of all the people, it struggled for the national freedom of the Lithuanians, too. The incarnation of such a national freedom would be the establishment of a democratic republic of Lithuania.

Finally, the desire to be independent of Russia was, to a point, a legacy from the past, reinforced by the nationalism of the PPS. Lithuania's existence as an independent state and then as one in union with Poland, before 1795, followed by Polish and Lithuanian uprisings against the Russians in the nineteenth century, were not forgotten by the founders of the LSDP.[7] Such a past may have fostered in them the kind of separate identity that was devoid of undue nationalism. Matulaitis suggests that Domaševičius and Moravskis, as residents of Lithuania (perhaps, too, as members of that country's aristocracy), sought to articulate the interests of a discrete local working class— in that sense, Lithuania's working class.[8] Admittedly, however, the precise bearing of these past experiences on their conduct is difficult to assess.

The Federalist Ideal

The early LSDP position on the national question was contained in three main documents, the draft program produced by the preparatory conference of 1895 and the two versions of the party program adopted by the congresses of 1896 and 1897. The first document, written by Domaševičius, has never been found, but contemporaries assert that it was virtually identical with the one approved in 1896.[9] The statement on the future of Lithuania, endorsed by the congress of 1896, included the following proposition: "An independent democratic republic, consisting of Lithuania, Poland, and other countries, based on a loose federation."[10] Further paragraphs indicate that this federation was to include Lithuania, Poland, Latvia, Belorussia, and the Ukraine.[11] In short, it was to be a federation without Russia. The founders of the party were not unanimous in their approval of such a separatist statement. In fact, a "rather sharp discussion" of the plank ensued, splitting the group into two factions.[12] Some delegates, including Birinčikas and Dzierżyński, preferred autonomy for a Lithuania that remained a part of the Russian empire.[13] However, the majority, which included Domaševičius, Moravskis, and the three promoters of socialist publications, opted for a federation that excluded Russia as one of its constituent states.

The Domaševičius-Moravskis formulation of the party's national objectives was thus initially supported by that group's preparatory conference of 1895, then weighed by all of its clandestine worker organizations, and finally adopted by its constituent congress in 1896. Yet the formally approved stand on the national question filled some party leaders with apprehension about possible rifts among the members of the LSDP. To avert such an eventuality, all party agitators were given another opportunity to express their views on the matter at a special meeting arranged for that purpose. There, on May 1/13, 1896, after lengthy discussions, a majority of those present endorsed the ruling of the congress.[14]

Formal settlement of the national question in 1895–1896 failed to quell the discord it occasioned among the members of the Lithuanian party. Early in 1897 a series of worker meetings were convened to discuss the party program and take a definite stand on it. Significant changes were in the making, creating a need for another congress to sanction a new consensus. Subsequent to a "very sharp" debate, the second congress of the LSDP, held on January 25 / February 6, 1897, altered the party program in one important respect. It no longer excluded Russia from possible membership in a future federal state. In addition, the individual members of the LSDP were said to be free to form their own views on this particular article in the platform.[15] Basically, the amended plank, which was further retouched in 1898–1899, evinced the party's willingness to federate with those neighboring countries which were ready to concede full autonomy to Lithuania.[16] Many felt that the Lithuanians, the Poles, the Latvians, the Belorussians, and the Ukrainians could coexist "without doing harm to each other." Conceivably, the Russians, too, could qualify for membership, but only if they renounced their policies aimed to russianize, amalgamate, and dominate the rest—a reversal of course which the progress of socialism among them might induce.[17]

The outbreak of the first large-scale strikes in Russian cities in 1896–1897, thought to be an indication of a growing revolutionary movement there, and concessions to the so-called internationalists within the party were probably the main reasons for the 1897 change in program.[18] It should be noted, however, that until 1905 most of the party decisionmakers, including some who later became communists,[19] adhered with more or less firmness to the original plan drafted in 1896.[20]

To the pre-1905 arbiters of the LSDP, the fruition of party policy on the national question appeared, if vaguely, as a two-stage process—the winning of independence from Russia, and then the creation of a federal state. This view, expressed in party statements and the writings of party leaders, was based on the conviction that the formation of a voluntary federation was predicated on a prior condition of independence for the member states.[21] It is incontrovertible, however, that independence was not the final goal. Although initially the idea of an independent Lithuania may have been proffered as a way of distinguishing that country's social democracy from the PPS, Moravskis and other founders of the LSDP soon realized that the indigenous revolutionary potential was simply not strong enough to aspire to a completely independent and separate Lithuanian state.[22] Unfortunately, party literature discussed neither the duration of the period of independence nor the mechanics of federation-making.

Separatist Perspectives

The ultimate objective of the LSDP, then, was the founding of a federal republic. Although federalism itself enjoyed a good deal of support, the composition of the future state presented problems. In that initially the list of possible members included Lithuania, Latvia, Poland, Belorussia, and the Ukraine, apparently the design was to reconstitute, on a different basis, the defunct Polish-Lithuanian state. (The inclusion of Latvia was probably motivated by its ethnic kinship with Lithuania.)[23] Later, the LSDP ceased to be explicit about the composition of the future state, although it remained wedded to federalism as the form which Lithuania's relations with the neighboring countries should assume. Deference to party internationalists and intensification of revolutionary action in Russia, as possible reasons for the change, were noted above.

Two additional reasons deserve consideration. First, failure to list the member states was partly due to insufficient interest in the proposed federation. The idea, it seems, evoked little or no favorable response from the Latvian, Belorussian, and Ukrainian social democrats.[24] Second, reluctance to be explicit on membership hinted at a mounting friction between the Lithuanians and the Poles. It appears that the quality of nationalism, on both sides, contained a measure of incompatibility. The Lithuanian national intelligentsia, including its socialist wing, was engaged in the process of nation-building. The leaders of the new Poland, who were used to viewing Lithuania as a Polish domain, refused to recognize the Lithuanian endeavor, or so the Lithuanians felt. In 1894–1896 some LSDP members apparently thought that union with Poland, on the basis of equality, was possible. But as optimism subsequently waned the LSDP deferred the question of membership to a future time.[25]

The significance of LSDP separatism needs to be evaluated on a two-dimensional scale of politics. On the scale of revolutionary politics, separatism tended to be divisive. First, socialist organizations that were affiliated with the Second International frowned upon the national tendencies of the LSDP. Although the LSDP considered itself bound by the decisions of the Second International, it gained admission to that body only in 1923, when party affairs unfolded in an entirely different setting. Second, the secessionist policy proved to be a source of perennial intraparty discord. The alienation of the Trusiewicz-Dzierżyński following in the 1890s was partly due to the national posture of the LSDP.[26] And in the years after 1905 those who stayed with the LSDP were again torn asunder—mainly, if not solely, by the national question.

On the scale of national politics, separatism elicited a more constructive sequel. In independent Lithuania of the 1918–1940 period the question of who pioneered Lithuanian independence became, perhaps excessively, one of controversy and concern. It attracted more attention than in the years before 1918. As late as 1894 Lithuanian independence was rarely an item on the agenda of the Lithuanian intelligentsia. To most it was nothing but an "empty dream." Except for individual views, the call of the LSDP for a break with Russia, or at least for a fundamental change in the basis of future Lithuanian-Russian association, was the first of its kind to issue from a Lithuanian political movement. Indicating an advanced quality in social democratic leadership, the action tended to politicize the essentially cultural character of Lithuania's national renewal.

Part II

The Politics of Assertive

Behavior, 1904–1905

4

New Vistas

The Wages of Failure

The revival of the LSDP set in motion at the turn of the century continued and intensified in 1903–1904. The party press informed its readers about recent contacts with Lithuanian workers living abroad; in 1903 local chapters of the LSDP were formed in the Latvian cities of Riga and Liepāja and, in Scotland, among the coal miners in the Glasgow area.[1] At home new primary party organizations were set up in various parts of the country, especially the western region, and in the summer of 1904 a conference of social democratic youth was held.[2] The financial position improved, too. The party budget for 1903 reached 1,981 rubles, an increase of almost 50 percent over the preceding year.[3] Another example of stepped-up activities was a joint effort by the LSDP and other groups to establish a special fund for the support of those who were being persecuted by the government for their political activities.[4] Finally, a number of prominent Marxists, including Birinčikas and Domaševičius, came home from distant parts of the empire to which they were exiled for political offenses in 1899–1900. They rejoined the party, contributing to its renewed vigor.

The character, scope, and pace of these routine political activities were significantly altered by momentous new developments in the Far East. These were the eruption of the Russian-Japanese war in February 1904, quickly followed by a succession of Russian military reverses—Japan's April victory on the Yalu, its May advances in the Liaotung peninsula, the destruction of the Lüshun (Port Arthur) naval squadron in August, the collapse of the September offensive along the Sha River in Manchuria, the loss of Lüshun in early 1905, and other disastrous setbacks later that year. Costing the two combatants an estimated 450,000 in killed and wounded, the war galvanized Russia's revolutionary movement into the kind of vehemence that wreaked political chaos and jolted that country's autocratic foundations.

The revolutionary agitation that was beginning to swell throughout Russia intensified in Lithuania, too. Early LSDP appeals attributed the responsibility for the outbreak of the war to the tsarist government and its upper class supporters, who were said to be the sole beneficiaries in the war. Since the ordinary people were presumed to have no stake in the war, they were encouraged to withhold their support of the country's war effort and, in the case of young men, to dodge the draft. Although some appeals advised the people to prepare for an eventual confrontation with the government, they generally refrained from calling them into action against the autocracy. These early Marxist efforts, then, could be termed refusal through civil disobedience to cooperate with the government. A number of men did in fact refuse to serve in the army, fled the country, or defected to the Japanese.[5] Although this behavior would seem to indicate compliance with the expected course of action, there is not enough evidence to gauge the net effect of the 40,000-odd appeals on war and mobilization (out of an approximate 1904 total of more than 63,000 copies of various appeals) attributed to the LSDP.[6] As a matter of fact, the LSDP itself was miffed by the absence of a forceful popular opposition to the draft.[7]

The views the party propagated through its written appeals resembled those it articulated in *Darbininkų balsas*, a leading party journal published in Germany and smuggled across the border into Lithuania. Its 1904 issues depicted the social democratic leaders as people who sensed the imminence of critical events but could not yet see clearly either the particular time of the revolution or its principal dynamics. They were filled with anticipation, formulating their own immediate objectives, weighing priorities, and planting seeds of assertive behavior in people's minds.

The general outlook of the LSDP first came into view in a lengthy lead article on the war published in *Darbininkų balsas*. The editors regarded the war as the inevitable result of two capitalist powers competing for markets in the Far East. Additionally, Russia's warlike disposition was presented as one way of deflating the revolutionary potential at home. Having denounced the capitalists, the bureaucrats, and the clergy for their alleged support of Russia's war effort, they advised the working people against such a course, for a weakening of the autocracy was bound to facilitate the quest for workers' rights. Their task, concluded the article, was to demolish government foundations.[8]

These initial LSDP reactions to developments in the Far East were followed by further analysis of the progress of the war and its consequences published in the spring of 1904. Some socialist observers now saw revolution in Russia as a foregone conclusion, regardless of the outcome of the war. They further envisaged the possibility of a domestic flareup while the war was still in progress, a preferred turn of events from their own perspective. A two-front war that forced the tsar to contend with both internal and external adversaries was likely to enhance the success of the revolution and lower its casualty rate. (When in May of 1904 the tsarist government lifted its unpopular forty-year ban on the publication or importation of Lithuanian books and periodicals printed in the Latin alphabet, the party press attributed this concession partly to the weakening of the Russian government caused by Japanese military successes.)[9] In their view, then, the immediate objective of the LSDP was to imbue the general public with revolutionary ideas, a task which it could accomplish by making the people aware of socialist political goals and by conducting a campaign against those holding moderate views.[10]

Socialist Concerns

A preparation for increased responsibilities spurred the LSDP to tackle a number of practical concerns, including such questions as social stratification and group receptivity to revolutionary change, transition to socialism, and possible future ties between the Russians and the Lithuanians. Concerning the cleavage of interests, the LSDP writers maintained that Lithuania was broadly stratified into three socioeconomic layers. At the top of the social scale were what the party propaganda often dubbed the rich people, e.g., merchants, manufacturers, and the landed gentry. The party was of the opinion that this social stratum, while not averse to the establishment of a constitutional monarchy, would take no action to bring about such a change.

At the next level down the social ladder, the LSDP found the farmers and the artisans. It classed this intermediate tier of society as the social base of the liberals. Although these groups had no liking for the tsarist government, their political objectives were nonetheless considered to be reformist in nature. To socialist critics, liberal support of the revolutionary movement was questionable since it hinged on both the feasibility of contemplated change and the material benefits it had in store for the middle class.

At the bottom of the social scale were urban wage earners, farm labor, landless peasants, and small landholders. As "soldiers of the revolution," members of this lowest class were thought to be destined to embark upon a struggle in which they had "nothing to lose and everything to gain."[11] The revolutionaries further hoped that a segment of the country's intelligentsia, such as doctors, teachers, lawyers, and labor advocates in general, would join them in that forthcoming struggle. The LSDP felt obligated to equip this class for its impending mission. The party's own membership was then estimated at 3,000— half of it in Vilnius.[12]

LSDP writers conceived of the transition to socialism as the end result of a country's progressive democratization.[13] Their analysis of contemporary forms of government yielded a typology that consisted of three main possibilities: despotic monarchies as in Russia, Turkey, and Persia; limited constitutional monarchies on the Austrian, English, German, and Swedish models; and republican governments like those in France, Switzerland, and the United States. Republics were in turn divisible into their aristocratic, bourgeois, and democratic subtypes, benefiting respectively the nobility, the educated and the rich, and the ordinary people.

The goal of the LSDP was the destruction of tsarist despotism followed by the founding of a democratic federal republic. It was assumed that in such a republic power would be vested in a legislature, elected by all adult citizens regardless of their sex, religion, nationality, education, wealth, or social origin. The nature of legislative enactments, so ran the argument, would depend on the composition of the legislature, while it, in turn, was bound to reflect the makeup of the electorate. Since the working people were presumed to constitute a majority of the population, workers' influence on government promised to be decisive. Responding to the needs of the people, lawmakers would then enact progressive legislation, replacing the army with a militia, increasing funds for education, protecting the needy, shortening the workday, introducing minimum wage, etc. Ultimately, as the

result of a gradual shift to public ownership of the means of production, the country would become socialist.

In addition to impressions of class attitudes and transition to
socialism, the national question reappeared as an important item on
the LSDP agenda. Considering different forms of coexistence between
the dominant Russians and their subject nationalities, party activists
put three images of their country's future on a scale of diminishing
aspirations.[14] The solution they clearly preferred was the original plan
announced in 1896–1897—a liberated Lithuania uniting with others
to form a federal state. Besides Lithuania, the contemplated union was
meant to include Latvia, Belorussia, and possibly Poland, Russia, and
the Ukraine.[15] Failing that particular solution, wide autonomy for a
Lithuania that remained within the confines of the Russian state was
held to be the next best alternative. Lastly, efforts at an extensive
democratization of the Russian government, without any structural
changes in relations among the nations within the empire, were presented as the minimal objective. It appears that on the eve of a marked
increase in revolutionary agitation the spokesmen of the LSDP evinced
the kind of pragmatism that was not averse to reconciling the desirable
with the possible. If the ultimate objective—the creation of a federal
state—proved to be beyond their reach, interim solutions such as the
attainment of Lithuanian autonomy or the democratization of Russian
government would still be seen as progress toward that eventual goal.

Bloodshed in the Capital

Increased revolutionary agitation, which was animated by staggering
defeats at the hands of the Japanese in 1904, was drastically changed
in character by a tragic occurrence in St. Petersburg the following year.
Early in January 1905 a seemingly minor labor dispute at the Putilov
Metal Works brought on a strike which rapidly spread to other factories employing large numbers of workers. The charged atmosphere
worsened when the controversial priest George Gapon, who inspired
and directed this strike action, divulged plans for a massive march on
the Winter Palace, where he hoped to present the tsar with a list of
grievances and demands. Among the latter were extensive economic
reforms and such basic modification of the existing system of government as the granting of civil liberties and the convocation of a constit-

uent assembly. On January 9/22, a day entered in the Russian annals as the Bloody Sunday, various processions of unarmed and generally peaceful demonstrators were met by cordons of troops. When the crowds refused to disperse, the troops opened fire. According to a conservative official count, 128 were killed.[16]

The repercussions of these events reverberated throughout the empire. In cities and towns mass action took the form of strikes and political demonstrations, while numerous agrarian disturbances plagued the countryside. Further, liberal opinion favored increasingly drastic solutions, discontent penetrated the armed forces, and terrorism intensified. Lastly, the spirit of rebellion spread to the borderlands of Russia—to Finland, Poland, the Caucasus, and other areas. Not surprisingly, the magnitude of revolutionary agitation produced a strenuous government counterdrive consisting of such disparate means as system-liberalization on the one hand and the use of punitive expeditions to suppress the riots on the other.

In Lithuania the news from St. Petersburg set off an initial wave of sympathy strikes and other types of activity. Within days large-scale strikes and demonstrations, supported by tens of thousands of participants, broke out in Vilnius and Kaunas, while lesser ones occurred in Šiauliai and Panevėžys. Lasting from January 11/24 to January 24/February 6, most of these strikes were instigated by the LSDP or the Jewish Bund, although other political groups were also variously involved. In Vilnius two political alliances were in the making; the PPS affiliate in Lithuania inclined toward the LSDP, while the RSDLP and the SDKPiL sided with the Bund. The main reason for their divergence was the Lithuanian party's advocacy of (and the other bloc's opposition to) Russia's conversion into a union of self-governing states.[17] Besides gestures in support of the St. Petersburg demonstrators, the strikers made numerous economic demands, including substantial pay raises, shorter workdays, disability and sick leave benefits, removal of objectionable foremen, and consultation over layoff decisions. The management would typically meet them partway, thus facilitating an early resumption of work. This labor unrest, as well as increased public activism generally, gave the LSDP an opportunity to circulate political messages as well. Mindful of the area's ethnic diversity, party activists published their political appeals and addressed their audiences in Lithuanian, Polish, Yiddish, and Russian.[18]

For many people these January strikes and demonstrations were first experiences in politicized activity, and as such, they produced mixed reactions and hinted possible corrective measures. For example, the LSDP was pleasantly surprised that the previously inactive Lithuanian workers were eager to show their dissatisfaction with the tsarist government and their affinity with workers of other nationalities. On the other hand, the party judged the Lithuanian action to be limited and uneven, suggesting that the people did not yet fully understand their own interests or the general situation. Party commentators noted, too, that inexperienced strikers and demonstrators, once out in the streets, did not always know what to do or how to sing revolutionary songs. Finally, joint efforts of the Lithuanians and the Jews produced somewhat ambivalent feelings among the former. For example, when the Russian governor suggested to the Kaunas workers that instead of striking they should beat up the Jews, whom he blamed for much of the labor unrest, the crowd failed to heed the advice.[19] In Šiauliai, however, misgivings chilled the Lithuanian demonstrators when they saw Jewish slogans imprinted on a red banner. Such a novel sight contributed to an untimely end of the demonstration. The incident, in turn, spurred the LSDP to work for better understanding between the two ethnic groups.[20]

Like many other critics of the old regime, the LSDP welcomed the revolution of 1905, thinking that it would lead to the collapse of tsarist despotism. Seeking insights into revolutionary dynamics, party analysts offered a comparison between the civil unrest of 1905 and the Polish-Lithuanian uprisings against the Russians staged in 1830 and 1863. In a style that mixed conventional analysis and Marxist notions, they remarked that the scene of revolutionary action had now shifted from the rural areas to cities and towns. Relying on the strike as the principal means of class action, the proletariat alone was said to possess the compulsive influence in inciting and stimulating people's efforts which was necessary for the success of the revolution. Finally, the leaders of the LSDP posited unity among Russia's subject nationalities as the only counterweight to the advantages which the highly developed weapons technology gave to the tsarist military establishment.[21]

Party Conclaves

Attempting to assume leadership of the revolutionary activity in Lithuania, the central committee of the LSDP convened to review the course of events and to lay down the party's immediate objectives. In a manifesto dated January 12/25, 1905, it articulated the following demands: an immediate end of the war; unity with the Russian workers in order to replace the autocracy with a constitutional government; freedom for Lithuania, Poland, Finland, the Ukraine, and other nationalities to negotiate an autonomous relationship with Russia; a league of nations in which Lithuania would exist as a distinct entity, with a government determined by its own *Seimas* meeting in Vilnius; a democratic Lithuania granting equal rights to its own national minorities; and the establishment of government agencies to look after the interests of workers, especially their right to guaranteed employment. To see to it that these demands were met, the manifesto envisaged the formation of a provisional Lithuanian government.[22] In the coming months the theses outlined in the central committee manifesto were propagated through public meetings, political demonstrations, party publications, mass-produced appeals, urban and rural strikes, talks with various political groups, and in other ways.

To take stock of the rapidly changing situation and to consider several practical questions associated with its revolutionary activities, the LSDP held a mid-May conference in Vilnius. Reports from the party's regional organizations convinced the conferees that, while agitation over the past several months was on the upswing, a further expansion and coordination of activities was needed. Concerned with the cost such an expansion of activities was bound to bring on (particularly with expenses incurred in the production of propaganda materials, the maintenance of a secret printing press, support of agitators, and the acquisition of firearms), the conference urged all party members and sympathizers to intensify their fund-raising efforts. Regarding firearms, it was decided that their use for self-defense was justified and that the party should make them available to both individual members and primary organizations. On two other matters, the delegates first instructed the central committee to prepare the draft of a revised party program for the next congress and then applauded the way it polemicized against the Kapsukas group.[23]

Of particular concern to the May conferees was the nature and extent of the party's involvement in provincial towns and rural communities. As reported previously, what troubled the LSDP leaders in the past was both the late start of their operations in the agricultural sector and the nature of their support there. In his memoirs Kairys noted that "the LSDP felt somewhat guilty about its delayed work in the countryside."[24] Further, when the party commenced its activities in the rural areas, it sought adherents wherever it could find them. As a result of such an indiscriminate drive, the party came to depend largely on young farmers for support, while its ties with hired help and the landless peasants were weak. Besides, Kairys also conceded that, as far as inroads on the rural labor were concerned, the LSDP lagged behind the Kapsukas-led *Draugas* group with which it was about to unite.[25]

The adoption of the "penitence resolution," as Kairys later termed it,[26] meant that the May conference set out to correct these strategic flaws. Having readily admitted that their propaganda campaign in the countryside was until now aimed primarily at the farmers, the delegates decided to concentrate their future efforts on the village proletariat, presumably including such low-income sectors of the rural population as farm labor, landless peasants, and the small holders of land. Alluding to sporadic rural disturbances, as well as to strikes which the party was planning to incite on large estates, the conferees further stipulated that these efforts should combine economic complaints and political demands. The latter included partial boycott of the tsarist government with a view to its ultimate displacement in Lithuania.[27]

In June 1905 party leaders again were summoned to Vilnius, this time to the sixth congress of the LSDP. Although no major new decisions were made there, a number of earlier policies and procedures were reviewed, amended, or clarified. Apart from several technical matters, the resolutions of the congress fell within four themes: aspects of historical development, national aspirations, leadership of the revolutionary movement, and methods of revolutionary action.[28] In a concise statement on the stages of historical development, the delegates said that, since only the advance of capitalism could lead to an increase in the number of workers and in class antagonism, both of which were considered desirable outcomes, they rejected all vestiges of feudalism, including redemption payments, use of unpaid labor, peasant land leases, and other burdensome past practices. Although the conferees appeared to welcome the escalation of class strife, their pledge to support the democratic aspirations of other social groups imparted a sense of moderation to their stance. Relatedly, while the congress frowned on the survivals of the feudal past, it was nevertheless opposed to the partition of landed estates among the peasants. Instead, it merely said that expropriated land and forests should become the property of the Lithuanian nation. Presumably, the contemplated confiscation applied to the land which the Russian state owned in its Lithuanian provinces. While generally the LSDP favored the abolition of private ownership in land, it stopped short of fomenting discord between the poorer section of the peasantry and the estate owners, a tactic that may have been due in part to the influence of West European social democratic parties whose agrarian programs neglected the question of large landownership.[29]

Concerning future ties with Russia and other states, the congress restated the party's maximal ambition formulated in 1896–1897—the establishment of a democratic republic of Lithuania which would then band together with other neighboring countries to form a federal union. Relatedly, the beginnings of social democratic activity in Belorussia prompted the delegates to express their hope that this particular neighbor would join such a federation as one of its member states.

The congress made a number of decisions bearing on the direction of the revolutionary movement. Viewing the LSDP as an organized revolutionary force capable of providing the needed leadership, it dismissed the idea of a special committee to oversee revolutionary activities in Lithuania. (However, to assist the party in raising funds and purchasing arms, the congress agreed to set up a subsidiary body which would function in foreign countries.) Basically, with respect to attitude toward other Marxist parties in the area, the LSDP seemed well-disposed toward the Kapsukas group and the Jewish Bund but kept its distance from the PPS and the RSDLP. First of all, the congress instructed its central committee to hold talks with the Kapsukas splinter group aimed at reuniting it with the LSDP. These particular efforts ended in success when, in the fall of 1905, the group discontinued its operations, while its members joined the ranks of the LSDP.[30] As for the Bund, the LSDP readily conceded a large measure of autonomy, in matters of both party organization and goal specification, to this Jewish organization. On the other hand, the LSDP expected the Bund members, as Lithuanian residents, to support and help achieve the Lithuanian national aspirations formulated by the LSDP. The LSDP offered the view that only in a future democratic Lithuania, federated with other area states, would the Jewish proletariat be able to fulfill its economic and cultural needs. It propounded its theses in a special appeal intended for the Jewish nationals, asking for their backing.[31] When, later in December, a member of the Bund rose to address the Grand Diet of Vilnius and wish it success in closing ranks for the good of their common cause (which, incidentally, he did in flawless Lithuanian), the mass audience responded with warm applause.[32] As in the past, however, the parallelism of interests between the Lithuanian and the Jewish parties was genuine but limited. The two often united in a mutually supportive action aimed at organizing strikes and anti-government demonstrations, procuring propaganda circulars, preventing mob violence against the Jews (even through suggested killing of its perpetrators), and reviewing innumerable practical questions.[33] Yet they could not bridge the gap left by the national question. The followers of the Bund, who generally regarded themselves as Russian Marxists, never endorsed the LSDP advocacy of Lithuania's partial dissociation from Russia. It is true that some Jews regretted the Bund indifference to the struggle for Lithuania's emancipation; they leaned toward Der Junge Bund (The Young Bund), a group considered to be free of RSDLP influence, and demonstrated their support of the Lithuanian cause.[34] But these were atypical cases.

The members of the congress were decidedly unenthusiastic about the Polish and the Russian parties. Calling the PPS extension in Lithuania divisive and its political program incompatible with that of the LSDP, they denied the validity of PPS operations in Lithuania, adding that the LSDP was capable of serving the needs of those Polish-speaking workers who lived in that country. Incidentally, the PPS affiliate in Lithuania, which leaned toward the LSDP, soon brought its activities to an end, thus increasing the Lithuanian party's membership rolls and widening the range of its political life. The leadership of the LSDP was augmented by the inclusion of such merger advocates as Pranas Eidukevičius (1869–1926), Kazimierz Pietkiewicz (1861–1934), Petr Shumov, and other former members of the PPS.[35] The last of these Marxian groups, the RSDLP, was judged detrimental to the interests of Lithuanian workers. In the eyes of the LSDP, the denial in practice of the right to national self-determination and a centralized mode of party operations earned the Russians their unfavorable assessment.

The June congress also dwelt on the manner of party operations. From a strategic view, it insisted that everywhere people's economic demands be linked with political solutions formulated by the LSDP.

The congress further stipulated that the urban and rural proletariat was to constitute the party's main social base. Finally, explicitly rejecting the use of economic terror, the leaders of the LSDP hoped to revolutionize the populace by such peaceful methods as persuasion, agitation, boycott, strikes, increased support of the party, and the like. Only in regard to exceptional cases did the congress authorize recourse to terror as a means of self-defense. In the discussion which follows, we shall seek to review some of the methods advocated, namely, strikes, demonstrations, and written appeals.

In retrospect, the nature of LSDP decisions in January, May, and June, 1905, mirrored the optimistic cast of mind which distinguished the early period of the revolution, when autocracy was in retreat. Commitment to psychological modernization, democratization of the political system, a reordering of relations between Russia and its increasingly self-conscious nationalities, faith in a revolutionized people, and willingness to assume leadership of the revolutionary forces in Lithuania all attest to a brightened outlook that enveloped the policymakers of the LSDP. Theirs was an exuberant, if momentary, authenticity.

5

Strikes and Demonstrations

Urban Unrest

Touched off by the January convulsion in St. Petersburg, the urban unrest in Lithuania continued intermittently throughout the spring and summer of 1905, culminating in demonstrations, general strikes, and politicized funeral processions in the closing months of that year. The general strike which paralyzed the Russian cities early in October reverberated in Lithuania's municipalities.[1] In Vilnius, where the crowds of demonstrators swelled to 40,000 people, it lasted from October 13/26 to October 22/November 4. In the interval between October 16/29 and October 24/November 6, general strikes erupted in Kaunas, Šiauliai, Panevėžys, and several smaller towns. Before the October strikes drew to a close, eighteen people were dead—sixteen of them in Vilnius and two in other parts of the country. The Lithuanian casualty total for the entire year included at least forty-two fatalities.[2]

Urban strife recurred on a smaller scale in December in conjunction with the attempted armed uprising in Moscow. A six-day general strike started in Vilnius on December 11/24 and in Kaunas on the following day. Other types of political action took place in various provincial towns.[3] Ordinarily, various locally prominent revolutionary groups shared in the coordination of strike activity in October and December. In Vilnius, however, political direction issued from two sources; the LSDP and the PPS in Lithuania set up one joint committee, while the RSDLP, the SDKPiL, and the Jewish Bund formed another. As noted earlier, this bifurcation of political leadership stemmed from differences over the ultimate goals of the revolution.[4] Consistent with the program of the LSDP, the followers of the first committee urged the creation of a federal state, but those supporting the second group sought the convocation of an all-Russian constituent assembly.

The 1905 strikes indicated the unsettling character of that year in at least three respects: the number of people who participated in the stoppage of work, the dispersion of strikes, and their penetration into agricultural areas. Although the total of some 29,000 urban workers involved in economic strikes was not very large, its significance increases when it is compared with the low numbers of strikers during the years both preceding and following 1905. (Figure 1 gives approximate numbers of workers who engaged in economic strikes between 1895 and 1914.) For example, the total number of strikers for the ten pre-revolutionary years came to only 15,970, roughly one half of the 1905 figure. The importance of the 1905 total increases further when participants in the so-called political strikes, estimated at 46,300,[5] are added to the number of those making primarily economic demands. According to one estimation, as much as 82 percent of the total labor force in the Kaunas and Vilnius guberniias took part in strike activity during 1905.[6] While typically the local chapters of various social democratic parties would join together in an attempt to direct this urban unrest, the role of labor unions needs to be recognized, too. The

Figure 1.   Participants in Economic Strikes, 1895–1914. *Source:* Adapted from E. Griškūnaitė, *Darbininkų judėjimas Lietuvoje, 1895–1914 m.* (Vilnius, 1971), pp. 97, 254, 258, 260, 287, and 292.

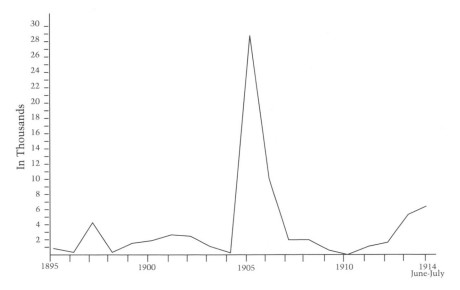

organization of workers intensified in the closing months of 1905, resulting in the formation of twenty-five authorized labor unions by the following year.[7]

The dispersal of strikes over a relatively wide area was another sign of the exceptional nature of labor unrest in 1905. Excluding the outbreaks of 1901 and 1902, which may have been related to the worsening of economic conditions throughout the empire, some 87 percent of strikes during the pre-revolutionary years, as table 1 indicates, occurred in the city of Vilnius. Only in 1905 did they spread to other Lithuanian towns.[8] The penetration of the outlying towns was bound to modify the social character of that body of workers which was induced to participate either in political action or in the struggle for its material well-being.

Agricultural Strikes

The year 1905 witnessed yet another unusual phenomenon, the agricultural strike. Although available statistical information about strikes in the agricultural sector is incomplete, several tentative observations are nevertheless possible. Throughout the course of that year there must have been approximately 166 rural strikes in the Kaunas

Table 1   Number of Strikes, 1895–1904

Year	Number of Strikes	Percentage of Total in Vilnius
1895	58	96.55
1896	24	87.50
1897	53	75.47
1898	18	83.33
1899	12	75.00
1900	23	91.30
1901	21	47.62
1902	28	53.57
1903	22	86.36
1904	7	100.00
Total	266	80.07

Sources: E. Griškūnaitė, Darbininkų judėjimas Lietuvoje, 1895–1914 m. (Vilnius, 1971), pp. 92, 97–98 and 137; V. Merkys, "Vilniaus darbininkų streikai 1895–1900 metais," in Lietuvos TSR Mokslų Akademijos Darbai, ser. A, no. 1 (1959), p. 173.

guberniia and the Lithuanian parts of the Suwałki guberniia. Unlike the dwindling industrial strikes, the agricultural ones continued to occur throughout 1906, reaching an annual total of 141 for the two guberniias. Their total for 1907, however, declined to 16. Agricultural labor in the Vilnius guberniia was also engaged in limited strike activity, but information about strikes there is virtually nonexistent. The grand total of known agricultural strikes for the entire revolutionary period of 1905–1907, including those in the Lithuanian districts of the Vilnius guberniia about which information is available, was 328. Of these, about 73 percent resulted in full or partial satisfaction of labor demands, while in the rest of them the outcome favored the landlords or remained undetermined.[9]

Almost all of the strikes in the countryside took place on large landed estates. (The few isolated strikes against medium farmers were omitted from the above totals.) Reportedly, the LSDP had hoped that strikers' demands for higher pay, shorter hours, better food, elimination of piecework, and improved medical care and educational opportunities would make estate farming unprofitable, thereby inducing their owners to sell land to the smallholders at prices the latter could afford.[10] Initially many farmers were behind the LSDP strike initiative, hoping to cash in on the adversities of the struck estates: "The workers will strike, the landlords will go broke, and we will buy their land."[11] However, the realization that agricultural workers could extend the strike campaign to take in all farms relying on hired help soon dampened their enthusiasm for action against the landed nobility.

Rural strikes were typically led by local social democratic organizations, initially by the Kapsukas group and later, after its merger with the LSDP, by the latter party in the Kaunas and Suwałki guberniias, while the RSDLP displayed at least a token initiative in the Vilnius guberniia. To assist the progress of the agricultural strikes in 1906, the LSDP dispatched twelve organizers to the two guberniias, five to Suwałki and seven to Kaunas.[12] Consistent with party policy, LSDP organizers and other leaders did their best to prevent unauthorized behavior, such as arson, plunder, theft, drunkenness, and the destruction of property. Due to heavy emphasis on a pacific settlement of disputes, only a few manor houses were looted and burned in Lithuania, which was so unlike the conflagration in other Baltic regions or the guberniias of central Russia.[13]

Clearly, the presence of party activists tended to politicize the agrarian strike movement. Social democratic leaflets, political speeches, red banners, and revolutionary songs and slogans often accompanied workers' economic demands.[14] Yet, in spite of LSDP intentions, a purposeful correlation of political and economic activities was not always achieved. After all, as some have pointed out, the economically motivated rural strikes, which broke out during the busy season in the summer of 1905, were not timed to coincide with the height of political action attained in the fall of that same year.[15] Similarly, a major LSDP directive to rural laborers issued in mid-1906 was devoid of any political content.[16]

Political Demonstrations

In addition to strikes, revolutionary action assumed the form of political meetings and demonstrations. What follows is an overview of these activities in the Lithuanian countryside, i.e., in provincial towns and villages exclusive of larger cities. According to one estimate that may have erred on the side of caution, at least 240 political meetings and demonstrations occurred in 1905.[17] (Increased government repression soon brought these rallies to a virtual end; their incidence in 1906 was so low as to warrant their omission from this review.) As figure 2 indicates, demonstrations during the early months of 1905 were very few, adding up to only 4 percent of that year's total by the end of May. The total for the following three months, however, rose to 15 percent. Higher frequency of demonstrations probably reechoed the revolutionary disturbances that broke out in many parts of the empire, particularly in neighboring Latvia. Additionally, two domestic factors quickened the energies of local activists, the resolve of the June LSDP conferees to revolutionize the country and the influx of students after the end of the academic year. When autumn came, political demonstrations tapered off to a stop, but then resumed in October and peaked in November and December. November alone represented 53 percent of the year's total, while together the last two months of the year accounted for close to three-fourths of such political manifestations conducted in 1905.

The year-end outburst of antigovernment activity was caused, first of all, by the proclamation of civil liberties incorporated in the tsar's manifesto of October 17/30, a move which led many to believe that Russia was evolving into a constitutional monarchy. Another

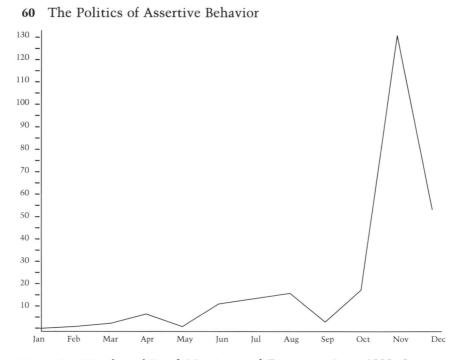

Figure 2.   Number of Rural Meetings and Demonstrations, 1905. *Source:* Adapted from A. Tyla, *1905 metų revoliucija Lietuvos kaime* (Vilnius, 1968), pp. 222–25.

major catalyst in the Lithuanian resistance to Russian authorities was the Grand Diet of Vilnius, an unprecedented two-day convention which met on November 21/December 4 to consult on the state of affairs in Lithuania and impart direction to that country's political efforts. Its 2,000-odd delegates represented various political groups and points of view, including that offered by the LSDP. Calling the existing tsarist government "our fiercest enemy," the convention urged the people of Lithuania to work, together with others, for the overthrow of absolutism. The delegates further demanded autonomy for Lithuania, including a separate legislature that would sit in Vilnius. Somewhat incongruously perhaps, they also said that future relations between Lithuania and other subject nationalities should be put on a federal basis, clearly a gesture toward an LSDP ideal. Finally, the Grand Diet recommended the following immediate steps: boycott of administrative and judicial agencies of local government, refusal to pay taxes, opposition to the draft, keeping children away from Russian schools, the closing of government liquor stores, and organization of urban and rural strikes.[18] The unanimous consent accorded to these resolutions grew out of numerous compromises designed to consolidate all political groups and individual activists into a common front to oppose the Russian autocracy.

Some of the delegates to the Grand Diet took part in two other meetings whose decisions went further than the relatively moderate resolutions of that Vilnius convention. Influenced by the formation of the Peasants' Union in Russia earlier in July, about eight hundred representatives convened on November 22/December 5 to found their own counterpart. Like the Grand Diet itself, the Lithuanian Peasant Union was emphatic about self-government by a legislature in Vilnius. Moreover, it demanded the restitution of the land which the Russian government seized in 1863 and recommended specific means for wrecking the apparatus of government.[19]

On November 23/December 6, the day following the adjournment of the Grand Diet, the LSDP arranged a separate meeting attended by some two hundred representatives of rural laborers and small holders of land who had been participating in the work of the convention. The meeting first endorsed the decisions of the Grand Diet and then, under the sway of radical opinion, urged the acquisition of firearms and the establishment of a militia designed to protect the rebellious populace from the tsarist police, pro-government mobs known as the Black Hundreds, fake socialists, and other perils. Departing from LSDP policy made at that party's congress in June, the meeting also called for the formation of local revolutionary committees which, in the event of a popular uprising against the tsarist authorities, would assume governmental powers and, in consultation with the LSDP, continue to exercise them until the convocation of a Lithuanian legislature in Vilnius. Finally, it issued explicit instructions for dismantling the existing organs of government and creating new ones.[20]

The resolutions of the Grand Diet (and of the two ancillary meetings) flooded the Lithuanian countryside. They were read, discussed, and acclaimed at public meetings and during political demonstrations which reached their climactic point toward the end of 1905. Insistence on native languages, rather than Russian, as the media of instruction in Lithuania's schools, opposition to military draft, refusal to pay taxes, election of new government officials to replace the tsarist incumbents, and other types of dissidence all indicated an increasingly defiant local behavior.[21] Numerous reports circulating among tsarist officials suggested that "laws were openly violated" in various parts of the country, that in some areas "complete anarchy" was achieved, and that opposition to constituted authority "turned into an open revolution." The city of Vilnius was said to have been in the hands of the revolutionaries.[22]

A review of some ninety-odd political meetings and demonstrations reported in *Darbininkų balsas* and *Darbininkas* (The Worker)[23] leads one to believe that an overwhelming majority of them was sponsored by the LSDP, probably the only Marxist party having a network of primary organizations in the rural interior of Lithuania. In some cases, however, the initiative emanated from the Democratic party or the Jewish Bund. Other sources also established a positive correlation between the level of social democratic activity in a given area and the number of such political manifestations there.[24] An LSDP nucleus in the countryside was typically reinforced by an assortment of area activists consisting of high school students and urban laborers assigned various tasks there. Further, prompted either by appeals for help or by their own sense of obligation, many Lithuanian students attending institutions of higher education in Moscow, St. Petersburg, Tartu, Warsaw, and elsewhere interrupted their studies in the closing months of 1905 for the purpose of joining the revolutionary movement in their own country. Finally, the LSDP was variously aided by prominent individuals favorably disposed to its efforts, by members of the professional class, and by organizers newly recruited from the lower-income sectors of the rural population.[25] These individuals and groups taken together constituted the local core of revolutionaries.

Strange Spectacles

On the basis of reports published in the two newspapers cited above, several additional observations are offered. To the Lithuanian rural interior political demonstrations were a strange spectacle. Unknown agitators, red or black banners displaying slogans inscribed in letters of gold, and shots fired in the air all initially produced a reserved or even openly hostile popular reaction. People's apprehension, however, was tempered with a touch of curiosity. When the assembled spectators realized that the "sermons," as the harangues of agitators were dubbed, dealt with their everyday concerns, an enthusiastic reception usually dispelled their initial misgivings. As the year progressed and people learned more about socialist "preachers," political demonstrations generally became welcome occurrences.

Not surprisingly, the Catholic clergy was ill-disposed toward socialist-inspired political rallies. When clerical attitude was reported in the press, it was generally found to be negative, while actions sympathetic to the protest movement were few and far between.[26] The newspaper accounts used in this survey, as well as the content analysis of socialist appeals presented below, suggest that in 1905 the anti-socialist opposition of the clergy was more intense than the LSDP challenge to church-supported values.

Violence, as a concomitant of these political demonstrations, was relatively restrained. Its occurrence could be linked to some extent with intervention of the police. Although police intrusion itself did not evince any kind of a pattern, when it did materialize, violence usually followed. Some accounts, however, seemed to indicate that the presence of the police acted as a deterrent to excessive crowd behavior. Occasionally, the eruption of violence was completely unrelated to interference of the authorities. Responsibility in such cases usually lay with the demonstrators who felt that, under the circumstances, manhandling the police was the proper course of action. A higher incidence of violence, finally, may have resulted from a divergence between the leaders of the LSDP, who cautioned against extreme forms of action, and some of its local functionaries who knew no moderation. These were known to have felt that servants of the tsarist regime should either be wiped out or taught a lesson.

In terms of programmatic import, the political messages which the demonstrators displayed on their banners, heard from their speakers, or propagated by means of printed leaflets were broadly divisible into two categories. The first and clearly the more popular category constituted a verbal protest against the autocratic regime. This protest was essentially negative in the sense that it opposed the tsarist political system or its component parts. For example, some political messages decried an assortment of government injustices, while others urged the people to withhold their support of the government. Most messages, however, demanded the end of autocracy itself. Political statements found in the second category, although communicated with a lower frequency than those in the first, were the more positive of the two, for they sought to impress the general public with selected images of the Lithuanian future. It seemed that the availability of constructive alternatives was needed to impart greater meaning to the revolutionary endeavor. The main attributes of that projected imagery were three: government by the people, a legislature in Vilnius, and freedom and independence for Lithuania.

6

Written Appeals

L ike other revolutionaries, the Lithuanian social democrats employed written appeals as a means for disseminating their views
and galvanizing the public into purposeful activity. The following content analysis results from an examination of twenty-two such
statements issued by the central organs of the LSDP. (See List of LSDP
Appeals compiled in appendix B.) Except for one document dated May
1906, all of them came out between the start of the Russian-Japanese
war in February 1904 and the elections to the first State Duma in
March 1906. Twenty-one of these documents were authored by the
LSDP, while one was signed by four area parties—Belorussian, Latvian,
Polish, and Lithuanian. The available total, although somewhat less
than all-inclusive, comprises all of the most important LSDP manifestos for the above period. Four of the twenty-two documents were
produced and circulated soon after the outbreak of the Russian-Japanese war in 1904, while another four came out in 1906. The remaining
fourteen were released in 1905, one as the consequence of Bloody
Sunday in January, the rest during the middle and the second half of
that year. These appeals and their local adaptations were reproduced
in numbers of copies whose total was estimated to be close to 450,000.

The analysis seeks to determine the relative emphases given to
different subject-matter categories in LSDP appeals. Where appropriate,
it attempts to show direction as well, that is, to indicate whether the
communication concerning the particular subject is given favorable
(positive), neutral, or unfavorable (negative) treatment. The unit of
analysis is the word, including word compounds and their synonyms.
When the relevant words were counted, arranged, and translated into
percentages, twenty-one subject-matter categories were summated

Table 2 Classes and Categories of Political Objects (Percentages)

Class		Category	
System as		Existing System: General References	10.0
General Object	17.0	Existing System: Physical Character	1.0
		Existing System: Integrative Change	1.0
		Modification of System: Political	2.2
		Modification of System: National	2.4
		Modification of System: Ideological	0.4
Component		Constituent Units	6.0
Parts of the System	63.0	Central Government	1.4
		Local Government	8.2
		Other Structures	3.5
		Ethnic Groups	4.8
		Social-Occupational Groups	17.1
		Policies and Decisions	22.0
Self as Object	20.0	Content or Quality of Personal Power	2.7
		Content or Quality of Personal Rights	0.2
		Content or Quality of Personal Obligation	0.1
		Sense of Personal Competence	0.3
		Belief in Change	0.8
		Strategies of Access to Influence: Minimal	7.3
		Strategies of Access to Influence: Moderate	6.4
		Strategies of Access to Influence: Maximal	2.2
Total Percentage	100.0		
Total Number	4,428.0		

into three classes of political objects: the political system as a whole, the component parts of the system, and the self as political actor. Developed by Gabriel A. Almond and Sidney Verba,* this classification of objects was altered to fit the needs of the present study.

Table 2 arranges a total of 4,428 recording units according to classes and categories of political objects. Evidently the component parts of the system taken together formed the main focus of LSDP attention, representing 63 percent of the relevant aspects of the content. Emphases given to the other two classes of objects were considerably lower—17 percent to the system as a whole, and 20 percent to the self. As for the

*Gabriel A. Almond and Sidney Verba, *The Civic Culture* (Boston and Toronto: Little, Brown, 1965).

subject-matter categories, the frequency with which the policy items appeared in the content (22 percent) points up a major concern about issues. In addition, relatively high distribution scores accompany two other categories, the social-occupational groups (17.1 percent) and the clustered strategies of access to influence (15.9 percent). These two scores are symptomatic of both a pronounced class-mindedness of the LSDP and its preoccupation with the means of revolutionary change, attributes associated with Marxist parties generally.

Table 3 has additional data on the system as the focus of LSDP attention. It shows that the combined score on the three existing system categories accounts for 70.7 percent of the class total, while that on system-modification constitutes 29.3 percent. Within the former grouping, a very high incidence of such system symbols as "tsar" or "tsarist government" makes general references to the existing system a category of overwhelming LSDP preoccupation. Additionally, of the 59 percent of references to this category, the percentage of positive attitude indicators is nil. References to other aspects of the existing system, such as perceptions of its strength or its self-perpetuating initiatives, are likewise highly negative. Of the subject-matter categories dealing with system-modification, the frequency of occurrence of ideological characteristics, such as socialism, is the lowest—2.2 percent. Mention of political changes, or democratization, reaches a total of 13.1 percent, while references to various forms of Lithuanian separatism make up 14 percent. As expected, the proportions of items favoring system-modification average in the vicinity of 100 percent.

Table 3   System as General Object, by Category (Percentages)

Category		Direction Within Category	
	Positive	Neutral	Negative
Existing System: General References 59.0	0.0	3.4	96.6
Existing System: Physical Character 6.0	8.9	0.0	91.1
Existing System: Integrative Change 5.7	2.3	2.3	95.4
Modification of System: Political 13.1	96.0	1.0	3.0
Modification of System: National 14.0	100.0	0.0	0.0
Modification of System: Ideological 2.2	100.0	0.0	0.0
Total Percentage 100.0			
Total Number 756.0			

Table 4   Component Parts of the System by Category and
Subcategory (Percentages)

| Category | Subcategory | | Within Subcategory | | |
			Positive	Neutral	Negative
Constituent Units	Russia	11.6	3.2	61.3	35.5
9.6	Lithuania	71.2	47.4	52.6	0.0
	Others	17.2	69.6	30.4	0.0
Central Government 2.3	Legislative, Executive, Judiciary	3.2			
	Bureaucracy	96.8			
	Law Enforcement	0.0			
Local Government 13.1	Legislative, Executive, Judiciary	9.6			
	Bureaucracy	76.2			
	Law Enforcement	14.2			
Other Structures 5.5	Church	1.3	0.0	50.0	50.0
	Military	59.5			
	Political Parties: LSDP	39.2	90.0	10.0	0.0
Ethnic Groups 7.6	Belorussians	2.8	66.7	16.7	16.6
	Jews	21.6	93.5	4.3	2.2
	Latvians	5.7	91.7	8.3	0.0
	Lithuanians	44.1	96.8	1.1	2.1
	Poles	4.2	88.9	11.1	0.0
	Russians	10.8	47.8	17.4	34.8
	Others: Lithuanian-American	3.3	42.9	57.1	0.0
	Others: Japanese	7.5	56.3	43.7	0.0
Social-Occupational Groups 27.1	Clergy	1.1	0.0	12.5	87.5
	Rich	11.5	1.2	1.1	97.7
	Oppressors	7.4	0.0	0.0	100.0
	Poor	3.8	93.1	6.9	0.0
	Capitalists	2.8	4.8	9.5	85.7
	Merchants	1.1	0.0	0.0	100.0
	Intelligentsia	1.1	62.5	37.5	0.0

| Subcategory | Direction | | |
Distinctions	Positive	Neutral	Negative
Existing	0.0	0.0	0.0	0.0
Future	100.0	50.0	0.0	50.0
Existing	93.4	0.0	10.5	89.5
Future	6.6	100.0	0.0	0.0
Existing	0.0	0.0	0.0	0.0
Future	0.0	0.0	0.0	0.0
Existing	8.6	33.3	0.0	66.7
Future	91.4	90.6	9.4	0.0
Existing	24.8	0.0	0.0	100.0
Future	75.2	63.6	36.4	0.0
Existing	96.2	0.0	2.0	98.0
Future	3.8	100.0	0.0	0.0
Existing	70.3	6.3	20.3	73.4
Future	29.7	100.0	0.0	0.0

Table 4 (continued)

| Category | Subcategory | | Within Subcategory | | |
			Positive	Neutral	Negative
Social-	Peasants—				
Occupational	General	4.5	91.2	8.8	0.0
Groups	Landless				
27.1	Peasants	0.5	100.0	0.0	0.0
(continued)	Smallholders	1.7	92.3	7.7	0.0
	Medium				
	Farmers	0.0	0.0	0.0	0.0
	Large				
	Landholders	5.8	6.8	38.6	54.6
	Artisans	0.4	100.0	0.0	0.0
	Workers—				
	General	30.5	97.0	2.2	0.8
	Urban Workers	1.3	90.0	10.0	0.0
	Rural Workers	8.7	98.5	0.0	1.5
	Soldiers	9.5	62.5	8.3	29.2
	Others	8.3	79.4	20.6	0.0
Policies &	Foreign	3.9			
Decisions					
34.8	Domestic	81.3			
	Nationality	6.2			
	Military	3.2			
	Other: Russian-				
	Japanese War	5.4	0.0	34.6	65.4
Total Percentage	100.0				
Total Number	2,789.0				

Data on the component parts of the system are summarized in table 4 which, in addition to subject-matter categories, introduces a series of subcategories, with or without further distinctions. As already indicated, the percentage totals point to the heavy emphasis on policy questions (34.8 percent of the class total) and on social-economic groups (27.1 percent), while scores on other categories are significantly lower. Regarding issue-orientation, the high subcategory percent of 81.3 attests to LSDP absorption in domestic policies. Further, the highly positive mention of future policy direction exceeds references to the existing policies, most of which are negative.

| Subcategory | Direction | | |
Distinctions	Positive	Neutral	Negative
Existing	97.4	0.0	2.7	97.3
Future	2.6	100.0	0.0	0.0
Existing	31.5	1.2	3.2	95.6
Future	68.5	98.9	0.7	0.4
Existing	40.0	0.0	0.0	100.0
Future	60.0	86.1	2.8	11.1
Existing	87.1	0.0	22.2	77.8
Future	12.9	100.0	0.0	0.0

Scores on the different subcategories of social and economic groups provide a measure of importance attributed to workers. Considered as a whole, they produce 40.5 percent of the category total. Quite obviously, this professed social base of the LSDP registers very high approval scores—90 percent or better. The cohort of groups (clergy, capitalists, merchants, large landholders, and such amorphous types as oppressors and the rich) which the LSDP dubbed supporters of the regime and portrayed disapprovingly represent approximately 30 percent of the category total. Incidentally, at a time when many Catholic clergymen pursued a moderate or conservative course of action, the relative frequency of references to them (1.1 percent) must be regarded as surprisingly low. Equally interesting is the omission of references to medium farmers. The LSDP communicators may have been in a dilemma. As Marxists, they may have found it ideologically inappropriate to give the medium farmers positive scores but, as politicians who enjoyed a measure of support by this particular segment of rural society, they must have been equally averse to alienating them with negative ones.

Table 4 further records a 9.6 percent measure of emphasis laid on various constituent units of the system and another 20.9 percent given to the combined categories of government institutions and other structures. Clearly, the attention fixed on bureaucracy is much greater than that focused on other government institutions. Whether central or local, the existing bureaucracy is perceived in highly negative terms. Concerning such other structures as the church, the military, and political parties, which together hold a relatively low measure of emphasis (5.5 percent of the class total), it is interesting to find the LSDP as the only political party to which textual references are made. This failure to mention other revolutionary parties probably means that the LSDP communicators sought to improve their party's visibility and enhance its leadership role. Finally, various ethnic groups are given 7.6 percent of the class total, with the Lithuanians and the Jews registering relatively high frequencies of occurrence, while the Russians receive less mention. Scores on the remaining groups are low. References to Jews, Latvians, Lithuanians, and Poles are highly positive, whereas those naming Belorussians and particularly the Russians have significant neutral and negative attributes. For convenience, references to Lithuanian-Americans and to Japanese are entered here as special subcategories, the former as an addressee to whom one LSDP appeal was particularly directed, the latter as another way of gauging the LSDP outlook on the Russian-Japanese war. A glance at the policy and ethnic group categories suggests that references to that war are either negative or neutral, while scores on the people of Japan are either positive or neutral. These somewhat asymmetric measures of bias arise from the LSDP assessment of the nature of the war and its impact. Since the ordinary people were presumed to have no stake in the war, there are no favorable references to it. By contrast, because the Japanese were viewed either as victims of Russian imperialism or,

Table 5 Self as Object, by Category (Percentages)

Category		Direction Within Category		
		Positive	Neutral	Negative
Content or Quality of Personal Power	13.7	83.5	0.0	16.5
Content or Quality of Personal Rights	1.1	30.0	0.0	70.0
Content or Quality of Personal Obligation	0.4	100.0	0.0	0.0
Sense of Personal Competence	1.7	86.7	0.0	13.3
Belief in Change	3.9	100.0	0.0	0.0
Strategies of Access to Influence: Minimal	36.5	99.0	0.0	1.0
Strategies of Access to Influence: Moderate	31.9	100.0	0.0	0.0
Strategies of Access to Influence: Maximal	10.8	97.9	2.1	0.0
Total Percentage	100.0			
Total Number	883.0			

when triumphant, as agents of system-destabilization, there is no unfavorable mention of them.

Finally, consider the data in table 5 which focus attention on the role of the individual and the types of strategies designed to improve access to influence. Although such themes as personal power and belief in change receive some mention, it is obvious that the authors of LSDP appeals were concerned primarily with the recommended course of individual behavior. Various minimal strategies (36.5 percent of the class total) include references to assertive personal behavior, the intermediate ones (31.9 percent) usually advert to boycott of the tsarist government, while maximal alternatives (10.8 percent) mention revolution or the use of arms. The proportions of items favoring these strategies are exceptionally high.

___

Image and Control

___

Popular Skepticism

The preceding analyses which have been mainly under review here have perforce depended more on the perspectives of party insiders than on those of the ordinary persons to whom their communication was directed. In the discussion which follows, we shall take a brief look at the reverse effusion of people's reactions to the socialist arrival. Of particular interest to us will be the conflicting images of socialists and the party's capacity to exercise directing influence over the energies it helped to unleash.

The descent of the socialists upon the Lithuanian countryside, which began soon after the outbreak of the Russian-Japanese war in 1904 and intensified until it came to a climax toward the end of 1905, elicited the kind of negativism that is commonly associated with ignorance and fear. The initial popular response betrayed an utter misconception about the nature of social democracy. In the eyes of some people the socialists were nothing but a band of horse thieves, robbers, murderers, and arsonists. Others viewed them as someone likely to steal bacon and loot the granaries. Finally, there were those who damned them as licentious heathens.[1]

Popular skepticism about the socialists also derived from their "atheism." To a conservative clerical mentality, the socialist world view was a threat to the established order, while "atheism" was a political slogan used to stir up hostility against those who propagated that view. A product of a liberal education that had shed its theological underpinning, the socialist philosophy was said to promote agnosticism among the younger generation, weaken the foundations of Christian morality, and generally disturb the tranquillity of Lithuania's rural way of life. Further, LSDP adherence to such programmatic objectives as freedom of conscience, the separation of church and state, and equality of all faiths before the law aroused resentment of the church hierarchy, which in turn communicated it to the ordinary parishioners.[2] At the grass roots of political action, then, the socialist frame of mind and socialist operatives combined to jeopardize the authority of the parsonage. Branding the socialist agitators and strike leaders "atheists," the body of religious functionaries (especially its senior members) thus sought to prod the faithful to reject socialist initiatives. Years later Kairys recalled that, as far as the parsonage was concerned, the socialists were "always a plague."[3] Considering the undereducated and clerically molded character of rural Lithuania, it was not surprising to find people who believed that socialists worshiped the devil as a god and were intent on setting churches afire.[4] Needless to say, by means of written statements and oral agitation alike the party sought to allay such fears and correct wrong impressions.[5] It is entirely possible that the relative infrequency of references to the clergy in the mass-produced written appeals also stemmed from the need to skirt the religious issue.

Yet another strand of negative perception suspected the social democrats as somebody else's agents. For example, when the socialists warned the rural workers not to plunder the large estates, rumor had it that they were bribed by the landlords.[6] When the party decried the manhandling of the Jews, some accused it of selling out to that particular minority.[7] Similarly, the epithet of "horse thieves" applied to the socialists was interpreted as a crude code designation disguising the fears of the middling farmers.[8] The social democrats became the victims of bias transplants. To be sure, these adverse reactions indicated that LSDP policy directives, such as rejection of economic terror and defense of the Jews, were beginning to penetrate remote points in the countryside, but they also meant that the party's success in breaking through prejudice and social animosity was only partial.

A final type of emotive behavior directed against the social democrats issued from one of Lithuania's minorities, the Russian. Here and there members of that particular group urgently appealed for help, saying that the rebellious crowd was "threatening to slaughter the Russians" or "beat up the Orthodox," or that "two thousand armed socialists [were coming] to kill the Muscovites."[9] Apparently, a premonition of danger was felt not only by those holding various positions in the local administration but also by ordinary Russian residents. The LSDP, assuredly, did not inspire any mistreatment of the ethnic Russians; their intimidation could be ascribed to what might be termed as guilt by ethnic association with the hated Russian bureaucracy.[10] Yet on the other hand, the party was not as protective toward the Russian minority as it was toward the Jewish.

Euphoric Mood

The foregoing overview sought to identify both the sources and the types of negative feedback. Although it is difficult to estimate the volume of this adverse citizen reaction, there is enough reason to think that the socialists initially met with a mixed reception. Gradually, however, people's ambivalence in attitude and behavior toward the socialists underwent a change. When the successes of the revolutionaries in Russia and the efforts of their counterparts in the nationality areas began to loosen the grip of the established political, religious, and social authorities, approbation seemed to supplant much of the suspicion and disapproval. The process of image reversal affected diverse social strata which may have included even the Catholic clergy.[11] Elevating the socialists to champions of the common people, the new mind-set invested them with ample deference and authority.[12] By mid-1905 some ventured to suggest that "power [was] in the hands of the socialists,"[13] a palpable overstatement, to be sure, but one that signified the direction and scope of attitudinal change.

People now sought advice from the socialists, wanted to enlist in their ranks, and followed their directions, while socialism exalted the popular imagination to new flights of fancy. People were eagerly awaiting socialist "preachers." When none came to their communities, they went out of their way to find them. As socialist speakers addressed the crowds, people stood motionless as though trying to take in the meaning of their words. And when the threat of police intervention materialized, the people offered them protection. Socialists were needed to help organize strikes, resolve local disputes, and avenge mothers whose daughters were seduced by police officers.[14] In the end the LSDP had to caution its supporters against an excessive entanglement of the party in such local affairs.

Increased public acceptance of the social democrats engendered willingness to affiliate with the LSDP.[15] The urban strikes and demonstrations of 1905, particularly in October–December, roused the workers to political participation, tending many of them in a socialist direction. To be sure, workers' party affiliation was often inconstant, but partisanship, especially in 1906, was clearly on the rise.[16] In rural areas, too, the year 1905 brought an increase in the number of socialist adherents. According to one report, thousands of landless peasants declared themselves socialists, each paying the agitators thirty kopecks for the privilege.[17]

In a parallel manner, the people clothed the socialists with quasi-governmental power.[18] For example, some communities insisted that the supply and sale of firewood carry the seal of LSDP approval.[19] Similarly, when government liquor stores were smashed and their cash receipts confiscated, the records were made to show that specified ruble amounts were appropriated by the social democrats.[20] When government officials wondered why taxes were not being paid, they were told by the peasants that "someone" had forbidden them to do so.[21] Finally, in some parts of the country the social democrats themselves collected taxes, gave out receipts stamped with the party seal, and reprimanded those who persisted in making payments to the established tsarist authorities.[22]

People's euphoric mood gave rise to a loose, or even naive, interpretation of the socialist promise. To some, socialism was a therapeutic force working to relieve social tensions.[23] To others, notably the village poor, it meant first and foremost the prospect of getting land. Regardless of LSDP reserve where agrarian reform was concerned, the poorer sections of the peasantry were convinced that they would obtain land. Although they were not sure who would parcel out the large estates, evidence suggests that they placed their trust increasingly in the social democrats, offering them their support in return.[24] Finally, as the following belief betrays, there were those whose conception of socialism filled them with utterly utopian hopes: "Whoever adheres to this faith will receive twenty kopecks a day and will not have to do any work."[25]

Beyond a doubt the Lithuanian social democrats helped infuse the local populace with the spirit of radical change. A fairly large nucleus of devotees trained in the ways of underground operations, a distinct pattern of organizational procedure, the frequency of structured meetings to discuss and determine the needed course of action, the great breadth of programmatic objectives, and the ability to elicit increased support from the general public all tended to project the LSDP as a party which confidently aspired to disrupt the existing political and institutional structure so that it could then build an entirely new one. In truth, however, the leaders of the LSDP were never completely free from doubt as to whether they could master the principal dynamics of such a change. Was the party ready for the "revolutionary harvest," Kairys wondered in retrospect?[26] Did it have the means to channel the passions of the revolution into purposeful activity? Anxious deliberation weighed upon the leadership when it stood on the threshold of the revolution, just as it did when the tsarist counterdrive dimmed the socialist prospects. Thus, the social democrats referred to 1904 as the year that suddenly thrust the party into the leadership of an increasingly assertive Lithuanian opposition to the tsarist authorities. However, as the party leaders were about to assume the position "fated" to be theirs,[27] they were aware of numerous shortcomings, including doubts about the party program, poor coordination of party organizations and their work, delayed production and distribution of written appeals, failure to conduct political demonstrations, and problems with economic agitation.[28] In 1908, when tsarist resurgence counseled avoidance of past mistakes, the recent problems were brought to light anew. The social democratic organizations were said to have been newly formed, inexperienced, and few in number, while their veteran leaders were so busy that they each had to be in ten places at the same time. As a result, the party relied on newcomers who were often unprepared and immature, erroneously believing that even the one-eyed leaders could show the way to a blind populace.[29]

Two problems were selected to focus attention on LSDP capacity to direct the forces which it helped stir into activity. Centering upon the national level of Lithuanian politics, the first problem considers a challenge to the party leadership growing out of a major initiative displayed by a concerned citizenry. The second takes a brief look at local politics, where the LSDP was threatened by a perversion of socialism.

A Challenging Initiative

The development that turned the social democrats off-balance was the convention of November 21–22/December 4–5, 1905, subsequently designated as the Grand Diet of Vilnius (Didysis Vilniaus Seimas). As mentioned before, it was an assemblage of close to 2,000 delegates who converged to confer on Lithuania's present condition, reflect on its future, and recommend an agreed course of action. The idea of calling such a convention together first occurred to Jonas Kriaučiūnas (1880–1967), an editor of a newspaper, when news of the October Manifesto reached Vilnius by telegraph on the morning of October 17/30. When two days later some twenty prominent personalities endorsed the idea, conditions seemed propitious for its fruition. Unexpectedly, however, the two Lithuanian political parties, the Democrats and the Social Democrats, came out against the project. While the lesser of the two parties, the Democratic, was forced by internal splits to moderate its stand, the LSDP persisted in its determined opposition. Only when they realized that their disapproval could not dampen the public's intense interest in the convention did the party leaders decide to participate in its work.[30] What caused their opposition to the plan?

Pranas Klimaitis (1883–1940), a secretary of the convention, advanced two theses designed to clear up the socialist contention against the Vilnius assembly.[31] In the first place he attributed it to LSDP intent to prove its Marxist purity by preserving the distance from the nationally minded middle-class groups and their endeavors. In the past socialist dogmatists like Rosa Luxemburg, of the SDKPiL, disparaged the LSDP by comparing its socialism with radical patriotism.[32] This contorted imagery discomfited the Lithuanian party and drained its support by those affiliated with the Second International. Dissociation from national causes like the Vilnius Diet, so ran the argument, was needed to rehabilitate that party in the eyes of its critics.[33] The argument, however, must be dismissed as a dubious assertion. While not entirely immune to foreign opinion or, for that matter, to divergent views within its own ranks, the LSDP had no qualms whatsoever about propagandizing its main national goal—the liberation of Lithuania from Russian control followed by the formation of a federal union of neighboring states. Had it been so inclined, it could have just as remorselessly given its blessing for the idea of a national convention.

The reason why the LSDP was not inclined to promote the idea could be found in the second proposition: A broadly representative convention augured a wide distribution of authority. When the Russian revolution broke out, the LSDP emerged as a major local force vitalizing the antigovernment sentiment of the Lithuanians. Large numbers of people who plunged into the insurrection sought to legitimate or coordinate their actions through at least a nominal association with the party. As a result, the real membership of the LSDP was greatly surpassed by its ostensible numerical strength. The prestige of the party soared to the point where its influence was seen by some as a "moral dictatorship" tinged by arrogance.[34] "We'll do without you," was the way Klimaitis summed up the initial LSDP retort to those who climbed the bandwagon and aspired to direct the course of events.[35] A national convention, seen at the time of its inception only as a "chance episode" unworthy of more than a casual interest, was not what the LSDP plans called for.[36] The party hoped to provide the needed leadership by means of revolutionary committees whose formation it advocated and whose activities it expected to coordinate.[37]

To the LSDP, then, the Grand Diet of Vilnius was a challenge issued by those segments of Lithuanian society whose new vitality the party helped to inspire. Since the social democrats never flirted with the possibility of transforming their moral dictatorship into a political one, they eventually agreed to take part in the work of the convention. There, as in any other consensus-prone forum, compromise became the hallmark of constructive participation. The socialists managed to make changes in the agenda of the convention, to influence the choice of its presiding officers (specifically, to have Kairys chosen as one of them), to include some of their methods of revolutionary agitation in the decisions of the convention, and generally to make their views known. On the national question, however, they acquiesced in a broad group consensus which called for Lithuanian autonomy, relegating the LSDP-conceived federation to a remote and vaguely stated possibility. In short, the party blunted the problem by political interaction and ultimate deference to majority sentiment.

Conduct Unbecoming

While contention about the general questions of leadership and goal-specification was mitigated by the give-and-take methods of political adjustment, serious problems at the local level of LSDP operations threatened to corrupt the meaning of socialism. The problems in question related to an alarming increase of arbitrary action. Unsparingly perhaps, some critics said that socialism degenerated into banditry.[38] The LSDP was as concerned about the violation of party discipline and authorized procedures as were its opponents. It discussed cases of improper behavior at its central committee meetings, dispatched troubleshooters to deal with them on the spot, and repeatedly placed them on the agenda of its conferences and conventions at both national and regional levels.[39] These and other actions signified the scope of irresponsible conduct by strayed revolutionaries.

There was every reason to feel concern about a dangerous drift toward abdication of control. Reports from the Suwałki guberniia, where the LSDP boasted one of its main regional organizations, amassed ample evidence of conduct detrimental to the socialist reputation. Kapsukas described the situation there as "an awful mess," and said that everybody acted as he pleased.[40] Reported transgressions included intimidation of private persons, demands for extortion money, and willful destruction of property. Further, some local activists altered party tactics, robbed post offices and government liquor stores, and destroyed government documents. The "revolutionaries" conducted their own kangaroo courts and inflicted punishment on convicted offenders, murdering a suspected spy in one place, flogging a loose woman in another—all on behalf of socialism.[41] Unfortunately, a general tendency to use force in settling local disputes probably meant that conditions in other provinces were not much better than those in the Suwałki region.[42]

An inquiry into the causes of this deviant behavior centers on three aspects of Lithuanian social democracy, its ability to provide competent leadership, the nature of its following, and the state of party organizations. As already indicated, doubts about their capacity, or readiness, to direct the course of revolutionary activities in Lithuania weighed on conscientious party leaders like Kairys and Kapsukas. The shortcomings attributed to the LSDP were certainly as serious as they were numerous. However, the utility of such brooding introspection is limited, for it implies the need for what may well be an unattainable state of readiness. Are political parties ever completely prepared for a revolutionary action, and can such action be devoid of excesses? Committed as it was to a program of revolutionary change, the LSDP had to embark upon such a course not when it felt duly equipped to do so, but when the occasion called for its initiative. It was true in a sense that the eruption of the revolution in Russia "fated" the LSDP to leadership in much of Lithuania.

To say that readiness to lead may not always adequately explain the actual assumption of leadership is not to sidestep commentary on the quality of that leadership. One important ingredient of a successful leadership is the character of party following. The LSDP congress which met in June 1905 provided for two kinds of membership. The first referred to membership in the party, while the second specified membership in party organizations. To be considered member of the party, a person was expected fully to accept the party's program and, to the extent possible, support its activities. Membership in local or central organizations, on the other hand, entailed the additional requirement of active participation in the work of the party.[43] To those who connected the causes of licentious practices with the party's recruitment and admissions policies it became readily apparent that at the height of revolutionary agitation the criteria of membership were either loosely applied or disregarded entirely.[44] For all practical purposes, the party opted for an open admissions policy. In some cases it was enough for a person to come out against the government or to refuse to take off his cap in front of a priest to be dubbed socialist, while in others a favorable disposition toward the party promised admission to its ranks. Large numbers of peasants professed socialism simply to obtain land. By contrast, there were those who were surprised to learn that they were listed as social democrats.[45] As Kapsukas had caustically remarked, such lax admissions procedures opened the doors to newcomers who knew about socialism as much as a pig did about the sky.[46] Finally, problems connected with an indiscriminate choice of members were compounded by the difficulty of dissociating the social democrats from the self-styled revolutionaries who proceeded to act on their behalf. As a result of these parallel problems, the host of LSDP supporters included an element which, when tested, succumbed to undisciplined behavior.

Yet another cause of improper behavior deserves some consideration, the condition of LSDP organizations. The conclusion emerges that at the end of 1905 and the beginning of 1906, when the tsarist authorities commenced their punitive operations, the party's regional and local units lay in a state of great destruction. As a result, its ability to direct local activities was seriously impaired. Some leading members of the LSDP, notably Antanas Garmus (1881–1955), Jonas Glemža (b. 1887), Pijus Grigaitis (1883–1969), Vincas Kapsukas, Pranas Mažylis (1885–1966), Juozas Rimša (1875–1970), and Jonas Zakarevičius (1883–1906), were arrested; others had to leave the country to avoid a similar fate. Among the latter were Kipras Bielinis, Andrius Domaševičius, and Jonas Grinius (1877–1954). An estimated total of over one thousand political prisoners were confined in Lithuanian jails at the time.[47] As for the party's regional formations, they were broken up in the areas of Suwałki and Šiauliai,[48] while the sight around Ukmergė and Panevėžys was "pretty sad," too.[49] The Vilnius organization persevered, but LSDP connections with the districts of western Lithuania had been severed.[50] Finally, aided by the workers affiliated with the Christian Democrats, the government authorities nearly decimated the Kaunas organization in the latter half of 1906.[51] For a short time the individual party members and their fellow supporters were left to fend for themselves.

By mid-1906, however, as the party struggled out of destruction, its campaign against disorderly conduct intensified. The central committee passed down directions to the party members banning extortion of money or private property, and further specifying a series of other measures intended to reduce the danger of unauthorized behavior.[52] Meetings were held to thrash out party tactics, discipline, banditry, and other questions.[53] Resolutions adopted by various national and regional conferences likewise condemned intimidation of private persons and seizure of their property. In addition, party functionaries were instructed to see to it that disreputable practices were not repeated.[54] Finally, one local chapter of the LSDP is known to have been disbanded due to undisciplined behavior of some of its officers.[55] Ultimately these efforts of a rebuilt party organization, together with the reimposition of tsarist authority in general, combined to reduce the incidence of licentious activity.[56] Yet students of social disorganization may still think about the problem as an opportunity to observe a political party as it sought to cope with the perilous side effects of actions which it helped to inspire.

Part III

Social Democracy in

Retreat, 1906–1914

8

Changing Prospects

As 1905 was drawing to a close, the tsarist authorities intensified their efforts to recover the ground. The end of the general strike on October 21/November 3, the arrest on December 3/16 of all of the deputies attending a meeting of the St. Petersburg Soviet, the suppression of the armed uprising attempted in Moscow on December 10/23, and the reestablishment of control over the rebellious soldiers in the Far East and at various other military bases all indicated a marked recrudescence of government authority. As for the western borderlands, the Russians made important concessions to Finland but restored their complete domination in Poland and the Baltic regions. In Lithuania, where some 55,000 government troops were stationed,[1] the old local administration was reinstated by the spring of 1906. Punitive expeditions sent to that country brought its overt resistance to an end.

Wishful Thinking

Like the leaders of other revolutionary parties, the men of the LSDP were reluctant to concede their defeat right away. According to a party conference held in January 1906, their activities were only "temporarily interrupted."[2] The Marxist rhetoric continued to insist that, despite the tsarist comeback, the revolutionaries were "unceasingly undermining the bases of despotic government."[3] The supposedly temporary tsarist rebound, which it dubbed "victory of the knout," was thought to be twofold.[4] In the first place, defeat of the revolutionaries was outer-inflicted in the sense that alien Russian forces removed the administrative personnel chosen by the people at the height of the revolution. These forces also wreaked punishment on the seditious local population and its leaders, driving the opposition parties underground. In addition, victory over the revolutionaries caused inner aggravation which put the LSDP on the defensive in relation to its domestic adversaries. Simmering political and social discord, curbed in 1905, surfaced the following year, when the revolution began to fade. As the LSDP defined the problem, the workers and the smallholders were still unwilling to surrender to the enemy, but the well-to-do sectors of the rural population were abandoning the cause. Moreover, together with the clergy and the capitalists, they were becoming increasingly hostile to the social democrats.[5]

Even though they were still unreconciled to bitter realities, the revolutionaries were clearly dispirited by the tsarist show of force. As they recalled the recent past when the momentum of events impelled the emperor to issue his manifestos and grant true freedom, the heavy vengeance that now fell upon them seemed doubly painful. Pain then gave rise to apprehension, as the socialists now wondered if anyone would have the strength to stop this Russian "gendarme of Europe" who was trampling on their "most sacred rights."[6] Yet having brushed all such memories and apprehensions aside, the LSDP decision makers repeated their refusal to accept the present adversity as the end of their expectations. On the contrary, they ventured to suggest that the revolution, which they termed "inevitable," will recur "sooner than we think."[7] Accordingly, in early April 1906 the central committee made a series of decisions intended to recoup party operations. It completed preparations for the publication of *Naujoji gadynė* (The New Era), a government-authorized newspaper edited by Kapsukas and Matulaitis from May through December 1906. Further, special agents were dispatched to various districts to oversee their efforts at party reconstruction. Lastly, the central committee planned to extend the party work to the Lithuanian community in East Prussia, perhaps even to Switzerland.[8] By midyear the arrangements for a party congress, scheduled for July or August 1906 (but then postponed until August 1907), were nearly complete.[9]

The belief in the recurrence of the revolution rested on the following train of thought.[10] An important reason for the recent setbacks was said to be the uneven development of class consciousness in different parts of the empire, resulting in a poor coordination of labor assault upon the autocracy. It was incumbent upon the class leadership to correct these flaws. Yet heightened labor awareness and organization, though essential, would not spark the proletariat to revolution. Rather, it was the approaching economic bankruptcy of the regime that would be the catalyst in a new uprising. Repayment of war debts, enlargement of the internal security apparatus, the need to "bribe" the armed forces in order to gain their support, and aid to poverty-stricken provinces all suggested the necessity of heavy borrowing from foreign lenders. Deep indebtedness, so ran the argument, was bound to cause large gold transfers abroad, precipitating a crisis in industry and agriculture. The ultimate result of this series of events would be total economic collapse. This is when the workers and the peasants would jointly effect a fundamental change in political and economic organization. In terms of its disequilibrating effects, this future economic breakdown was seen as the indispensable functional equivalent of the Russian-Japanese war.

The themes of the inevitable renewal of revolutionary action and of a stepped-up preparation of the working class for its future role, which were articulated at party conferences and in underground publications, recurred constantly in *Naujoji gadynė*. Although its publishers, editors, and contributors were harassed with fines and jail sentences, this newspaper persisted in thinly veiled seditious utterances. That the government tolerated them for eight months was partly due to Mykolas Itomlenskis (1883–1960), the chief censor who, as a Lithuanian-Russian, understood the local national movement and favored a moderation of the regime.[11] Was the LSDP prognosis justified at the time, and was it believed by those who made it? Perhaps it was, but only partially. Kairys, the author of many of the editorials and articles on political subjects published in *Naujoji gadynė*, intimated in retrospect that party reasoning, expectably, was tinged with factors other than observation or a carefully factual presentation.[12] In the first place, Kairys said that the images of optimism and determination may have been a function of their own age. Presumably the deliberations of the relatively young LSDP activists were not as sound as those of a more mature leadership would have been. In addition, conviction entered the decision-making process. The as yet "unextinguished belief" that the revolution would ignite anew seems to have been widely held. Lastly, Kairys testified that the LSDP sought to maintain the revolutionary mood of the public. In short, informed judgment and a combination of relative inexperience, conviction, and a sense of obligation shaded into each other as the social democratic brain trust tried to comprehend the changing situation and chart the LSDP course for the months ahead.

A Reluctant Concession

When the party leaders convened for their next conference in September 1906, they seemed to restate their thinking formulated earlier in the year. Having generally conceded that "the revolution had quieted down" and that "it was not that easy to wreck the tsarist government," the delegates felt nonetheless that another armed uprising would come in the near future. Yet it was a significantly modified restatement. Unlike the previous rationale, which elaborated on the political effects of the expected economic disintegration, the amended version dwelled on the reasons why an early outbreak of the civil conflict was no longer a certainty. The class awareness of the various segments of the population was said to be badly underdeveloped. Further, the industrial crisis, which at one time seemed to threaten an economic disaster, had measurably abated. As for the desperate plight of the farmers, the central committee suggested that their adversity could be counterproductive, for a worn-out peasantry was not likely to embark upon an organized class struggle.[13] In September, then, the memory of one season lingered as the portents of another dawned.[14] Not surprisingly, the conferees unanimously adopted a resolution urging the party members to get ready for the final test of strength. They advised the rank-and-file to popularize the idea of an armed uprising, form their own combat squads, infiltrate the army, and put up funds for all these activities.[15] That their scheme died stillborn only indicated the air of ambiguity that enveloped these deliberations at this transitional point. More important, perhaps, the delegates also awoke to the realization that now was the time to equip themselves for the long haul from the euphoria of the revolution to the ordeal of intensified persecution.

As the passage of time lessened the possibility of an economic crisis, then seen as a prerequisite for the rebirth of revolutionary action, the socialist frame of mind sustained further changes. Frequent professions about the temporary nature of the tsarist comeback or an early resumption of the fight with the autocracy faded from the party literature. What replaced them were increasing references to the decline of the revolutionary movement and the ubiquitous persecution, torture, and destruction of former insurgents.[16] At the beginning of 1908 the leaders of the LSDP openly acknowledged that "the enemy had defeated us in the first battle."[17] The further question of the next battle became a nebulous one. To some party followers its resumption seemed a distant possibility, perhaps decades away.[18] Others were content simply to voice a hope that "repression will not last forever," and that the socialist "fighters for a better future" will "ultimately" attain their goal.[19]

Except for regional variations, the impairment of the LSDP noted by these commentators was generally corroborated by reports from local activists in the field. Memoirs, available collections of LSDP periodicals, and excerpts from the Lithuanian press in the United States give a fair idea of the state of affairs at the intermediate level of the party organization from the beginning of 1907 to the middle of 1908. Lying between the party's national apparatus and its primary organizations, the intermediate tier comprised eight regional organizations and their district subdivisions. For the year and a half under consideration, the evidence in hand mentions a total of twenty-two regional and district conferences held by the Kaunas, Panevėžys, Šiauliai, Suwałki, and Vilnius organizations.[20] Regrettably, information about the party conferences in the three remaining regions of Białystok, Brest, and Grodno, where a considerable social democratic activity is known to have existed,[21] is either unavailable or inadequate. It is possible that the recent expansion in areas which formerly were the preserve of the PPS affiliate in Lithuania did not give the LSDP enough time to integrate the information gathering there with its own channels of communication.

An overview of these parleys indicates that each of the five regions had at least one conference, with Suwałki holding a total of ten. The number of participants in each conference ranged from nine to twenty-six, averaging out to sixteen. Performance reports presented by regional or district committees and by chapter representatives formed the main focus of attention. Equally important, it seemed, were a series of organizational concerns, including the structure of various agencies, the election of officers, and relations between the party's national and regional bodies. A somewhat lower emphasis was given to regional finances, involvement in cultural activities, and representation in the State Duma. Finally, the conferees usually devoted some time to discussing controversial policy issues, the conditions of agricultural workers, the formation of labor unions, the campaign against unauthorized behavior, and the intensification of work among women and the Jews.

The regional survey further shows that in Kaunas, where the party counted about two hundred followers but where its roots never ran deep, many of its backers had cooled on political action. What especially gnawed the LSDP were the inroads of the moderate groups, notably the Christian Democrats, on the area wage earners. Years later the miffed revolutionaries would remember the city as "that rock of reaction against the labor movement."[22] The disruption of the Panevėžys and Šiauliai organizations by the tsarist counterdrive was followed by a creditable recovery around the middle of 1907, which then faltered at the turn of the year. There were more than three hundred party members in the Panevėžys area during the summer of 1907. Subsequently, membership started to fall, the payment of dues became irregular, and the regional committee reported only small accomplishments. Similarly, with a combined membership that climbed to 236, the primary party organizations of Šiauliai were almost back in shape. However, the arrival of 1908 visited heavy reverses on them, as a "heavy mood" dampened people's enthusiasm in public affairs and reduced the membership roster to sixty-nine names.

The prospects in the Vilnius area were brighter. Here the approximate membership of the LSDP (excluding that attributed to its allies in the PPS) stood at 1,020 in late 1906, decreased to 817 by mid-1907, but then rebounded again to 941 in the early part of 1908. Although the dearth of education obtained by the Vilnius laboring class hindered the expansion of political activity, the party analysts were pleased to find a heightened class awareness among that city's workers. Lastly, government repression inflicted heavy losses on the Suwałki LSDP. Its following, which still comprised about 250 members in the second half of 1906, was steadily weakening in numbers and other resources. By the middle of the next year, however, the process of decline had been contained and then reversed, with the membership now hovering around 195, or higher. Later reports for the first half of 1908, which refer to increases in the number of primary party organizations, good attendance at monthly meetings, a fairly regular payment of membership dues, and the formation of women's chapters, further suggest that the LSDP managed to keep its Suwałki organization on an even keel.

In all, then, the resilience of regional organizations, especially in the Vilnius and Suwałki areas, enabled them to keep alive, and perhaps even to extend into the post-1908 period, a respectable political activity. Unfortunately, the newspaper *Žarija* (Ember), a vital part of the LSDP communications fabric, was obliged to discontinue publication in June 1908. The impact of its shutdown was such that neither the former revolutionaries nor the students of the social democratic movement could reconstruct the contours of a lost subsequent endeavor.[23] Yet although the years following the demise of *Žarija* were lean on political news, the possibility of an unrecorded local activity cannot be ruled out entirely.[24] After all, a newspaper ceased to function, not the party organizations.

Political Eclipse

Despite the problems of documentation, the period lasting roughly from 1909 to 1912 is believed to have brought a virtual cessation of activities, similar to the disruption of the party after the punitive action of 1899. If the LSDP congress held in January 1909 could still speak of a "considerably weakened" state of party organization, the conference which met in May 1912 registered the bitter truth—the revolutionary movement during these three years had been silenced. Increasing references to the "might of the counterrevolution" supplanted the earlier thoughts of the "next battle." The main task set for the party was to rally the energies of the proletariat in order to face the twin threats of capital and reaction.[25] Euphemism aside, the task was simply to survive under severe political conditions.

Arrests, exile, resettlement abroad, and absorption in professional pursuits temporarily removed most of the best-known members of the LSDP leadership group from practical work in the field. Kipras Bielinis was arrested in 1907 while attending a meeting of the Riga party committee. After the completion of a four-year prison sentence, he was sent away to the Irkutsk guberniia.[26] Apprehended in mid-1909, Zigmas Aleksa-Angarietis (1882–1940) languished in tsarist jails until 1915, when he was exiled to Siberia.[27] When ordered to leave his country in late 1906, Jonas Jaks-Tyris (1877–1938), a Lithuanian of

Tartar descent, resettled in Turkestan.[28] Vincas Kapsukas, who was captured in May 1907, spent his next six years in Lithuanian, Polish, and Russian prisons. After the escape from confinement at the end of 1913, he eventually came to Germany but then relocated in Austria. In April 1914 he conferred in Kraków with a group of Lithuanian social democrats. The conference was also attended by Lenin.[29] Aiming both to go to college and evade the police, Vladas Požela headed for Estonia, where, in 1906, he enrolled in the University of Tartu. The police locked him up in 1908. After his release in 1912, Požela soon returned to that country to forestall another arrest. Lastly, Antanas Povylius (1881–1961) was imprisoned three times between 1906 and 1911, while Jurgis Smalstys (1881–1919), who escaped from tsarist jails in 1907, eventually moved to Belgium.[30]

Apart from those under confinement, some party activists left the country either to avoid possible arrest or for personal reasons. During 1908–1912 Juozas Paknys (1883–1948) was studying commerce in St. Petersburg. Fearing seizure by the police, Jonas Šepetys (c. 1885–1942) departed Lithuania for western Europe in 1908. He resumed his political activities the following year, when he surfaced among the Lithuanian social democrats in Scotland. Šepetys returned to his country in 1913, only to be drafted for military service.[31] For similar reasons, both Konstantinas Jasiukaitis (1882–1941), in 1907, and Pranas Mažylis, in 1908, hastened off to various European countries.[32] Attempting to escape the consequences of a failed strike which he led in 1909, Pranas Eidukevičius spent a year in the United States. He was arrested in 1913, but received permission to go abroad, whereupon he crossed the Atlantic for the second time.[33] Finally, Steponas Kairys considerably reduced his own participation in party politics. After the conclusion of the LSDP congress in Kraków, Kairys resumed his studies at the St. Petersburg Technological Institute. Following their completion in 1908, he settled in the Samara guberniia and stayed there until his return to Lithuania in 1912. Back home, according to Mykolas Biržiška, "he was busy and tired, as usual," reluctant to plunge once more into underground revolutionary activity.[34]

The remaining members of the party elite similarly shied clear of deep engagement in the social democratic action. Vladas Sirutavičius put politics aside for the time being, while Alfonsas Moravskis may have been reassessing his very commitment to socialism.[35] Andrius Domaševičius faced imprisonment for his revolutionary activities in

1905 but was ultimately cleared of all charges, possibly as a result of a bribe and a friction between two security agencies which removed his case to the higher authorities in St. Petersburg. While practicing medicine in Vilnius, he engaged in various cultural activities but shunned immersion in politics.[36] Similarly, when a hundred-ruble bribe caused the law enforcement officers to drop the case against him, Stasys Matulaitis confined himself largely to the practice of medicine. Years later he admitted that the defeat of the revolution shattered his ideals and drove him to despair.[37] Finally, tired of the usual party routine, Augustinas Janulaitis turned to law practice and historical research. From time to time his party colleagues chided him for "chasing after women" and shirking all service obligations.[38]

In summary, what emerges is the picture of a significantly weakened condition which prevailed at the highest level of the LSDP elite throughout the course of 1909–1912. It is not surprising, then, that as early as 1907–1908 reports from various localities registered a diminishing supply of organizers, speakers, trained personnel, and intellectuals.[39] Were it not for the loss of these leading members of the party, the rebuilt local organizations would probably have prolonged their curtailed existence through the coming years. Most of these LSDP notables would soon converge toward Lithuania, or reemerge from political eclipse, to resume their leadership roles under conditions which the outbreak of World War I would change in a fundamental manner. In the meantime, however, only Biržiška and Eidukevičius, with the occasional participation of others, struggled along to preserve a modicum of organized political activity.

Hopeful Portents

The 1912 massacre of the striking miners in the Lena goldfields renewed labor unrest in Russia. The number of strikes there increased from 200 in 1910 to 2,000 in 1912, and then jumped to 4,000 during the first half of 1914—a hopeful portent of a new socialist beginning.[40] To the Lithuanian delegates attending the 1912 conference of the LSDP, the news from Russia meant the awakening of the working class. As far as the central committee of the party was concerned, the period of reaction had come to an end.[41] The Lithuanian conferees saw the reanimation of class spirit in Russia as a historical necessity arising out of the economic and political oppression of that country's wage earners. For their part, the leaders of the LSDP resolved to vitalize the Lithuanian members of the empire's lower classes and impart a socialist direction to their anticipated political revival.[42]

The revitalization of the LSDP in 1912 commenced with work stoppages and strikes in Vilnius, Panevėžys, and Šiauliai, which were designed as protests against the Lena killings.[43] To facilitate communication between the Lithuanian party and the socialists of other countries, a foreign bureau was established in Austria. Its operations eventually fell under the direction of Kapsukas.[44] Party recovery continued with the efforts of Požela and Biržiška—the one barely out of prison, the other willing to resume political responsibilities—to arrange for the publication of a socialist newspaper. Initially, they hoped to put one out jointly with the liberals in Šiauliai. When these plans failed to materialize, they came out with *Vilnis* (The Wave), a publication issued in 1913–1914 by the Lithuanian socialists living in the Latvian city of Riga. Finally, one might also mention a conference of the rural youth which the party convened in mid-1913.[45] These, then, were the harbingers of a slow and halting awakening that went on in the LSDP. The renewal of suspended party life witnessed the customary forms of action—conferences, strikes, written appeals, transient publications, and the like. However, this conventionality of form was enveloped in a new psychology that sensed the immensity of conflicts impending over the nations of Europe.[46] The likelihood of war and its disequilibrating effects seemed to animate those who pondered the varied images of their country's future.

A disastrous experience usually begets a critical insight. Not surprisingly, the collapsing hopes and expectations, which distinguished the years from late 1905 to 1912, enveloped the Lithuanian social democracy in a psychology of failure. A tendency to stress errors and imperfections burdened the party conscience with the thought that the LSDP was somehow partly responsible for the heavy reverses visited upon the revolutionaries. Consequently, in an effort to prop up the faltering revolution, or to prepare themselves for its expected second wave, the leaders of the LSDP proceeded to make a series of political adjustments. In the discussion which follows, we shall seek to review this partial redirection of LSDP endeavors. Our presentation begins by looking into the possible convergence of area Marxist parties and the attendant changes in party organization. It then takes up the controversy over the resolution of the national question and continues with a review of the party's socioeconomic base. The final chapter reflects upon the fragmentation of Lithuanian social democracy.

9

Unity Efforts

The Kapsukas Accession

The unity of Marxist parties that sprouted up across the empire was an often discussed goal, yet one whose attainment was only partial. However, the political impact of the Russian-Japanese war, the new responsibilities which the revolution thrust upon its harbingers, signs of tsarist recovery, and the weaning of the moderates and the conservatives away from the socialists all presaged a renewal of interest in the consolidation of Marxist forces. To be sure, practical collaboration among the several area groups was already considerable (if somewhat neglected in scholarly accounts), but many people thought that a further enhancement and coordination of their common efforts depended on the achievement of greater organizational unity.

After their failed uprisings against the Russians in 1794, 1831, and 1863, a number of Lithuanians relocated in neighboring Latvia. Looking for work, many of them gravitated toward that country's industrial centers, including Jelgava. Sheltering some 800 Lithuanians prior to 1914, the town grew into a cultural and political center, while its high school, or gymnasium, continued to enroll both area students and those from Lithuania proper.[1] Of the students here who developed a socialist orientation, Kapsukas was perhaps the most prominent one. As indicated previously, he first leaned toward the LSDP but then, due to both policy differences and personality conflicts, opted to form his separate Lithuanian Social Democratic Labor Party. It concentrated on work among the members of the village proletariat, favored guerrilla-type operations against the tsarist government, and sought the establishment of a Lithuania that would be federated with its neighbors. In September 1905, having found their differences insubstantial, the two parties merged to form a united LSDP. The agreement, however, provided for a rediscussion of the national question and the party's name at the next congress.[2] A fulfillment of these requirements at the Kraków congress in 1907 formalized the adhesion of the Kapsukas following.

The absorption of the Kapsukas group must, on balance, be considered a gain for the senior party. According to Kairys, Kapsukas brought some unease to a party that, until then, was relatively free of personal rivalry and backhanded intrigue. Even after he was seated on the central committee, Kapsukas stayed at personal odds with such members of the party core as Janulaitis and Sirutavičius.[3] Yet Kairys also underscored the positive effects of their political partnership. In the first place, the LSDP success in inspiring and piloting the agricultural strikes of 1905–1906 must be attributed to the attention which the Jelgava graduates fixed on the rural workers. In addition, their affiliation procured for the LSDP a number of educated young men whose energies enhanced the party potential. Like Kapsukas, Juozas Paknys and Vladas Požela were in touch with the LSDP even before the fusion of the two parties. Others, including Bronius Kareiva, Petras Klova, Kazys Mažonas, Petras Prapuolenis, and Jonas Šepetys, must be regarded as newcomers.[4] Most of them, however, earned a measure of distinction for their actions in 1905–1906, or at the time when the party was gasping under the weight of political repression, or during and after the revolution of 1917.

The Polish Connection

Our discussion presently shifts to changes in the relations between the Lithuanian and the Polish parties—the LSDP and the PPS. As already indicated, some of the inspirers of the Polish national revival visualized a Polish-dominated commonwealth arising out of the old *Rzeczpospolita* and comprising its various member nationalities. Those who cherished such hopes generally deplored the development of Lithuania's own identity. Not surprisingly, the PPS, too, initially aspired to extend its operations not only over Poland proper but across Lithuania as well. To facilitate its penetration of that country, the Polish party formed a regional affiliate called the PPS in Lithuania (PPS na Litwie). However, the limited nature of its inroads on the Lithuanian community, coupled with the changes which the revolution injected into the total complex of interacting relations, led to a gradual rapprochement between the two parties. Their convergence reached the point where, in 1905, the PPS subsidiary assented to the national aspirations of the LSDP, the convocation of a constituent assembly to arrange Lithuania's membership in a family of federated area states.[5] In addition, disapproval of the PPS incursion into outlying national areas by that party's left wing (or PPS-Lewica), abandonment of the PPS for the locally more popular LSDP by some members of the Polish party, and support of unity efforts by such former partisans of the PPS as Pranas Eidukevičius, Kazimierz Pietkiewicz, and Petr Shumov all combined to create a climate favorable to interparty negotiations.[6]

The exchange of unity proposals commenced toward the end of 1905. The PPS in Lithuania initially suggested a prior agreement on a new program, to be followed by the merger of the two groups into a single party having its own name.[7] The Lithuanians demurred. Their party conference of January 1906 voiced a strong support of the consolidation effort, but said that it lacked the authority to obligate itself to such drastic changes as those advanced by its would-be partners. By way of a counterproposal, the conference fell back on the formula used to incorporate the Kapsukas group; it urged its Polish colleagues to enter the ranks of the LSDP more or less unconditionally, deferring the resolution of their differences until the next party congress. Specifically, the January conferees invited the Vilnius, Kaunas, and Grodno chapters of the PPS to enroll in the corresponding LSDP organizations. As for the units in such towns as Białystok and Suwałki, their strong economic ties with Poland made their merger with the LSDP seem inadvisable.[8] At a later conference in September the LSDP essentially repeated its January proposals. Only the question of the southern limits of party operations was left unresolved.[9] The PPS in Lithuania, which had a strong Polish and Jewish following in such border towns as Białystok and Brest, sought their affiliation with the enlarged party. The LSDP, on the other hand, was concerned that their inclusion might reduce the influence of the Lithuanian members.[10]

Recognizing both the similarity of their interests and the harm that a further delay in their unification would do to the labor movement, the PPS in Lithuania readily agreed to the terms set forth by the LSDP. The union of the two parties, which had the blessing of the parent PPS, occurred in November 1906.[11] A joint central committee was formed to conduct the party affairs until its next congress. When that congress met the following year, it unanimously ratified the accomplished partnership. On the territorial extent of party operations, the congress was vague, too. Basically, it preferred to carry on the party work wherever it was possible.[12]

The leading members of the LSDP viewed their linkup with the Lithuanian branch of the PPS as a significant, if not an unqualified, political victory for their nation and their party. The assent of the PPS to the fusion of its affiliate into the LSDP was interpreted to signify its recognition of both Lithuania's quest for autonomy and its territorial objectives. According to the Kairys memoirs, the ten-year rivalry over the greater Vilnius area came to an end.[13] Considering the flare-up of the Lithuanian-Polish dispute over Vilnius during the years between the two world wars, the Kairys retrospection certainly seems flawed.

On the scale of party politics, the LSDP registered a mildly favorable balance. The unification, in November 1906, of the local social democratic organizations in Vilnius, Kaunas, Panevėžys, and St. Petersburg was a definite gain, for it gave added strength to party work in those cities.[14] Another accomplishment was the inclusion of several additional districts of the Grodno and Vilnius guberniias in the sphere of LSDP operations. Expansion in these new areas, however, created a problem—a shortage of party officers fluent in Polish, the language spoken by the bulk of the population there. The LSDP of necessity expended greater energies on the Lithuanian-speaking supporters than on its Polish friends. Ultimately, a distance between the central committee and the local organizations developed in some places, while only minimal activities were conducted on others.[15]

The adherence of the PPS group reinforced the leadership of the LSDP. In addition to Eidukevičius, Pietkiewicz, and Shumov, several veteran activists—such as Witold Abramowicz, Jan Czerniawski, Aleksander Djakonow, Stefan Michniewicz, Czesław Silwanowicz, and Menachim Wajner—offered it their services. On the other hand, the LSDP soon realized that many other local stalwarts of the PPS, including Jan Piłsudski, remained aloof from the Lithuanian party.[16] Lastly, the LSDP proponents of separatist solutions in relation to the Russians, who had hoped that the former members of the Polish party would support them against their malleable colleagues, got less from

the merger than they expected.[17] It is true that some arrivals from the
PPS, like Czerniawski, were hardliners, but others, including Eidukevičius, were prepared to make extensive concessions.

Outlook on the Jews

For the Lithuanian social democrats, inroads on the local Jewish community were a two-pronged endeavor. One aspect of it entailed a
discussion of the proper relationship with the Jewish Bund. The other
pertained to the nature and scope of their activities intended for the
Jewish nationals who considered themselves members of the LSDP.
Regarding their intergroup ties, the Lithuanian and the Jewish parties
settled into a compatible parallelism. Unlike its rivalrous attitude
toward the other Marxist parties in the area, the LSDP outlook on the
Jewish Bund has been positive. Historical records are replete with
instances of cooperation between members of these two groups, while
only a few sharp disagreements are registered.[18] Yet it was a mutually
beneficial cooperation between two distinct political parties. The ex-
ploratory talks between the leaders of the Lithuanian-Polish and the
Jewish groups, held in the 1890s, were probably the only serious effort
at the formation of a single party designed to unite the Lithuanians
and the Jews for work in Lithuania. A divergence of opinion on the
type of political organization intended for the ethnically diverse area
proletariat doomed these early efforts. Instead of one regional party, a
number of Marxist groups were founded, including the LSDP and the
Bund. The LSDP then adopted a position to which it adhered in the
subsequent years. It affirmed that the Jewish wage earners were entirely free to pursue their national interests and determine the nature
of their own organization. As Lithuanian residents, however, they
were expected to acknowledge the political program of the LSDP. The
Jewish workers were further asked to join their Lithuanian counterparts in a struggle for the actual fulfillment of that program.[19] Despite
these pleas, however, the idea of an autonomous Lithuania federated
with other area states never received the kind of endorsement the
LSDP expected of the Bund. According to Trusiewicz, when the contemplated federation of Poland, Lithuania, and Belorussia was first
broached in 1895, the Jewish forerunners of the Bund, presumably
Gozhansky and Kopelson, refused to support the idea.[20] Although their
successors continued to withhold that support, the LSDP and the Bund

remained on good terms with each other throughout the pre-1914 years.

Enlisting individual members of the Jewish community under its banner was another aspect of the LSDP desire to radiate its influence throughout the ethnically diverse segments of Lithuania's population. In addition to the advantages normally accruing to political parties when their membership increases, the Jewish presence in the Lithuanian party had symbolic value. For a party seeking to represent the interests of the entire area proletariat, regardless of its linguistic or religious preferences, the diversity of its membership was one measure of success. According to one conservative estimate of the LSDP numerical strength, the total of 2,310 members represented at the 1907 party congress included 380 Jewish followers.[21] The Vilnius and Grodno organizations had 150 Jewish members each, while the remaining 80 belonged to the Białystok and Brest Litovsk chapters.

Although generally work among the Jews was not a priority project for the LSDP, a modicum of its energy was nevertheless expended in various tasks directed primarily toward this particular group. Further, when the merger with the PPS branch in Lithuania caused an increase in the number of Jewish members, additional responsibilities devolved upon the LSDP. One example of these new tasks was associated with the 1907 reorganization of the party's administrative structure in the city of Vilnius. Of the five districts into which the Vilnius organization was divided, one was designated as a citywide Jewish national district.[22] This exceptional method of party organization, which granted the Jewish chapters an autonomous status in the Lithuanian party, was consistent with the terms of the merger agreement between the LSDP and the local affiliate of the PPS.[23] The enlarged party made arrangements for a Jewish committee entrusted with responsibility for conducting work among the members of that nationality. The committee's charge included the supervision of agitators, provision of Yiddish literature, and plans for conferences of Jewish organizations.[24]

Other activities aimed at the Jewish audience included the issuance of several written appeals and the distribution of some 10,000 leaflets during the 1906 elections to the first State Duma or that year's preparations for the second. They also saw the publication, in 1906–1907, of such short-lived periodicals as *Sozialistische Flugblatt* and *Arbeiterstimme für Lite.*[25] Meeting in 1907, the Kraków congress of the LSDP was unimpressed with these accomplishments. Its planned formation of the Jewish committee, the decision to publish a weekly newspaper in Yiddish, and exhortations to local party agencies to step up the united activities of Christian and Jewish workers suggest that the LSDP meant to bridge the gaps between the Lithuanians and members of other ethnic groups.[26] However, mounting government repression, which palled on the revolutionary movement throughout the empire, stalled the implementation of these plans.

Problems with the Russians

Unlike the favorable termination of the dialogues with the Kapsukas and the PPS factions, both of which either had a Lithuanian orientation or developed one, unity talks between the LSDP and the RSDLP were largely unproductive. The political and psychological climate that facilitated negotiations with the two former groups simply did not exist to assist the progress of the latter parleys. The LSDP and the RSDLP represented, in the last analysis, two different social democratic movements, a Lithuanian and a Russian, a reality which the intermittent feelers and consultations could not explain away. While charting the resolution of the national question or the defense of class interests, the policymakers of the LSDP sought a tangible acceptance of their Lithuanian identity. When the Russians failed to accord them the desired measure of recognition, the two sides aborted the union of their parties. That other obstacles also stood in the way of the contemplated unity only heightened the impossibility of its attainment.

Connection between the two parties was first seriously considered by the LSDP at its conference in September 1906.[27] The question of merger was twofold; it involved relations between the RSDLP and the LSDP organizations operating outside Lithuania proper, as well as bonds between the RSDLP and the LSDP themselves. With respect to the status of its branches in the Lithuanian diaspora, the conference allowed these outlying organizations to decide whether to maintain their membership in the LSDP or to join the RSDLP. However, those planning to enlist in the RSDLP (or, for that matter, in any other area party) were advised to be in contact with the Lithuanian party about agitation, propaganda, and cultural matters.[28]

The LSDP was particularly concerned about the future of its chapters in St. Petersburg, where some 30,000 Lithuanians lived prior to 1914, and in such Latvian centers as Riga, Jelgava, and Liepāja. In the imperial capital the Russians put out merger feelers. They suggested that the LSDP organization there blend into the RSDLP, retaining only a separate group of Lithuanian propagandists functioning under the auspices of the Russian party. However, stressing the positive aspects of its separate existence and citing differences in their political programs, in March 1906 the LSDP rejected these merger terms.[29] Subsequently the Lithuanian position softened. A conference of LSDP organizations in St. Petersburg, which met in October 1906, decided to sign up with the RSDLP, but without leaving the LSDP. When the Russians vetoed this idea, the possibility of union was rediscussed at a later conference held in March 1907. Expressing the pro-merger sentiment of the 170 party members in the St. Petersburg area, the conferees agreed to sever their ties to the LSDP. However, their readiness to enroll in the RSDLP was predicated upon two desired, but unrealized, concessions: the right to establish a cultural center for the purpose of conducting agitation and propaganda among the Lithuanians, and the right to campaign in favor of Lithuanian autonomy. These remaining differences between the Russians and the Lithuanians brought their unity efforts to a standstill.[30] Eventually the LSDP strength in St. Petersburg began to wane. The educated members vegetated in their own chapters, while workers' groups disintegrated. The more active members of the latter groups joined the RSDLP, the rest avoided political activity. Referring to 1908–1909, a concerned member of the LSDP said that his colleagues in St. Petersburg were simply "groping in the dark."[31]

Unification in Latvia was relatively smooth. In Riga, whose Lithuanian population increased to a 35,000 total by 1913, the inception of Lithuanian social democracy in the 1890s was linked to the activities of Vincas Mišeika, Antanas Zabūras, Juozapatas Jančevskis, Juozas Girjotas, Pranas Eidukevičius, and others. On the eve of the 1905 revolution the LSDP organization in Riga totaled approximately 150 adherents. At the time of the revolution its thirty-seven chapters counted five hundred members.[32] Their incorporation into the city's Latvian social democracy, itself an affiliate of the RSDLP, occurred in May 1907. The Lithuanian socialists retained the right to pursue their own cultural activities, e.g., to establish small-scale libraries, distribute newspapers, study the living conditions of the Lithuanian workers employed by area industries, and the like. On the other hand, they surrendered both their party funds and their responsibility for political agitation and propaganda to the Latvians.[33] Kipras Bielinis, a prominent member of the LSDP who was elected to the Riga party committee, testified that the everyday course of political operations following the merger created no undue problems between the Latvians and the Lithuanians.[34] The situation in other Latvian towns was not markedly different from that in Riga. For example, the Liepāja members of the LSDP entered the local Latvian social democracy in 1906. Here, too, the direction of Lithuanians' nonpolitical activities was entrusted to their own cultural center.[35] Whether in Russia or in Latvia, however, the Lithuanian social democrats seem to have kept in touch with the parent LSDP.

Differing from the LSDP organizations in Latvia, those functioning in various other countries were reluctant to combine with the nationally dominant Marxist parties. For example, at a conference in July 1907 the LSDP extension in Scotland voted to postpone indefinitely the question of enrolling its 73 members in the local British party.[36] In the United States, the Lithuanian Socialist Union, whose membership rose rapidly from 348 in 1905 to more than 3,000 a decade later, similarly delayed its affiliation with the American Socialist Party until 1915.[37]

Possible integration of the Lithuanian diaspora organizations into the Russian party (or its territorial affiliate) was one side of the unity question. Its other side concerned the attempted merger of the RSDLP and the LSDP themselves. Efforts at cooperation between the Lithuanians and the Russians had a bad start. Insisting on a prior commitment to federalism as the form of possible association between their countries and their parties, the LSDP declined to attend the first congress of the RSDLP held in 1898.[38] Relations between these two parties then worsened to the point where, in mid-1905, a congress of the LSDP denounced the work of the Russian party as "detrimental to the interests of the Lithuanian proletariat." The Lithuanian conferees cited two main reasons for such a critical appraisal, the centralized nature of the Russian party and its failure to acknowledge in practice the right to national self-determination.[39] Before long, however, the harsh tone which the LSDP adopted in the early months of the revolution was tempered with a more conciliatory stance. A heightened sense of isolation following the association of the RSDLP with various Caucasian, Latvian, and Polish groups was one causative factor in the changed attitude of the LSDP.[40] Equally important, it seems, was the impulse to close ranks which frequently arises when individuals or groups feel a premonition of defeat, as the social democratic parties did at the moment of the tsarist rebound. "Once the common struggle had begun," said the LSDP in 1906, "it was no longer possible to live apart from others as before."[41]

Rhetoric aside, the LSDP position on the merger issue, taken at that party's September conference, was not likely to expedite the consolidation program; possible unity of the two parties was predicated upon the Russian acceptance of twelve conditions stipulated by the Lithuanians.[42] Adapting the pattern of the Latvian-Russian association to meet their own needs, the conferees projected the LSDP as an autonomous regional organization of the RSDLP, having extensive decision-making powers relating to party work in Lithuania. In a further effort to solidify those powers, the LSDP attempted to monopolize party operations in Lithuania by expecting all other Marxist groups in that country to combine under its umbrella. As for the resolution of the national question, which the LSDP was about to weigh anew, the Lithuanians insisted on retaining the right to propagate their country's autonomy. Apart from one policy issue, which sought to give the Lithuanian party a free hand in settling the land question, the remaining conditions dealt largely with procedural matters. They described the future role of LSDP congresses, mentioned the participation of the LSDP in the organs of the Russian party, referred to the principle of democratic centralism, and requested the inclusion of LSDP members in the Russian delegations to the congresses of the Second International.

The unity scheme elaborated in 1906 was in most instances ratified by an LSDP congress convened in Kraków the following year. Eight of its twelve conditions were made public; these differed only slightly from the corresponding demands made a year ago. The other four conditions remained undisclosed. Presumably they dealt with various measures designed to improve the position of the LSDP in relation to the other groups, for the more explicit earlier references to intraparty linkages involving the Jewish, Lithuanian, and Russian parties were deleted from the published portions of the 1907 document.[43] Taken together, the purpose embodied in the two documents of 1906 and 1907 was to secure to the Lithuanian party (and, through a parallel retouching of the national question, to the Lithuanian people as well) the highest degree of self-government consistent with the concept of autonomy.

Talks between the Russians and the Lithuanians began toward the end of 1906. Initially these were informal contacts established through the St. Petersburg organization of the LSDP. However, when a member of that party's central committee later arrived in the Russian capital, the formal negotiations commenced. In November the Lithuanians met with the central committee of the RSDLP, at which time they apprised their Russian colleagues of the LSDP position on the unity issue. Apparently, their disagreement was such that the merger of the two parties was considered to be impossible.[44] A month later the central committee of the Russian party submitted its written reply to the Lithuanians. The document stated that it was too early for the Russians to scrutinize the Lithuanian plan, or to make a counterproposal, since they had little knowledge of the LSDP. Additionally, such actions would be devoid of any practical significance, because the central committee did not have the authority to effect conditional mergers. As for the possibility of forging closer ties between the two parties, the central committee said that it intended first to gather as much information about the nature of LSDP activities as it could.[45] The negotiations reached a standstill.

Kairys next raised the question when he addressed the London congress of the RSDLP on April 30/May 13, 1907. Having first wished the Russians success in moderating the factional strife within their party, Kairys turned to the contemplated union of the RSDLP and the LSDP. He set forth briefly the changing character of Lithuanian national objectives and then alluded to the failed St. Petersburg initiative, including the recent rebuff by the central committee of the Russian party. Since that party organ had no right to agree to an autonomous type of affiliation sought by the Lithuanians, Kairys asked the congress to put the unity item on its own agenda.[46] Although Georgii Plekhanov, the presiding officer, reciprocated the Lithuanian greeting and a number of delegates applauded the Kairys speech, consolidation of the two parties was left undiscussed.

The question of interparty collaboration fell into abeyance. Quite obviously, the Russians lacked enthusiasm for the kind of union the Lithuanians had in mind. For their part, the policymakers of the LSDP were averse to forging a partnership if it imperiled their endeavors to attain their national objectives or to preserve the autonomy of their party. While the association with the RSDLP found considerable support in the middle tier of the LSDP hierarchy, the senior officers of the Lithuanian party were wary of the Russian connection. Kairys, although initially impressed by the Russian, Jewish, Latvian, and Polish brain trust attending the London congress, was so saddened by its absorption in theoretical arguments and factional strife that he lost interest in intensifying his search for unity. The then nationally minded Kapsukas was also skeptical of any ties to the Russian party, fearing that they could entangle the Lithuanians in the rivalry between the Bolsheviks and the Mensheviks.[47] Even more serious reservations about the attempted merger were voiced by other prominent party figures, including Domaševičius, Matulaitis, and Moravskis.[48] All these fears and reservations, as well as the unanimity with which the bases of the unity move were adopted by the 1907 congress of the LSDP,[49] underscored the great differences between the Russians and the Lithuanians on the convergence of their parties.

The unity question, however elusive, continued to arise in the subsequent years. At the end of 1907 or the beginning of 1908 a joint Lithuanian-Russian commission managed to hammer out a compromise. Suggesting a softening of the Lithuanian position, the commission report designated Lithuanian autonomy as an open question, but left the LSDP free to conduct its agitation and propaganda in an autonomous vein. A conference of the Lithuanian party, held in February 1908, then accepted the report after a lively debate. The project, however, ran aground. When the next party congress met, in January 1909, it stated that the LSDP did everything possible to effect a merger with the RSDLP. It closed the matter by instructing the central committee to continue negotiating with the Russians along the lines determined by the 1907 congress and the 1908 conference.[50] Its reference to the strongly autonomous will of 1907 seemed to imply that there was some dissatisfaction with the commission report presented to the party conference a year ago.[51] When the LSDP convened for another conference, in May 1912, the entry in the party record for that year was similar to the one for 1909. The central committee was said to have done all that it could do to hasten the coming of the union, but there was no indication of any progress.[52]

In conclusion, when the Russians rejected the self-protective Lithuanian proposals of 1906–1907, the intermittent unity talks that followed deepened the breach within the LSDP. Some members of that party urged renewed contacts with the Russians and were willing to modify their earlier posture, as the commission report indicated. However, the more nationally inclined LSDP politicians hedged against absorption by the Russian party. As the social democrats were coming out of a three-year slump, the unity question resurfaced in 1912. Its resolution at that time, however, was further complicated by the echoes of Russian-style factionalism penetrating the Lithuanian party. Although not looking to others for the guidance of their conduct, Požela and Eidukevičius, at least on some issues, tended toward the Bolsheviks, while others sympathized with the Mensheviks.[53] As Kapsukas had feared, the great schism introduced new complexities into the small world of Lithuanian Marxist politics.

Structural Contours

Party Organization

Merger with the Kapsukas and the PPS factions and efforts to enroll individual members of the Jewish community in the LSDP resulted in a modification of that party's organization. Its structural contours are best described as a triangular party organization surrounded by two support environments, shown in general form in figure 3. At the apex of the party pyramid were the national formations: the party congress, the party conference, the central committee, and a number of other agencies.[1] The party congress was the supreme organ of the LSDP. Prior to 1914, a total of eight congresses were convened. With only two exceptions, all of them were held in Vilnius. Although the word *congress* often connotes a very large gathering, the congresses of the LSDP, like some of their early Bund or RSDLP counterparts, were small conclaves. The number of delegates attending them ranged from thirteen to twenty members representing the party's regional organizations, the central committee, and the editors of LSDP newspapers. The regional delegates were supposed to be selected by their own territorial organizations, but in practice they were sometimes designated by the central committee.[2] Congresses were usually dominated by educated party members, although workers were also represented.

The central committee usually consisted of three or five members and several alternates elected by the congress. (An overview of individual service on the committee is shown in figure 4.) Its purpose was to direct the activities of the party between the congresses. In the interval between the congresses the central committee convened national party conferences to discuss questions of party policy or to clarify

Figure 3.   Party Organization and Its Support Environments

controversial planks in the party platform. Finally, the list of central agencies included the Jewish committee, the party court, the editorial boards of party newspapers and journals, and various ad hoc policy or investigating commissions.

In 1907 the intermediate tier of the apparatus comprised eight regional organizations (*apskritis*) and their several district (*rajonas*) subdivisions. Including representatives of the local chapters and members of the existing district executive committees, district conferences coordinated the activities falling within their jurisdiction and then elected new district committees. The district organizations also selected their delegates to the regional conferences. These dealt with the affairs of the region and elected regional executive committees. As noted earlier, the regional organizations were expected to supply the delegates to the party congress. Lastly, when necessary and feasible, the regular regional organs were supplemented with such auxiliary bodies as party courts, libraries, study groups, and schools of agitators.

At the bottom of the hierarchy were the primary party organizations. They were formed in factories, craft shops, and rural villages, on

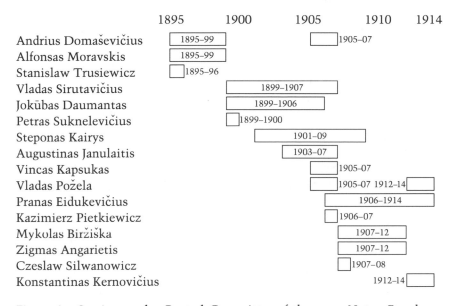

Figure 4. Service on the Central Committee of the LSDP. *Notes:* Based on fragmentary accounts, the indicated timelines are only approximations of actual service records. Even when they are shown as continuous, they do not necessarily mean an uninterrupted service on the committee, because arrest, relocation, and other forms of disengagement often resulted in merely nominal membership. The three-man team chosen in 1895 was not yet formally called central committee; one of the three former members of the PPS in Lithuania who were briefly seated on the committee in 1906 remains unidentified; and alternate members are omitted from the figure. *Sources:* Z. Angaretis, "Iz deiatel'nosti s.-d. p. Litvy v gody reaktsii," *Proletarskaia revoliutsiia*, no. 11 (1922), p. 76; Bielinis, *Penktieji metai*, pp. 29 and 114; Biržiška, *Lietuvių tautos kelias*, II, 163; Biržiška, *Keleivis*, September 13, 1950, p. 5; *ibid.*, September 20, 1950, p. 5; *Encyclopedia Lituanica*, II, 505; Griškūnaitė, *Darbininkų judėjimas Lietuvoje...*, pp. 179 and 209; Griškūnaitė and others (eds.), *Lietuvos TSR istorijos šaltiniai*, II, 476 and 509–10; Institute of Party History, *Lietuvos komunistų partijos istorijos apybraiža*, I, 67, 171, 206, 224, 241–42, and 250; Jurginis and others (eds.), *Lietuvos TSR istorija*, II, 175; Kairys, *Lietuva budo*, pp. 323 and 303; Kairys, *Tau, Lietuva*, p. 46; Kapsukas, *Raštai*, IV, 373; *ibid.*, VII, 596, 629, 631, 648, and 654; *ibid.*, X, 103; *ibid.*, XI, 386 and 400; *Lietuvių enciklopedija*, IV, 373; *ibid.*, V, 105; *ibid.*, X, 253; *ibid.*, XXVII, 506; *MLTE*, I, 672; *ibid.*, II, 126 and 396; Polska Akademia Nauk, *Polski Słownik Biograficzny*, XXVI (Wrocław, 1981), 157; Juozas Vilčinskas, personal letter to author, July 13, 1987.

great landed estates, and among soldiers, intellectuals, and members of
the Jewish community. Party cells held meetings where they elected
their own officers and picked those who represented them at the
district conference.

The numerical strength of the LSDP depended on the condition-
ing nature of exogenous forces. The estimates for 1907, when the
liberating effects of the revolution were already nearly smothered
but the triumph of reaction was not yet fully achieved, placed the
party total anywhere between 2,310 and more than 3,000 members.[3]
Ideally, these were the people who accepted the party program and
the by-laws, carried out the decisions of the party congresses,
belonged to one of the party organizations, and paid their dues. In
actuality, however, members were not always as dedicated as the
1907 by-laws would have them appear. In the years immediately
prior to 1905, affiliation with the LSDP was relatively simple: Any
person who acted in the spirit of the party program and tactics
qualified for membership. There was no formalized selection process
for new members.[4] Admissions handled at the time of the revolution
ranged between extremes of laxity and firmness. As already indicated, in some cases the criteria of membership were ignored in an
effort to enroll various activists in the party. Similarly, membership
in an LSDP-dominated labor union was sometimes equated with
membership in that party.[5] In other cases, however, the eligibility
requirements were strict. To take one example, Jurgis Šaulys (1879–
1948), a signatory of the Lithuanian Declaration of Independence in
1918, could not join the LSDP in 1905 because his scholarship award
had obligated him to contribute to a magazine sponsored by the
Democrats. In the opinion of the party's central committee, the
submission of articles to the publications of other political groups
was inappropriate to the members of the LSDP.[6] An uneven application of eligibility standards, the need to specify who had the right
to participate in the election of party officers, and the fear that
lax admission policies may have contributed to an increase in
undisciplined behavior impelled the party leaders, first in 1905 and
then in 1907, to determine the eligibility criteria with greater
precision. However, the impending disruption of LSDP operations by
the government deprived these efforts of any practical significance.

Due to a dearth of information about the rank-and-file members
of the LSDP, no quantified assessment of their social origins or occupa-

tional structure can be made with any degree of certainty. The available analyses of the party's social composition likewise suffer from insufficient data.[7] As for the higher and lower levels of the party leadership during the first decade of LSDP operations, 163 persons have been identified, a total that was 92 percent male. In terms of occupation, the information for 114 members of this group indicates that about 59 percent of them held, or aspired to, various middle class positions. Workers accounted for approximately 32 percent of the leadership corps, while farmers trailed with only 9 percent of the total. Finally, information available for 93 members of this circle of party leaders shows that their average age, in 1907, was twenty-nine.

Support Environments

The LSDP organization proper was surrounded by two support environments. The first, or inner, circle consisted of individuals and groups which gave tangible support to some aspect of party operations. Attracted by the party's nationally tinged activism or its ideological bent, a diverse entourage—college and high school students, the educated farming strata, allies in the splintered labor movement, soldiers receptive to socialist propaganda, liberal intellectuals, selected members of the professional class, and numerous local activists—converged at various times to broaden the LSDP range in the Lithuanian provinces. When the LSDP Grodno organization suggested that its small membership had the means to influence the labor behavior in all of the area's factories and shops, where decisions made by the party were virtually irrevocable, it provided an example of the kind of support that issued from the inner circle.[8] Similarly, a 1908 claim that the 941 members of the party organization in Vilnius had varying degrees of leverage over an additional number of 2,700 people also alluded to the inner ring of the support environments.[9] A numerous and vitally important part of the LSDP effort in 1905, this particular support element significantly weakened in its allegiance to the party during the years of the counterrevolution, but it did not disappear entirely. Groups of former revolutionaries, concerned students, members of various labor unions, and leftist intellectuals continued to harbor or to acquire socialist political attitudes.

The Lithuanian social democracy was also helped by what may be termed an outer support environment, the category of voters and identifiers that a political party will rally when nonthreatening conditions of political life give it the opportunity to do so. During the "days of freedom" in 1905, when the socialists were in the process of establishing their so-called moral dictatorship, thousands of peasants were known to have professed their allegiance to them. Two years later such a favorably disposed public helped elect five Lithuanian socialists to the second Duma. (Like most Marxian parties, the LSDP boycotted the 1906 elections to the first Duma. Only one area socialist deputy was elected to the third Duma and none to the fourth.) Finally, support of that type resurfaced at the time of the 1920 elections, when some 87,000 voters (13 percent of the total) sent twelve social democrats to Lithuania's Constituent Assembly.[10] However, in the interval between 1907 and the restoration of Lithuania as an independent state in 1918, this amorphous body of voters and identifiers gradually dwindled away to political insignificance.

Party Funds

Efforts to establish the financial position of the LSDP run into a number of difficulties. First, the party system of classifying, recording, and summarizing financial transactions was flawed. As a result, virtually nothing is known about party funds before 1902 and after 1908. In the mid-1890s Domaševičius was probably the only person who had knowledge of the group's financial affairs. Dubbed the minister of finance, he alone knew how to raise the needed sums of money and was usually successful in doing so.[11] Second, the known budget totals often did not include the frequent but undisclosed contributions by various members of the LSDP elite. Domaševičius in particular, but also Biržiška, Daumantas, Kairys, and many others, represented the kind of commitment to the cause that exacted financial sacrifices from its devotees. The money value of their donations may never be determined. Modern Lithuania provided further instances of altruism to which some of these idealists adhered. The agrarian reform laws enacted there after World War I provided for grants of land to individuals whose services to Lithuania were deemed to be exceptional. Suggesting that their labors in behalf of their country were not motivated by personal gain, Kairys declined the offer outright, while Biržiška accepted it as a way of raising funds for the construction of a hospital, which he handed over to the local government.[12] Finally, the assessment of LSDP finances was complicated by the use of single-purpose funds. Monetary contributions to an arms fund, aid to the victims of government persecution, money for the acquisition of a secret printing press, and coffers of the party's regional organizations—all constituted subsidiary sources of income.[13] Their accumulated totals were not included in the regular budget.

The party's regular annual budgets prior to 1905 hovered below the 2,000 ruble figure: 1902—1,324 rubles; 1903—1,981 rubles; 1904—1,459 rubles. The budget totals rose to approximately 5,000 rubles in 1905, and then swelled to 29,439 rubles the following year. With the defeat of the revolution, however, political money began to decline sharply. The last available figures indicated a 3,000-ruble amount projected for 1908.[14]

Some 70 percent of the 1906 total came from abroad. Socialist supporters among the Lithuanian community in the United States donated 19,282 rubles, those in Great Britain contributed 1,020 rubles, and sales of LSDP publications brought in 309 rubles. The rest of the money was raised in Lithuania.[15] Close to one-half of the 1906 budget expenditure was for party organization, agitation, and the acquisition of arms. The other half was expended on the publication and distribution of various LSDP materials—pamphlets, newspapers, written appeals, newsletters, and workers' calendars. According to a central committee report for 1906, the sixty-eight issues of various periodicals, twenty-one pamphlets, and twenty-six written appeals—published in Lithuanian, Polish, Yiddish, and Russian languages—comprised a total of over half a million copies.[16] Appendix A contains some information about the party periodicals for the other years.

Images of the Lithuanian Future

The Need for Another Look

The LSDP plank on the national question remained basically unchanged since its formulation in 1896–1897. As already indicated, it sought the establishment of a democratic republic of Lithuania which would then voluntarily unite with various neighboring countries to form a federal state. What occasioned a reappraisal of that particular conception in 1906–1907 was, in part, the realization that neither the moderate political groups nor the other socialist parties showed much enthusiasm for such drastically separatist solutions. Autonomy was what the Lithuanian moderates stipulated as their immediate objective when they met in Vilnius in 1905. As for the socialists, the Latvians did not raise the question of their country's independence, the SDKPiL tended toward Rosa Luxemburg's antinationalist position, the Bund sought mainly cultural autonomy for the Jews, and some of the leaders of the Lithuanian PPS who joined the LSDP when the two groups coalesced shied from Lithuanian separatism.[1]

More basically, the attack upon the autocracy which shook Russia in 1905 further caused considerable soul-searching in Lithuania. To the architects of the LSDP who affirmed their country's Western orientation, the thesis concerning Russia's social and political underdevelopment was an article of faith. They were convinced that the allegedly backward character and low class consciousness of the Russian workers doomed the heroic liberation movement of the intelligentsia to noble futility. Such dire images and predictions further strengthened the belief, current among many socialist leaders of the subject nationalities, that neither the betterment of their national lives nor the emancipation of their working classes was possible without freedom from Muscovite control. An array of nationality spokesmen who at one time or another harbored such views included Andrius Domaševičius, Alfonsas Moravskis, and Vincas Kapsukas (Lithuanians); Bolesław Limanowski, Stanisław Mendelson, and Józef Piłsudski (Poles); Anton and Ivan Luckevič (Belorussians); and possibly Mikhel Goldman and Aaron Weinstein (Jews). The dramatic events of 1905, however, prompted the kind of reassessment of these beliefs that, according to Mykolas Biržiška, grew to a crisis in the LSDP.[2] The political demonstrations following Bloody Sunday, the October general strike, the formation of the Soviet of Workers' Deputies in the nation's capital, and the December uprising in Moscow all made a profound impression on Lithuania's ethnically diverse urban population. As a result, the reverse process of fascination with Russia's revolutionaries intensified, causing some people to overestimate that country's revolutionary potential and making others lessen their concern about its domination of the outlying border nationalities. While many of the veteran leaders of the LSDP continued to adhere to the ideals forged in 1896–1897, the party's newcomers, especially the students who were markedly affected by the Russian revolution and its intellectual precursors, seemed to undervalue Lithuanian separatism as a nebulous goal. Additionally, since a number of party activists viewed their separatist stance as a major obstacle to closer ties between the LSDP and the RSDLP,a goal which they favored for reasons of both class solidarity and the hoped-for success of the revolution, a reconsideration of the position on the national question became unavoidable. Its discussion proceeded publicly in the party press, as well as behind closed doors at party meetings.

The volatile issue of national priorities burst into the open when Jonas Šepetys, a twenty-one-year-old member of the LSDP, published an article in the April 1906 issue of *Darbininkų balsas.*[3] The Šepetys contribution was an attack on the 1896 statement. The author considered merger with the RSDLP as the principal immediate task facing the LSDP leadership and further suggested that the original party stand on the national question was the main hindrance to the realization of this objective. Šepetys conceded that a modification of the 1896 position occurred at a party conference held in January 1906, when the initially conceived "federation of neighboring countries" was reformulated to mean "Russia as a union of federated republics." The writer added, however, that the LSDP did not go far enough. He urged his colleagues to free the LSDP from the "remnants of patriotism" by further diluting the Lithuanian party's national program. Specifically, instead of advocating Russia's conversion to a federal state, he simply wanted the LSDP to seek broad autonomy for various parts of Russia.

The Šepetys article was noteworthy in two respects; it was a clue to a previously undisclosed reconsideration of the national question at the January conference and a portent of an incipient wrangle between the so-called Federalists and Autonomists. The published account of the January conference contained nothing that would indicate a retouching of the national question. Presumably the 1897 amendment, which provided for Russia's possible inclusion in the projected federation, was still party policy. Besides, important changes in the party program were usually made by party congresses, not conferences.

Despite these questions of competence and omission from public record, the Šepetys intimation of the January changes cannot be brushed aside. There is reason to think that a discussion of the national question did take place, and the different views divulged by Šepetys were probably expressed at the conference. The national question may have been reopened for two reasons. First, as Šepetys put it, the original statement on Lithuania's future was but a "nice spot" on the party platform, a "utopian element" there.[4] As an abstract idea without any sense of urgency, it did not unduly worry the LSDP leaders. However, as the eruption of the Russian revolution heightened party activism in Lithuania, the precise meaning of the LSDP position on the national question became a matter of considerable importance. According to Šepetys, some party adherents harbored doubts about the old formulation, vacillated, or were generally at a loss for a solution under drastically changed conditions.[5] Others viewed various articles of the LSDP program, including those on political subjects, as unclear or unfinished, venturing to say that the LSDP "was not quite ready for battle."[6] Concerns of that type may have caused a rediscussion of the national question at the January conference.

Increased interest in the country's political future on the part of other prominent individuals and political groups may have been an additional reason to put the national question on the agenda of the January conference. It should be pointed out that the Grand Diet of Vilnius, a 1905 convention that included leading members of the LSDP, projected Lithuania as an autonomous part of the Russian state, a goal far less ambitious than that incorporated in the 1896–1897 documents. To those who attended that convention autonomy seemed a more realistic objective than the separatism of the LSDP. This group consensus may, in turn, have prompted the LSDP January conferees to take another look at their own stand on the national question and its practical consequences.[7]

Federalists and Autonomists

These terms designate two factions of the LSDP which, in 1906–1907, confronted one another on the national question. The Federalists favored Russia's transformation into a union of states in which Lithuania would have virtually complete control over its internal affairs. The proponents of such a solution included Domaševičius, Kapsukas, Matulaitis, Moravskis, and Suknelevičius.[8] The Autonomists, on the other hand, sought the establishment of a democratic Russian republic that would grant Lithuania an autonomous status. The core of their leadership consisted of Angarietis, Eidukevičius, Požela, Sirutavičius, and possibly Biržiška and Kairys.[9] The intraparty debate between these two camps continued unabated.[10] In the summer of 1906 the Suwałki, Kaunas, Šiauliai, Panevėžys, and some of the other regional organizations supported the Federalists, but those in Vilnius and St. Petersburg tilted to the Autonomists.[11] The national question was thrashed out anew at a conference in September 1906, although its final resolution was deferred until the next party congress, which was scheduled for August 1907. The confrontation in September offered the two sides an opportunity to expound their respective views on the sought relationship between Lithuania and Russia. Reflecting dissension in the ranks of the party, the fifteen conferees found the national question so divisive that they could not agree even on a single draft intended for next year's congress. Instead, they decided to publish both proposals in the party press, hoping that their constituents would peruse them and thereby facilitate the resolution of the matter in 1907.[12]

The Autonomist document envisioned the formation of a truly democratic Russian republic in which an autonomous Lithuania would be conceded its own legislature. The extensive but undefined lawmaking powers of that body were to comprise the following areas of public policy: cultural activities, local administration, the judiciary, labor and agrarian policy, and fiscal matters.[13] The supporters of the Autonomist position explained the need for such an all-Russian solution by insisting that, regardless of ethnic differences, the Lithuanian proletariat was but a part of the entire working class, which was said to be united by common interests. What the Lithuanians had to do first was fight for political freedom and the establishment of a democratic republic in the country as a whole, and then participate in a joint struggle for socialism. Having thus stressed the commonality of class action and interest, the Autonomists next proceeded to rationalize their quest for Lithuanian autonomy. Quite apart from their general preference for political decentralization in such a large and diverse country as Russia, the Autonomist spokesmen maintained that Lithuania differed culturally and economically from other ethnic units comprising the Russian state. Autonomy, they concluded, would enable the Lithuanians to frame political institutions appropriate to their own particular needs.

The Federalist design was to transform the absolutist Russian state into a federal democratic republic within whose confines Lithuania would possess the widest possible autonomy. Its authors envisaged first of all a federal all-Russian legislature with preponderant powers in such areas as constitutional construction, foreign relations, defense, and various sectors of the national economy. For local lawmaking, however, they proposed the formation of a Lithuanian legislature. The fields they assigned to the latter body included education and cultural activities, the adoption of civil and criminal laws, agrarian policymaking, and the establishment of courts and organs of administration. In addition, the Federalist plan contained qualified concurrent powers; both governments could levy taxes, enact labor legislation, consider questions of military service, and oversee transportation and communication. Lastly, the Lithuanian lawmakers were empowered to seek continued democratization of the federal constitution.[14]

The Federalist demands were yet another way of reconciling presumed class interests and national aspirations. Federalist spokesmen maintained that the attainment of socialist objectives depended on the degree of a country's economic and cultural development; an advanced state of development augured the kind of democratization that would lead to class differentiation, enhance labor consciousness and organization, and improve workers' ability to provide for their material and spiritual needs. Since the Federalists assumed that Lithuania progressed to a more advanced stage than Russia (a recurring motif in Lithuanian Marxian literature), their insistence on home rule for their country seemed to them the right solution.

The Federalist reasoning also adduced national considerations.[15] It contended that in a multinational state, such as Russia, the bourgeoisie of the dominant nationality, said to be the ruling class under capitalism, aspires to hegemony. The ensuing enmity between the dominant Russians and the oppressed national minorities entangles the working class in ethnic conflicts, blunting its sensitiveness to its own class interests. An ethnically distinct Lithuania, if granted wide autonomy, would presumably avoid such dire consequences.

Reduced to terms set forth briefly in the Federalist and Autonomist drafts, the national question continued to hold the attention of the party's leadership and its local chapters during the months following the September conference.[16] Early in 1907 Stasys Matulaitis, a Federalist proponent, published two articles in which he elucidated different types of autonomy, clearly suggesting the type the Federalists intended for Lithuania.[17] Using as his criterion the degree of self-rule granted to regional governments, Matulaitis reviewed three types of autonomy. The political system of France, where the legislature of the *département* could only adapt national laws to meet local requirements, typified the most restrictive division of powers between the central and local authorities. The more extensive powers that Austria conceded to the legislatures of Bohemia or Galicia represented an intermediate type of systemic arrangement. Finally, the author cited Germany, Switzerland, and the United States as examples of the most permissive type of autonomy that is generally known as federation. It is some variant of this federal pattern that Matulaitis and his Federalist colleagues hoped the Russians would accept as a way of healing national rifts in their far-flung state. If adopted, it would recast Russia into a union of states in which the member nationalities would have virtually complete control over their internal affairs.

Showdown in Kraków

In the continuing altercation between the Federalists and the Autonomists in 1906–1907 the latter were on the upswing. An apparent agreement with the country's moderates viewing autonomy as the more feasible goal for the Lithuanians to pursue, a reduced emphasis on demand for a Lithuanian constituent assembly in favor of an all-Russian constituent assembly in the party slogan, a slackening of conditions for a possible merger between the LSDP and the RSDLP, and the nature of central committee instructions to socialist members elected to the Imperial Duma—these all indicated an erosion of Federalist strength.[18]

Settlement of the factional conflict over the national question was a priority item at the August 1907 congress of the LSDP. Held in Kraków, a Polish city then under Austrian control, this nine-day gathering included twenty delegates and two guest participants representing the party's central committee, the editorial staff of its publications, and seven regional organizations. Several other prospective conferees—including colleagues from Riga and St. Petersburg, as well as a representative of Lithuanian socialists in the United States—failed to arrive.[19] Initially, the Autonomist-controlled congress voted down the Federalist proposal. However, the fear of a possible Federalist walkout made the conferees take up the national question anew. Following a suggestion offered by Angarietis and Czerniawski, this time they focused not on the "federalist" or "autonomist" labels but on the desirable content provisions. The upshot of the breach was the adoption of a resolution introduced by Kairys, a "peacemaker" on this particular question. The decision put the party on record as favoring the establishment of a democratic Russian republic and seeking political autonomy for Lithuania. The matters over which the Lithuanian legislature was expected to have jurisdiction comprised cultural activities, land policy, area economy and administration, taxation, courts, and militia.[20] On the face of it the Kairys initiative elevated the Autonomist proposal into party policy.

The modification of the original party program of 1896–1897 was probably due to two main considerations. A descent to realism was one of them. It reflected the popular view that, as matters stood, autonomy was all that Lithuania could hope to achieve.[21] A majority of delegates at the Kraków congress apparently concurred in such an assessment of possibilities and, unlike their senior colleagues a decade ago, were content to designate it as their political aim. Besides, those still wedded to the more assertive statement of 1896 could always interpret autonomy, and indeed many of them did, as the first step in the right direction. To them it was but a transitional stage.[22]

A resurgence of tsarist power in 1906–1907 led many revolutionaries to believe that it was vitally important for them to close ranks, a perceived necessity that also influenced the Kraków solution. "Closing ranks," in turn, subsumed a number of related concerns. For example, some members of the party wanted to impart a stronger sense of class-mindedness to their various programs.[23] Others felt that a consolidation of their ties to the working class would better equip them for intensifying polemics against the moderates and the conservatives who relied on other social strata for support.[24] Most important perhaps, the LSDP conferees meant to pave the way for a possible tie-up with the RSDLP, as the SDKPiL, the Jewish Bund, and the Latvian social democrats had done at the Russian party's Stockholm congress in April 1906. It was hoped that a particular prominence given to the commonality of class interests, coupled with a damper on Lithuanian separatism, would help them pursue these unity efforts.[25] Considerations of that type were rife in the LSDP, especially among members of its Vilnius organization.

What the Compromise Meant

Who won the laurels in Kraków, the Federalists or the Autonomists? For a number of years immediately following the 1907 congress the national question lay dormant. There was no concerted effort to reverse or reinterpret the formal ruling. What caused considerable afterthought, however, was a subsequent communist historiography, which invariably presented the Kraków outcome as an Autonomist triumph—perhaps even a "final victory."[26] The Autonomists, in turn, were portrayed as the internationalist precursors of Lithuanian Communism.

While the Communist interpretation contains an element of truth, it nevertheless minimizes a number of complicating factors that obfuscate any final assessment. Communist authors do not give enough weight to the strongly democratic character of the LSDP as a deterrent to that party's entanglement with the RSDLP. They also underrate the breadth of autonomy sought by both factions, the motives of those who considered autonomy as only the first step toward increased national separatism in the future, and the radically changed contours of area politics in 1914–1918 as the more important determinant of people's affiliation with, or opposition to, Communism than the Kraków decision. By and large Kairys was probably correct when he suggested that, generally, throughout most of the pre-1914 period the direction of the party's central organs was in the hands of those whose embrace of socialist doctrine was compatible with the development of their Lithuanian identity.[27] On the other hand, national individuality and its practical significance appear to have been a lesser concern of the LSDP rank and file, especially in the ethnically diverse Vilnius and its environs.

A final comparison of the Autonomist and Federalist positions stated in September 1906 and resolved in August 1907 reveals not only points of disagreement but also significant parallelism between the two. The reasoning contained in both statements gave due regard to workers' national and sectional interests alike; that is, the delegates acted both as spokesmen for a particular class and as members of an increasingly distinct Lithuanian nationality. The attainment of their twin purpose at this time, however, became an internal all-Russian solution since both saw Lithuania as a part of a democratic Russian republic—a federal republic according to one project, a decentralized unitary state according to the other. Here, then, is a major programmatic change. The political aspiration of the LSDP in 1896–1897 was to establish a union of neighboring countries that would possibly include Russia. Its external solution of that time implied a staged progression from the recovery of Lithuania's "independence," to the convocation of a constituent assembly empowered to speak in its behalf and, finally, to the expected decision to join with others in a federal union of states. Ten years later the resolution of the national question was shifted to the general context of a radically restructured Russia that was expected to concede Lithuania a measure of self-government. Acceptance of an internal settlement of the national question distinguished the Lithuanian thinking until 1914–1918, when world conflagration, domestic upheavals in Russia and Germany, and Wilsonian idealism caused a revival of radical solutions—the formation of independent states in Central and Eastern Europe.

To be sure, the LSDP conferees differed on the definition of self-government they sought, but it does not appear that these particular differences were regarded as crucial. After all, in view of the expanse of self-government the Autonomists requested, one may well consider their program autonomist in form but federalist in substance. In effect, this was how Angarietis interpreted the Kraków compromise in one of his major works.[28] The initial impasse could also be attributed to a psychopolitical discord among the participants. Bent upon the unity of revolutionary action, some Autonomists viewed the restatement of a limited Lithuanian separatism as not pressing, others as perhaps not worth supporting. If Kairys could be said to have symbolized the former view, Eidukevičius personified the latter proclivity. By contrast, the Federalists were stronger backers of Lithuanian risorgimento who harbored a distrust of Russia, whether autocratic or democratic. Not surprisingly, they sought to promote their sectional and national interests by wresting an institutionalized recognition of a Lithuanian identity from the Russians in both interparty affairs and in the mode of coexistence between the two countries. In the end, due to a display of commendable politics, the controversy which threatened the unity of the LSDP dissolved into a compromise based on the idea of a wide autonomy.

—————

Realignment on the Land

Embrace of the Farmer

The men who set out to revive the battered Lithuanian social democracy at the turn of the century altered the recruitment policies in order to broaden the base of party operations. Without neglecting work in the city, they nevertheless decided to penetrate the low-income sectors of the rural population—the agricultural workers, landless peasants, and the small holders of land. The eventual success of this new strategy modified the very character of the LSDP, as the once urban group developed strong rural connections. More important, perhaps, as its incursion into the countryside progressed, it appears that the LSDP followed the routes which demanded a minimum of effort and promised a maximum of receptivity to its appeal.[1] As a result of such a drive for membership, on the eve of the 1905 revolution the socioeconomic base of LSDP support in the village was made up of farmers, their student offspring, and artisans.[2] By contrast, the political penetration of hired farm laborers and landless peasants, two rural strata whose combined total may have exceeded half a million people, had barely been started.[3]

Reliance on small and medium landowners had two main causes, the social background of the new party elite and the politicizing effects of education on the farmers. A socially dichotomized leadership of the 1890s witnessed the alliance between workers and artisans, on the one hand, and urbanized descendants of the Lithuanian nobility, on the other. But the people who converged to restore the party and extend its reach beyond the environs of Vilnius belonged to a different social group. A majority of them were either farmers or their student offspring aiming to become writers, lawyers, physicians, engineers, economists, or other members of the learned professions.[4] In some ways this new generation of leaders was still a part of the farm community; it retained strong family ties there, understood its economic interests, and knew both the rhythm of country life and the literary tradition that was beginning to enshrine it. Not surprisingly, when the new activists decided to communicate their message to the agricultural sector of the population, they first descended on the farmers.[5]

In addition to social affinity, a relatively advanced quality of the landowner's education facilitated the encroachment of the LSDP upon the farm territory. More than the uneducated and hardly accessible rural laborers, the Lithuanian farmers engaged in a clandestine instruction of their children, supported their country's cultural ferment, and were prone to resist the repressive Russian presence.[6] "So what if I'll have to share my property and wealth with the workers," reflected a farmer. "As long as there is justice in the world, as long as Lithuania is delivered from misery and slavery."[7] The LSDP was eminently successful in tapping such a farm sentiment, even if its strategy had gone amiss. The intended contacts with the village proletariat developed into temporary entrenchment in the rural middle class.

The convergence of the farmers and the social democrats resulted in a limited-purpose alliance. What held the two together was their increasingly assertive stance on a series of Lithuanian national aspirations. In other words, the justification of the partnership was primarily political, not ideological. The LSDP expected the rural sector to support its political agenda: convocation of a Lithuanian constituent assembly, formation of a federal state, democratization of public life, enactment of progressive labor legislation, etc. The farmers developed only marginal interest in the Marxist ideology, that coherent and consistent set of beliefs which constituted the sociopolitical program of the LSDP. In most instances the socialist doctrine was presented to them sparingly; when fuller treatment was attempted, its import often escaped the farm audiences. Kairys went so far as to suggest that the landowners were simply not a stratum suitable for Marxist agitation. However, since many social democrats regarded the political agenda of the LSDP as important as its ideological predisposition, ties to the farmers appeared to be a sensible strategy, especially when other groups did not yet have the capacity to mobilize this particular sector for political action.[8] At the time of the social democratic arrival upon the rural scene, neither the possible asymmetries of political and ideological objectives nor the stunted divergence of interests within the agricultural community itself seemed pressing enough to inspire an extensive discussion of potential problems.

Class Imperatives

The year of the revolution witnessed the start of a critical reassessment of rural coalition-building. Touching upon the relationship between policy and social status, this reexamination of alliance patterns was prompted by signs of increasing difficulties in reconciling the interests of the party's ideologically prescribed cohorts in the village, meaning the agricultural workers, with those of its actual supporters there, the small and medium farmers, artisans, and students. The agricultural strikes of mid-1905 and their political repercussions made interest aggregation a real concern to the LSDP. As noted earlier, these strikes occurred mainly on the large landed estates; presumably the owners of average holdings had no cause for alarm. Nevertheless, the strikes evoked unanticipated side effects. Their recurrence in 1906, indications of rural polarization based on ownership of land, the sharpening of ideological positions resulting from the "classes" which the jailed social democrats conducted for the hundreds of their fellow inmates, and the absence of countervailing forces committed to a reconciliation of interests all strengthened the impression that urban and rural workers, and not farmers, were the chief beneficiaries of socialist policies. The farmers began to desert the LSDP.[9] A pious rural populace shed its inhibitions and rallied to the socialists in 1905, when it thought they would help farmers obtain land. However, when that party's intentions toward the farmers were cast in doubt, as they were in 1906, agrarian support began to weaken. Farm disenchantment with the LSDP stemmed more from that party's tilt toward the village proletariat than from any possible religious backlash.

Faced with these disintegrative tensions, the party policymakers resorted to class-based solutions. Instead of a search for ways to prevent an open breach in its agrarian following, the LSDP avowed its primary devotion to the underprivileged sector; rural laborers, landless peasants, and small farmers. This was the gist of the decision made at a party conference in January 1906. Having admitted their previous neglect of the poorer section of the peasantry, the party conferees resolved to conduct their future operations primarily among these "true village proletarians."[10] Požela was pleased to inform Kapsukas that the strategy formerly followed by their *Draugas* Organization now prevailed in the LSDP.[11] But the January conferees did not intend to sever their party from the other groups completely. Rather, to facilitate the democratization of village public life the LSDP, while focusing on the rural proletariat, also aspired to place the political activities of farmers of small and medium holdings under its direction.[12] Incidentally, the proper place of the small farmers, owners of some fifty-four acres or less, was not firmly established.[13] They were classed among the true proletarians at one time but elevated to the intermediate tier the next. Only the large farmers and the landed nobility, as members of the upper social stratum, were beyond the pale of LSDP policy.

As the condition of the revolutionaries grew worse, LSDP recriminations against the farmers increased. These former followers of the party were called an "unsteady element" or "temporary companions" who scattered in different directions when a severe test came, while the laborers emerged as the most active and courageous builders of the new order.[14] Further, many of the young farmers who had flocked to the LSDP before 1905 were now designated as "revolutionaries rather than social democrats."[15] Finally, some have even caustically alleged that the farmers, as a group, tended to associate themselves with the winning party, the social democrats in 1905 or the tsarist authorities the following year. For their part, many farmers blamed the social democrats for the wrath of the tsarist government that has now enveloped them.[16]

According to the social democrats, the practical lesson to be drawn from recent experience was that the agricultural workers were capable of sustained revolutionary action, whereas the farmers were not. This viewpoint may prove to be valid, but fragmentary evidence and ideological predisposition so far have not suggested that it was. Describing the tenor of LSDP conversations held in January 1906, Kapsukas made the remark that the brunt of the tsarist punitive effort fell upon the farmers. Presumably it was the severities of political backlash, which included a pecuniary liability for the murder of local officials and public servants and the destruction of government property at the height of the revolutionary upheaval, that soured them on the socialists, not just their social status.[17] As for the laborers' capacity for unflagging action, experience did not always confirm preconception. In the first place, the rural workers were believed to have made only a modest contribution to the furtherance of the revolutionary cause.[18] In addition, one party caucus diagnosed a low degree of their class consciousness and organization, while a later conference found them developing a habit of caution that was bordering on timidity.[19] Perhaps Kairys left an accurate description of reality when he suggested that both farmers and workers displayed a limited capacity for endurance.[20]

Dubious Prospects

The question of which social group actually possessed the greatest revolutionary potential tended to become moot as the year of aggressive activism receded into history. Vivid impressions of the revolutionary experience, altered policy objectives, and an increased diversity of LSDP policymakers produced by various unity efforts had a stronger bearing on the realignment of social forces than the correct assessment of group behavior. As already indicated, the net result of these preferences and perceptions was disappointment in the farmers and an attendant recommitment to the true village proletarians. Most of the decision-making forums of the LSDP, notably the three congresses of 1905, 1907, and 1909 and such national conferences as those held in early 1906 and then in 1912, restated the primacy of effort among the rural poor.[21] In order of a diminishing ideological kinship, this low-income category consisted of hired laborers, landless peasants, and small landowners. Yet occasionally various leaders of the party still voiced the hope that the medium farmers and these proletarian groups would eventually coalesce for a common political end.[22]

In spite of repeated intentions to attend to the needs of the low-income sector, the success in forming primary party organizations on the large landed estates, or conducting other types of political activity there, was a modest one.[23] While the achievements of the Suwałki and Panevėžys organizations were considerable, progress in the Grodno and Vilnius guberniias was especially slow. According to the delegates to the 1907 party congress, recruitment from among the rural laborers there had not even been attempted prior to that time.[24] In more ways than one, it seemed, the world of the rural laborer was still unknown territory to many members of the LSDP. One obstacle to that party's drive for membership was the language barrier between its Lithuanian organizers and the many agricultural workers who spoke either Belorussian or Polish.[25] More important perhaps, there is reason to think that a segment of the LSDP continued to concentrate its efforts on the farmers, rendering the implementation of the new course a problematic issue. The LSDP proponents of the landowning interests generally distrusted the farmhands, were slow to enlist them in the party, and sought to shield the farmers from agricultural strikes. Further, to feign compliance with the new recruitment strategy, they may have inflated the number of agricultural workers in the party through a dubious designation of their occupations.[26] In short, many retained a greater affinity for the landowners than for the farm laborers.

The agricultural workers, for their part, were not always as receptive to socialist overtures as the party presumed them to be. The association of the local LSDP organizations with the interests of the farmers made the hired laborers dubious about the socialist concern for the rural have-nots. As a result, the workers were not eager to affiliate with the LSDP, and those who did enroll sometimes regarded themselves as second-class members.[27] Symbolizing an enhanced "labor" presence in the village, the city agitators who were charged by the party to direct the agricultural strikes eventually may have eased these workers' apprehensions about the farm-oriented local socialists.

13

Divided They Stood

The constellation of changed conditions, policies, and personnel mentioned in the preceding chapters modified the scope and character of LSDP operations from 1906 to 1914. These interrelated factors included the party's heightened class awareness, along with a revision of its national objectives. No less important than class ideals or issue conflicts was the changing nature of the party leadership caused by successful unity efforts, the emergence of regional activists, and a significantly reduced availability of the veteran LSDP elite for regular political assignment. Above all, the telling effects of government repression, though tempered with prospects of parliamentary activity, tended to redefine the terms of the party's structural integrity. These developments converged to beget disintegrative influences inside the LSDP apparatus. In the end the party lapsed into a state of fragmented existence. To be sure, a spirit of goodwill that existed between the former revolutionaries, their aversion to dogmatism, respect for customary party discipline, and a constant proximity of danger precluded the occurrence of irreparable breach. Yet the various clusters of individuals who persisted in the party work managed to preserve but a semblance of organizational coherence.

Dilemmas at the Polls

The series of imperial concessions intended to deflate the revolution of 1905 included the establishment of a bicameral parliament. Its upper house was known as the State Council, while the more representative lower chamber was called the State Duma. Although the compo-

sition of this parliament was determined on the twin bases of appoint-
ment and circumscribed elections, its establishment nevertheless
offered the prospect of Russia's evolution into a constitutional monarchy. Optimism particularly rested on the belief that no law was to be
passed without the consent of the Duma. To be sure, tsarist aversion
to the democratization of government soon tempered these great expectations, yet the coming of the Duma, the rapid approach of electoral
campaigns, and interest in the future work of the deputies all quickened people's political energies.

A total of four elections to the Duma were held during the course
of that body's existence. Controlled by the Constitutional Democrats,
a liberal Russian party, the first Duma endured from May 1906 to its
dissolution by the emperor later in July. The decision of the social
democrats and the Socialist Revolutionaries to drop their earlier boycott of the elections made the second Duma more radical than the
first; it lasted from March to June, 1907. The breakup of this Duma
and the issuance of a new electoral law, which arbitrarily reduced
the representation of the peasantry and of the national minorities,
dimmed the prospects for constitutional government. The sponsors
of the bill intended the future assemblies to be Russian in spirit and
submissive to the tsarist authorities. As a result of these structural
changes, the third Duma (November 1907 to June 1912) and fourth
Duma (November 1912 to February 1917) were dominated by various
conservative parties.

Seven ethnic Lithuanians were elected to serve in both the first
and the second Dumas, but their totals fell to four in each of the last
two Dumas. Like most revolutionary parties in the empire,those in
Lithuania initially arrayed their forces against the Duma. Representatives of all of the socialist parties active in the area, including those of
the LSDP, conferred in Vilnius late in December 1905 and unanimously
agreed on a policy of "active boycott."[1] The policymakers of the LSDP
still harbored a view that the current unrest was bound to create
conditions enabling the workers and peasants to overthrow the existing order. Participation in the elections, they said, would tend to divert
the people from a revolutionary course of action. And why bother, the
Duma itself would surely be washed away in a tide of discontent.
Clearly, what the LSDP had not anticipated were such asymmetric
developments as the resurgence of autocratic power and the election

of a large number of deputies who managed to use the Duma as the tribune of the people.[2] When they realized what happened, the policy of boycott was given short shrift.

The work of the first Duma elicited an ambiguous response from the LSDP. First, the party propaganda insisted that the Duma proceedings had nothing in store for the low-income sectors of the population. The need to have the consent of both the emperor and the upper house of parliament would tend to moderate the nature of Duma initiatives; a Duma that ventured on a bold legislative program could not expect to last a single day. While it thus minimized the possibility of that body's tangible contribution to working-class interests, the LSDP nevertheless urged the leftist deputies there to popularize various socialist ideas and criticize the tsarist authorities. Deputies were asked to help the people see the "bloody hands of the tyrants."[3] It was obvious the party hoped to use the Duma as a means for sustaining its revolutionary agitation.

LSDP involvement in the elections to the second Duma was a foregone conclusion. Joining the bandwagon needed little explanation; the Duma was to act as a forum in which socialist proposals could be aired and the people could be imbued with revolutionary doctrines. The party's chief immediate concern was the convocation of a constituent assembly to lay the foundations of a democratic government.[4] Their boycott mentality now a thing of the past, the LSDP activists plunged themselves into the electoral campaign.[5] Hoping to put their limited resources to good use, they converged upon the Kaunas guberniia, where Kairys, Kapsukas, Mažylis, and Požela each assumed responsibility for the coordination of campaign activities in districts assigned to them. Under their direction, district party organizations and their supporters carried the burden of the campaign. Finally, specific responsibilities devolved upon the local chapters of the LSDP, while individual party members were expected to contribute a day's pay to defray the costs of the effort.

The labors of these campaigners contributed to the election of five socialist deputies. One of them, Antanas Povylius (1871–1961), received some recognition when he attended the Grand Diet of Vilnius in 1905. He later joined the LSDP press bureau in that city. Pranas Gudavičius (1876–1956), another successful candidate, was a Berlin-educated physician who, as a Duma deputy, became adept in interpersonal relations. Vladas Stašinskas(1874–1944), a lawyer trained at the

University of Moscow, gained political visibility when he addressed
the Duma on such questions as education, land reform, and Russian
policies in Lithuania. Finally, the contributions of Povilas Kumelis (b.
1880) and Antanas Kupstas (b. 1881), two participants in LSDP activities, consisted of their service on the Duma committees.[6] While Kumelis and Kupstas apparently ended their involvement in government
affairs when the second Duma was dissolved, the other three deputies
continued their intermittent service in the public sector.

Socialist victory at the polls imparted a new dimension to LSDP
pursuits. The Duma delegation became the hub of a quasi-legal political activity which, for a short period of time, supplemented the party's
underground revolutionary operations. Seeking to coordinate the two
types of activity, the party named Kairys a liaison between its central
committee and the Duma group. Although the deputies chose Povylius as the officer responsible for their records and correspondence, it
was Kairys who became the group's actual secretary. He resided in
St. Petersburg, attended the consultations between the deputies, and
helped them maintain communication with their constituents.[7] In St.
Petersburg these five socialist deputies affiliated themselves with the
RSDLP fraction. However, when Duma politics revolved around the so-
called national question, all the Lithuanian deputies, including such
non-socialists as Andrius Bulota (1872–1941) and Petras Leonas
(1864–1938), usually met in a caucus.[8] A lively correspondence developed between the social democratic representatives and their constituents. According to Kairys, in the course of a single month the deputies
received 199 messages, including some bearing thousands of signa-
tures.[9] People offered various specific proposals, such as keeping the
draftees in their home countries or abolishing capital punishment.
They complained about high taxes, the injustices allegedly committed
by the landed nobility, or the excesses of punitive expeditions. In most
cases, however, they turned their thoughts toward land and freedom.

Communication between the legislators and their constituents
came to an abrupt end when the emperor prorogued the second Duma
and then put the Lithuanian socialists behind bars. What precipitated
government action against these social democrats was the publication
of an appeal which all of them had signed.[10] Addressed to Lithuanian
workers and peasants, the appeal was meant to apprise the reading
public of the position the delegates intended to assume in the Duma.
There they proffered a plethora of civil liberties, as well as comprehen-

sive social and economic reforms. Above all, the document mentioned their quest of an autonomous Lithuania existing within the confines of a democratic Russian state, an image of their country's future that cost the former legislators one-year prison terms.

The announcement of a new electoral law, which coincided with the dissolution of the second Duma, portended serious trouble for the parties of the left, especially those in Russia's ethnic borderlands. The advisability of participation in elections to the next Duma sparked a debate among the revolutionary parties. A majority of LSDP activists were inclined to stay in the race, but others, including Kapsukas, wanted to abandon it.[11] Awaiting a decision by the party congress, scheduled for August 1907, the central committee hedged, while several local party organizations weighed the question and took a stand. Their July and August conferences in Kaunas, Šiauliai, and at least one Suwałki district favored participation in the elections, but in Panevėžys the conferees opposed it. Even where majorities carried the day, the idea of boycotting the election elicited considerable support.[12]

The weeks of indecision ended when the party congress, held in Kraków, resolved to enter the race in order to agitate the people and propagate socialist views.[13] This time, however, Pranas Kuzma (b. 1877), a onetime metal worker at a shipbuilding company and then the Putilov factory in St. Petersburg, was the only Lithuanian social democrat who managed to get elected to the third Duma. (He was also the last member of the LSDP to serve in this Russian parliament, since none was elected in 1912.) Like his party predecessors, Kuzma cooperated with the Russian social democrats, while conferring with other Lithuanian deputies on matters affecting the interests of their country.[14] Directed by a conservative Russian majority, the third Duma elicited no favorable response from its social democratic critics. Instead, they dubbed it the Black Duma and said the Lithuanians, whether as members of working-class groups or those of a subject nationality, had no reason to expect anything positive from its deliberations.[15] This Duma shattered the illusion of support by the Russians that some minority reformers may have entertained. It was time for the LSDP to retreat into the Lithuanian fold.

The Vilnius Caldron

Conscious of the city's ethnic pluralism, its rich social democratic traditions, and a working-class following, the Vilnius organization evolved into a distinctive, if somewhat contentious, component of the LSDP. In 1905 its approximate membership stood at 1,500, but then fell to 1,100 the following year. (The mid-1906 membership figures for the Vilnius chapters of the other Marxist groups were as follows: The Bund—1,200, the RSDLP—800, and the PPS in Lithuania—300.)[16] At the time of the 1907 party congress, its five city wards comprised a body of supporters which included 817 members. In addition, twenty study groups facilitated the radiation of party influence by instructing many other wage earners on such questions as workers' economic demands, the nature of their struggles, and the attainment of socialism. Finally, like the RSDLP and the Jewish Bund, the LSDP infiltrated into local labor unions, both legal and illegal, and operated a school for political agitators.[17]

An opening phase of the friction between the party's top leadership and its strong Vilnius contingent came about in 1906–1907. Their disagreements revolved around issues associated either with the national question or with ties to non-Marxian parties.[18] In the first place, when the question of Lithuania's future brought on a clash of the Autonomists with the Federalists, Vilnius activists like Zigmas Angarietis, Jonas Janulevičius (1874–1941), and Jadvyga Netupskaitė (1887–1942) favored the former group, while the party's central apparatus initially leaned toward the latter faction. Relatedly, on merger with the RSDLP, the Vilnius coterie appeared to have fewer reservations than its cautious colleagues on the central committee. In addition to the problems bearing on Lithuanian-Russian relations, the advisability of collaboration with other groups caused mutual recrimination. Traditionally, the LSDP engaged in a limited type of cooperation (as well as continuous rivalry) with the Lithuanian liberals. Consultations over political strategy during the elections to the State Duma, mutually supportive journalistic endeavors, and aid to the victims of government repression were examples of the party's collaborative stance. The Vilnius critics generally frowned on such cross-ideological connections. For a while, then, these issues bred dissension in the ranks of the party, prompting the central committee to resort to political maneuvers which included the mediating efforts of such LSDP functionaries as Vladas Sirutavičius and Jurgis Smalstys. As a result of their mediation, and of such later developments as the formal resolution of the national question and the arrest or reassignment of the principal Vilnius opponents, these particular controversies eventually abated.

The fissures in the party grew sharper during a later phase of tensions rife in the Vilnius organization. Central to these political quarrels of the 1908–1912 period was Pranas Eidukevičius, a member of the central committee who acquired considerable prominence in party affairs. Unfortunately, a combination of such interacting factors as his national connections, character traits, and a narrow interpretation of LSDP activities tended to alienate him from his colleagues and reduce his political effectiveness. For years Eidukevičius was exposed to a variety of cultural and national influences—Lithuanian, Latvian, Polish, Belorussian, and Russian. His strong affinities with the Polish labor movement may have included a ten-year collaboration with the PPS, a party which he abandoned when its local branch merged with the LSDP. The supporters of the Lithuanian party who took up a rather ambitious national agenda must have been discomfited by the kind of amorphous ethnicity that Eidukevičius represented.[19]

Although a social democrat of long standing, Eidukevičius was only recently acquired by the LSDP. His election to its central committee in 1907 resulted from support by the dominant Autonomist faction, the need to provide the new partners from the PPS with representation on the central organ, and the dispersion of the previous elite. The reelection of Eidukevičius at the 1909 congress, on the other hand, stemmed from a parallelism of interests between his own urban loyalists and the rural delegates picked by Angarietis.[20] While in Vilnius, Eidukevičius assumed the responsibility for that city's party organization, a difficult task whose performance called for integrative skills he may not have acquired. New to the Vilnius political scene, Eidukevičius found it difficult to establish closer rapport with its seasoned party regulars, relying instead on the fringes of LSDP membership.[21] Regarding his political operations there generally, workers' professional concerns seem to have engrossed his attention, which displeased those who sought to broaden the scope of LSDP activities.[22]

Finally, a worsening of interpersonal relations between Eidukevičius and his party co-workers contributed to the predicaments of the Vilnius LSDP. The root of these particular problems probably lay in the personality of Eidukevičius. Although a practiced organization man, he was portrayed by Biržiška and other contemporaries as a rather ambitious, arbitrary, arrogant, and autocratic type of person, shunned by his fellow workers and intellectuals alike. These alleged character traits tended to estrange the city party loyalists, turn other social democrats away from the LSDP, and impair the coherence of central committee operations.[23] Due to these bad feelings and other differences, individual party leaders began to act independently of one another, rather than seek a consensus of opinion. For instance, one of the main reasons why Visuomenė (Society), a socialist monthly put out in 1910–1911, kept its distance from the regular party organization was the desire of its publishers to bypass Eidukevičius.[24] Clearly, it was an uneasy peace that prevailed among the Vilnius social democrats.

The Intellectual Luggage

If the regular Vilnius organization could be regarded as one center of LSDP activity, an array of such prominent party men as Biržiška, Domaševičius, Janulaitis, Kairys, Matulaitis, Juozas Paknys, and Antanas Purėnas (1881–1962) constituted another source of social democratic initiative. These were the party intellectuals. Whether they resided in Lithuania (as most of them did) or in some other country, collectively they now generated a good deal of quasi-political activity.

One of the group's distinctive characteristics was its deep involvement in cultural pursuits that often contained a socialist dimension. Publication of socialist newspapers and journals, provision of articles and reviews for various periodicals, studies of socialism in other countries, efforts to transmit socialist values and beliefs to the young, presentation of trend analyses, participation in learned societies, translation of foreign literature, and establishment of libraries and evening schools all provide examples of activities that engaged the group's attention. The first, and initially the most basic, reason for such an extension of party work to various cognate fields was an ideological one. When the 1907 party congress unanimously prescribed a broad cultural program for LSDP organizations and individual members, it reflected the view that education will facilitate the political socialization process. According to the delegates, new opportunities which were opened up in the wake of the revolution, coupled with the fear that other social and political groups will utilize them to wrest the loyalties of the laboring class to their own purposes, called for a widening of interests.[25] In an article published in early 1908, Kairys informed the party rank and file about the nature of the new direction and its causes.[26] Without disparaging conventional political functions, he clearly focused on the cultural thrust.

In time, however, this particular rationale developed into a variant justification of the cultural endeavor. What was once an ideologically motivated strategy became a precept of political realism. For many social democrats, cultural labor remained practically the only kind of activity possible under severe political conditions. These educated party notables involved themselves deeply in a revolutionary course of action when the situation warranted it, as it did in 1905–1907 and would do after 1912. Their intervening years, however, were spent chiefly on depoliticized projects. When the workers, students, and intellectuals lost their enthusiasm for politics, Biržiška recalled, the unheroic party work became "more complicated, versatile, [and] drab."[27] Its most significant attributes now were civic, cultural, and social responsibilities, not strict party politics.[28] It was this preponderant attention given to the cultural tasks that turned the party intellectuals into a faction within the LSDP.

In addition to ideological concerns and political conditions, the cultural bent of the party intellectuals must be attributed to their own academic interests and occupational goals.[29] Most of these men were products of various institutions of higher learning, getting to be well-known doctors, lawyers, engineers, scholars and other professionals. It is not surprising, then, that their interests went beyond the confines of routine political activity.

Besides their cultural propensities, cooperation with the liberals distinguished the party intellectuals as an autonomous entity. Due to the nature of psychopolitical commitment springing from a nation-wide dislike of Russian rule, the term *liberal* was more complex in Lithuania than in countries leading an independent existence. In the Lithuanian context liberals were educated individuals, or groups of individuals, favoring progressive reforms—cultural, socioeconomic, and political. When in politics, they gravitated toward the incipient Democratic party. Liberals shied off the social democrats because they demurred to that party's class-based ideology or could not fully support its revolutionary methods. However, they also kept their distance from the clerically inspired Christian Democrats; they doubted that party's reliance on papal encyclicals for its theoretical underpinning, disliked the conservatism of its senior clergy, and generally frowned on the entanglement of the church in public affairs. Liberals thus generally pursued a middle course of action. Yet the more cautious ones (the early Smetona type, for example) sometimes flirted with the Christian Democrats, while those radically inclined (the Grinius variety) would join hands with the social democrats—in the 1890s, during the pre-1914 years, and especially in 1926, when they formed a coalition government in independent Lithuania. For their part, the less doctrinaire Christian Democrats (like the Rev. Tumas-Vaižgantas) and similarly disposed social democrats (of the Biržiška stripe) were willing to collaborate with the liberals on various cultural enterprises. Unlike those who had written the post-revolutionary period off as sheer repression, the party intellectuals viewed it as a portentous stage in the development of society. Accordingly, they endeavored to understand the nature of the incipient changes and then reorient themselves to the challenges they might present. Broadly speaking, the party intellectuals foresaw the rise of an urban and rural middle class whose intellectual brain trust would seek to dominate Lithuania's public life.[30] In the marketplace of action and thought the participants in the mounting controversies dichotomized into "progressives" and "reactionaries," to use the crude labels of the period. The first group was an aggregation of liberals with the leftward tinge and persons of the socialist persuasion. The other camp consisted of clerically inspired Christian Democrats aided by those among the liberals steering a cautious and prudent course; its cultural program issued from a "realistic" assessment of possibilities.[31]

Cooperation with the leftist liberals facilitated (or, at a minimum, posed no threat to) the realization of three objectives. In the first place, the liberals, who were weakened by defections to the right, and the social democrats, now in the throes of a failed revolution, had joined forces against the conservatives—or the "black peril," as they put it.[32] In addition, collaboration with the liberals offered the party intellectuals an acceptable way of enhancing their country's cultural development, an important consideration to the socialist exponents of Lithuania's national renewal.[33] Finally, a partnership confined to a limited range of cultural endeavors did not preclude parallel efforts aimed at preserving and articulating a separate socialist identity, especially in politics.[34] Sometime after the 1907 congress Moravskis proposed to the party policymakers a substantial deepening of their cooperation with the liberals. Presumably fearing the impairment of their identity, the central committee

of the LSDP turned the idea down.[35] Conceptually at least, cooperation did not mean amalgamation.

The centerpiece of the party intellectuals was *Visuomenė*, a socialist monthly conceived by Domaševičius but edited by Biržiška and
Janulaitis.[36] Although authorized by the government, *Visuomenė* was
heavily censored by the authorities. According to Biržiška, the censor
was "almost dictating" the contents of its opening statement.[37] The
previous newspapers of the LSDP, such as *Naujoji gadynė*, *Skardas*
(The Echo), and *Žarija*, were party organs intended for the general
public. By contrast, *Visuomenė* was a product of the nationally minded
socialist intellectuals devoted to an educated audience, particularly
the students. Further, although edited by a member of the central
committee, the journal was free of party control. A satisfactory modus
vivendi enveloped the factious elements of the LSDP: *Visuomenė* sti-
fled its opposition to the party regulars, while Eidukevičius did not
obstruct the progress of the intellectuals.[38] This mutual tolerance was
entered in the party annals when a conference of the LSDP, held in
1912, embraced *Visuomenė* as the "first ray of light" brightening the
period of the counterrevolution.[39] *Visuomenė* was meant to enhance
the consciousness of students interested in socialism. Its publishers
further hoped to strengthen the work of the party with newly enlisted
supporters. Lastly, the party intellectuals sought to improve the visibility of socialists participating in their country's cultural and political
life.[40] There is reason to think that these efforts met with some success. A number of the newly prominent public figures are known to
have belonged to various student groups keenly interested in *Visuomenė*.[41] The journal may have sharpened their preoccupation with
public affairs.

The Party Professionals

In addition to the Eidukevičius group in Vilnius and the Biržiška-style
intellectuals, yet another cluster of individuals—the party professionals—exhibited the characteristics of a political faction. The two well-
known spokesmen for this particular orientation were Kapsukas and
Angarietis, although in some respects party men like Eidukevičius,
Mažylis, Požela, and Šepetys also favored a similar course of conduct.[42]

There were two main issues which separated this group from the
party intellectuals, accent on party organization and opposition to

flirtation with the liberals. Unlike Kairys, who expanded the LSDP interest in the cultural sector, Kapsukas remained preoccupied with the organizational dimensions of the task. As far as he was concerned, the socialist response to the challenges of the post-revolutionary period necessitated a determined effort to deepen the meaning of class consciousness, strengthen labor morale, enlist workers and smallholders in the primary party organizations, and above all, replenish the LSDP leadership corps.[43] Other party professionals equivocated. Šepetys, while doubting the feasibility of nonpartisan cultural projects, viewed them as a legitimate socialist alternative under the circumstances. For his part, Eidukevičius basically rejected the direction taken by *Visuomenė*. However, realizing the impossibility of political work among the laboring class, he did not interfere with the activities of the party intellectuals.[44] Demonstrating LSDP capacity for compromise, the two party conclaves of the period, the 1908 conference and the 1909 congress, reconciled the various preferred types of activity with the constraints of the moment. They resolved (futilely, as it turned out) to bolster the faltering party apparatus, but at the same time appreciated the merits of a broad cultural program.[45]

The party professionals were also unhappy with socialist ties to the liberal bourgeoisie, urging instead an exclusive dependence on the urban and rural working class. Kapsukas and Angarietis, despite their own occasional cooperation with the liberals, were rather emphatic about the need for such a dogmatically conceived course of action.[46] Initially Biržiška attributed their disapproval of the party intellectuals to misunderstandings caused by the dearth of information available to the two imprisoned revolutionaries; he even thought that a clarification of the position the intellectuals assumed had resulted in an adjustment of differences with Kapsukas.[47] However, as Kapsukas and Angarietis tended towards Bolshevism, their criticism of the party intellectuals hardened into vilification. In true Leninist fashion, they ultimately stigmatized their former colleagues as the "liquidators" of the LSDP.

Their embrace of Russian Bolshevism made the two men political outcasts in their own country, though not to its Communist fringe. After Lithuania's consolidation of its independence in 1919–1920, Kapsukas and Angarietis decided to move to the Soviet side (yet also remain immersed in Lithuanian affairs). They helped found the Communist Party of Lithuania and were always included in its leadership.

When the Red Army tried to export the Communist faith to the neighboring countries in the West, as it did in 1918–1919, both served as members of the short-lived Soviet government in Lithuania, Kapsukas as its head and Angarietis as commissar for internal affairs. The collapse of these Communist plans then led to their eventual resettlement in Moscow. There they lectured at various party schools, attempted to guide the Communist underground in their native country, and wrote extensively on both current events and the history of Lithuanian socialism. Finally, the two leaders worked in the executive committee of the Communist International, where, from 1921, Angarietis represented the Communist Party of Lithuania, while Kapsukas, who started in 1923, was eventually named head of a secretariat specializing in Baltic and Polish affairs.[48] Kapsukas died of natural causes in 1935, whereas Angarietis perished in the Great Terror when, in 1940, a firing squad carried out a sentence of death.

Psychological Differences

Going back to the pre-1914 fragmentation of the LSDP, one might also note the psychological overtones differentiating the organization men from the intellectuals. Party professionals like Kapsukas represented a heroic obduracy headed for failure. First, the post-revolutionary period, to them, was nothing but an unmitigated "black era," its social, economic, and cultural development devoid of any positive attributes. Wedded to the kind of political action the government resolved to eradicate, they dismissed a wide spectrum of activities which it was willing to tolerate. Having condemned the action falling within the range of possibility, they proceeded to ennoble their quest for the unattainable. A blinding commitment to the cause made them despise many of the life's ordinary pursuits. Thus, Kapsukas expected Kairys to quit his job and dedicate himself to reviving the party, scoffed at Domaševičius for helping found a local credit union, and feared the disruption of his own family life if his wife sought personal happiness through material comfort.[49] Second, while their narrow interpretation of the functions appropriate to the social democrats had elevated the role of the party machine and venerated the absorption in its operations, the party professionals at the same time undermined the future effectiveness of the LSDP by limiting its source of support to a single social class. Instead of aggregating a variety of related social and economic interests, they viewed themselves as the champions of a relatively small segment of the population. Not surprisingly, the combined weight of sectarian mentality and government repression kept the party professionals a marginal entity.

By contrast, party intellectuals such as Biržiška evinced the kind of resilience that enabled them to withstand the perils of the counter-revolution without permanent rupture. A constructive conception of reality saved them from a state of mental gloom, prompting them instead to take advantage of such opportunities as the dynamics of a changing society might offer. To them the party organization was always a means to the furtherance of socialist ends, never a substitute for them. When the maintenance of its administrative and functional integrity became a virtual impossibility, the organizational tasks were practically suspended until a mounting unrest in Russia permitted their resumption around 1912. In the meantime, the party intellectuals harnessed their aptitude and capacity for other types of labor which, in their estimation, bore some relevance to the socialist cause. Severed from the bulk of the former LSDP following, they maintained their ties to the leftist intelligentsia with whom they shared a similar outlook on a variety of public issues. Together they produced a respectable volume of work.

Conclusion

————

The onset of World War I in 1914 signaled the approach of a new age. The fall of the main monarchical systems on the continent, the triumph of Lenin-style Bolshevism in Russia, the advent of Wilsonian idealism, and the drive for national unification and freedom from foreign domination all converged to recast the organization of the European world. Amidst all the immense suffering the war caused, the hope for a better future was planted. The nations and peoples in Europe and beyond were readying themselves for a new beginning.

Lithuania, too, experienced both affliction and anticipation. From the moment the invading and retreating armies commenced their sojourns there, a group of Lithuanian leaders initiated a series of actions aimed first at helping those who suffered from the war and then at ridding their country of foreign occupations. Emanating from Vilnius, the campaign for Lithuania's reconstitution elicited ample support from various sections of the Lithuanian diaspora scattered in Russia, Western Europe, and the United States. Debilitating revolutions and other dislocations in both Russia and Germany, together with a determined Lithuanian effort that found some backing in the Western capitals, augured the success of these endeavors. In 1918 Lithuania regained its independence.

The victory of Bolshevism in Russia and the establishment of many independent national states in Central and Eastern Europe shook the entire socialist movement. Conflicting allegiances and ideological issues consummated its split into two mutually antagonistic types, evolutionary and revolutionary. Democratic socialism represented the former variety. Reflecting the belief that socialism could be achieved through gradual changes in individual nations, it fostered the development of numerous worker-oriented parties actively participating in the governments or politics of their respective countries. Despite the espousal of a common theoretical basis and other general similarities, these parties inevitably took on the national coloration of whatever indigenous environment enveloped their activities. In contrast, modern Communism was a movement whose advocates believed in the necessity of violent struggle to overthrow the capitalist order and impose their own system of social organization. In addition, they denounced the bourgeois nation-states, seeking their replacement by an international socialist commonwealth. Since the Soviet Union was pictured as a partial embodiment of Communist ideals and the catalyst in their ultimate attainment, Communists everywhere were expected to forgo their conception of party strategy, policy, organization, and procedure in deference to that of the Kremlin.

The split within the Marxian camp dealt the Lithuanian social democracy a severe blow, while strong enmity engulfed those on the opposite sides of the schism. Kairys, Bielinis, Biržiška, Požela, Sirutavičius, and a host of other LSDP leaders, ordinary members, and identifiers remained true to the kind of democratic socialism that sought the fulfillment of its class objectives within the context of an emerging Lithuanian state. But many others, including Kapsukas, Angarietis, Eidukevičius, and Šepetys, embraced Communism. Their association with Soviet Russia was so strong and close that the very idea of an independent Lithuania became anathema. Indeed, on two occasions the Lithuanian Communists sought to quench their country's independence in conjunction with the efforts of the Red Army to export the Russian Revolution to other nations. They failed in their initial attempt, in 1918–1919, but were successful in 1940. Finally, Domaševičius, a figure of towering prestige in the LSDP, appeared to avoid rigid commitment at this particular juncture. Absorption in revolutionary activity probably made him receptive to an autonomous type of Communism, but not to one warped by the interests of a foreign power. Whatever the motive, during the years following the consolidation of Lithuania's independence Domaševičius languished on the sidelines of political action.

The LSDP that took part in the politics of independent Lithuania never regained the stature it possessed in prewar times. The party sought to extend the boundaries of its influence by penetrating the labor unions, appealing to certain segments of the younger generation, and concentrating its efforts on the local government. Nationally, however, the number of seats it managed to win in the legislative elections of the 1920s ranged from 10 percent to 18 percent of the total. The LSDP lagged behind the Catholic bloc and the Populists.

The breach in the Marxist camp, as already indicated, was a major cause of LSDP diminution. Three other reasons deserve consideration. One important factor was Poland's annexation of Vilnius. Issuing from both colliding images of their respective national futures and diverging political interests, the friction between the Lithuanians and the Poles erupted in an armed conflict which, in October 1920, removed approximately a third of Lithuania's disputed territory from its jurisdiction. The dispute over Vilnius lasted until the outbreak of World War II. The city was seized by the Red Army in September 1939, after the Russian and German forces subdued the Poles. Finally, in October, having exacted from the Lithuanians the right to station its military bases in their country, the Soviet Union agreed to restore a part of the so-called Vilnius territory, including the historical capital itself, to Lithuania. During the two interwar decades, however, party politics was confined to a smaller, ethnically distinct Lithuania that Kaunas came to symbolize. Yet the Lithuanian social democracy was rooted in Vilnius. Having an appreciation of the area's social complexion, the LSDP managed to blend the disparate interests of its Lithuanian, Polish, Jewish, and Belorussian constituents in that part of the country. Losing this microcosm of a modern urban community hurt the party at the polls.

The second limitation on the effectiveness of the LSDP derived from its class approach to politics generally. When a political party seeks to advance the interests of a single social class, as did the LSDP, it often encounters difficulties in winning the support of those who identify themselves with other socioeconomic groups. This was a serious obstacle to the electoral success of the LSDP, for the laboring class in Lithuania was neither large nor solid. A leadership adept at interest aggregation could have tempered class polarization with a stable coalition of interests. But skilled politicians, unlike ideologues, were in short supply, and the so-called catchall parties had been slow to take root in East European politics.

The stress on class conciliation was the third reason for the weakening of the LSDP condition. The Marxian theory of historical change endowed the industrial proletariat with the task of effecting a social revolution that would replace capitalism by socialism. Fueled by the antagonism between social classes, such a succession from one mode of production to another was said to be a rational, progressive, and inevitable course of social development. But while this new Marxist faith, which had enhanced the role and power of the working class, animated the founders of the LSDP, it disaffected those who sought the consolidation of national energies. Concerned with national cohesion, they strove for an alleviation of class antagonism, not its aggravation.

National unification was meant in part to help the Lithuanians combat foreign domination before 1914 and defend their country's interests after its independence was finally achieved in 1918. At the same time, however, it was reinforced by various strands of nationalism, including an extreme postwar form found in European fascism. Nationalism in Lithuania received an increasingly systematic exposition of its meaning and purpose after liberal democracy and popular participation in politics were jolted there by a military coup in late 1926. Aided by the Nationalist Union and numerous other supporters, Antanas Smetona, installed by the military as president, proceeded to shape the contours of an authoritarian system that lasted until the country's occupation by the Soviet Union in 1940. As his prepossession with national unity presaged conversion of the pluralist Lithuanian society into a monolithic community, theories and practices which accented the conflict between discrete groups and interests fell by the wayside. Accordingly, censure faced all political parties save the Nationalist. While the Catholic groups and the Populists managed to preserve some vestiges of their activity, the ban against the social democrats was fully realized.

Lithuania thus pursued a course charted by President Smetona and his numerous followers who either formally enrolled in the Nationalist Union or simply coalesced to back the leader. Accepting certain aspects of philosophical reasoning, government organization, political symbolism, and policy direction which were commonly associated with fascist states, but rejecting their structural and behavioral extremism, the Lithuanian Nationalists moved toward the mid-century mark. The cataclysms of World War II, however, abruptly choked off their progress, as well as that of the country whose destinies they managed. The Hitler-Stalin pact (and the attendant secret protocols) negotiated in 1939 carved up various parts of Eastern Europe into

German and Russian spheres of influence. The ensuing increase in Russian military power and expansive propensity limited substantially the autonomy of East European states, but did not deprive them of their statehood. In contrast, to Lithuania, Latvia, and Estonia the Kremlin administered the ultimate sanction—outright annexation to the Soviet Union.

A century has elapsed since the time the Vilnius socialists registered their resolve to liberate their country and its working class. What, then, is the political legacy of social democracy to Lithuania's future generations? Does the LSDP bequest—purpose, method, and accomplishment—have any relevance to that country's present agenda? One might first reflect on the socioeconomic aspects of the socialist endeavor. On these the conclusion emerges that, although social stratification was as evident in Lithuania as in many other countries, the concepts of irreconcilable interests and class-determined politics have never penetrated the depths of its national psyche—nor are they likely to at a time of ideological defervescence. Rather, what has endured is the LSDP commitment to articulate and ameliorate the plight of the underprivileged sectors of the population. Clearly it was more than a symbolic coincidence that the socialist effort commenced in the Vilnius sweatshops and on the peripheries of landed estates, and not at theological seminaries or within the editorial boards of the leading journals. The kind of progressive legislation the party had in mind or on the table, during both the tsarist occupation and the period of Lithuania's independence, was intended primarily to alleviate the condition of the country's low-income groups. Encouragement of labor union activity, participation in urban and rural strikes, improvement of medical insurance, support of laws on better working conditions, and concern with eating houses and orphanages—they all, without in any way belittling the contributions of others, served to substantiate the LSDP proclivity.

Equally significant was the socialist effort in the field of ethnic interaction. A cardinal achievement of the LSDP was its demonstrated capacity to articulate Lithuanian national aspirations without an undue alienation of its Polish, Jewish, and Belorussian members and supporters. There was discord, to be sure, especially when the LSDP stressed the primacy of Lithuanian interests. Yet there was also constant bridge-building to link the various subcultures. Cross-pollination occurred in the 1890s, when members of the several nationalities made their first contacts with one another, formed local chapters, and discussed their tactics. Cooperation (and rivalry, too) continued in 1905, when they confronted the authorities in the streets of Vilnius, Kaunas, and Šiauliai, or attempted to free their jailed fellow revolutionaries. Finally, when the Populists and the social democrats formed a coalition government in 1926, they welcomed the participation of minority parties. A country with multicultural oases can ill afford to overlook such a record of accommodation.

Any assessment of the LSDP must, of course, conclude with politics. As the first major political party whose appearance spurred the formation of other groups, the LSDP has complemented Lithuania's national revival by supplying its cultural thrust with political organization. The early phase of the movement articulated the elements of national revival: reliance on the common people, care for the language and the religious heritage, recovery of the homeland, resistance to alien domination, and, perhaps, a longing for national liberation—at present an "empty dream," no doubt. Its later, or politicized, phase began to aggregate those elements and assert them with greater vigor and coherence. The "empty dream," once viewed as too unrealistic to be brought up for consideration, was now placed on the national agenda. The ideal of Lithuania's resurrection protruded from the party platform of the LSDP. It was thrashed out by that party's agitators and worker organizations, at its regional and national conferences, and in its press and other publications. Further, national liberation of Lithuania was discussed with the socialists of other nationalities— Jewish, Polish, and Russian. Finally, the question of Lithuania's future existence appeared as key planks in the policies of that country's other political parties and as a priority item in the Grand Diet of Vilnius.

National emancipation, whether at the end of the nineteenth century or of the twentieth, has been a struggle for distance between Lithuania and Russia. The founders of Lithuanian social democracy defined that distance as federation (1896–1905), while a later national consensus redefined it first as autonomy (1905–1914) and then as independence (1918–1940). Whatever the definition, the desired distance reflected efforts to recognize and preserve Lithuania as a distinct entity leading a more or less independent existence. In a way that proved to be prophetic, the founding generation of the LSDP articulated the belief that subjection to Russia—and it did not matter much whether that Russia was White or Red—was fraught with irreparable harm to Lithuania. So when, at the end of twenty years of independence, the Soviet Union annexed the three Baltic states in 1940, desperate efforts to reestablish that distance resumed. For those seeking to reverse the predatory Soviet action, as for the founders of the movement analyzed in this book, national liberation became a cardinal plank in their party platforms. In a decade-long guerrilla war that broke out in 1945, the Lithuanians lost more than 30,000 lives before they modified their opposition to Russian rule. However, the twin means of openness and reconstruction which Mikhail Gorbachev and his associates have employed in reforming Soviet public life have given a good deal of impetus to another overt quest for liberty. At joint conferences in Vilnius, Riga, and Tallinn, the independence fronts of Lithuania, Latvia, and Estonia resumed charting a course designed to distance the Baltic states from Russia. To the leaders of these fronts, reimposition of Soviet control is always a possibility, but so are various forms of a new relationship between Moscow and the Baltic capitals—statutory concessions, treaty-based ties, autonomy, and outright Baltic independence. The outcome of these strivings, of course, is bound to reflect the vicissitudes of power, policy, and purpose inside the Soviet Union and in other countries.

Appendixes

Appendix A Periodicals of the Social Democratic Party of Lithuania, 1896–1914

Title	Year	Country	Number of Issues	Language
Aidas Lietuvos darbininkų gyvenimo	1899	Germany	2	Lithuanian, Polish
Arbeiterstimme für Lite	1907	n.a.	5	Yiddish
Darbininkas	1905–1906	Germany	9	Lithuanian
Darbininkų balsas	1901–1906	Germany	36	Lithuanian
Darbininkų žodis	1908–1909	Lithuania	5	Lithuanian
Echo	1906	Lithuania	18	Polish
Echo życia robotniczego	1897–1898	Lithuania	9	Polish
Echo życia robotniczego na Litwie	1902–1906	Lithuania, Germany	9	Polish
Głos robotniczy	1908	Lithuania	2	Polish
Kowieński robotnik	1897	Lithuania	1	Polish
Lietuvos darbininkas	1896–1899	Switzerland, Germany	3	Lithuanian
Naujoji gadynė	1906	Lithuania	32	Lithuanian
Partijos žinios	1906, 1908, 1912	Lithuania	3	Lithuanian
Pirmyn	1905	Latvia	2	Lithuanian
Pisemko ulotne	n.a.	n.a.	n.a.	Polish
Robotnik litewski	1896–1899	Switzerland, Germany	3	Polish
Robotnik wileński	1905	Lithuania	1	Polish
Skardas	1907	Lithuania	21	Lithuanian

Sozialistische Flugblatt	1906	n.a.	4	Yiddish
Sparva	1905	Germany	1	Lithuanian
Topór	1906–1907	Lithuania	14	Polish
Vilnis	1913–1914	Latvia	23	Lithuanian
Visuomenė	1910–1911	Lithuania	20	Lithuanian
Žarija	1907–1908	Lithuania	48	Lithuanian
Žvilgsnis	1912	Lithuania	1	Lithuanian

n.a.: Not available

Sources: M. Baltasis [Mykolas Biržiška], "Socialdemokratų laikraščiai lietuvių kalboje 1896–1906 metų," Žarija, May 1/14, 1908, pp. 265–66; Griškūnaitė and others (eds.), Lietuvos TSR istorijos šaltiniai, II, 607–9; Kairys, Tau, Lietuva, pp. 326–27; Lietuvių enciklopedija, V, 328–29; ibid., XXIII, 48; Darbininkų balsas, no. 3 (March 1902), p. 2; Čepėnas (ed.), Vladas Požela . . . , p. 260; MLTE, I, 21, 361–62, 364, 456, and 580; ibid., II, 198, 371, 671, 770, and 863; ibid., III, 93, 214, 263, 778, 799, 874, and 948.

Appendix B   List of LSDP Appeals

1. Karė (War)   1904

2. Švęskime darbininkų šventę, pirmąją gegužės (Let's Celebrate   1904
    Workers' Holiday, May Day)

3. Vyrai! (Men!)   1904

4. Spauda leista! ([Freedom of] the Press Has Been Granted!)   1904

5. Ko mes reikalaujam (What We Are Demanding)   1905

6. Ko nori lietuviai socialdemokratai (What the Lithuanian Social   1905
    Democrats Want)

7. Šalin caro valdžia! (Down with the Tsarist Government!)   1905

8. Lietuvos inteligentija! (Lithuanian Intelligentsia!)   1905

9. Lietuvos valstiečiai, ūkininkai ir darbininkai! (Peasants, Farmers, and   1905
    Workers of Lithuania!)

10. Kaimo darbininkai ir darbininkės! (Rural Workers!)   1905

11. Kokią mes turime įtaisyti tvarką (What Kind of a System Must We   1905
    Establish)

12. Į kovą už Vilniaus Seimą (To War for the Vilnius Diet)   1905

13. Zapasnieji! (Reservists!)   1905

14. Lietuvos Socialdemokratų Partijos manifestas (A Manifesto of the   1905
    Social Democratic Party of Lithuania)

15. Vyrai, nesiduokim suvedžiot! (Men, Let's Not Get Deceived!)   1905

16. Vyrai, už ginklų! (Men, Take Up Arms!)   1905

17. Vyrai ir moters, prie darbo! (Men and Women, to Work!)   1905

18. Jaunieji kareiviai! (Young Soldiers!)   1905

19. Draugai! Apsisaugokim, nes caro valdžia nori mus apvogti (Friends!   1906
    Let's Keep Our Guard up Because the Tsarist Government Wants to
    Rob Us)

20. Ko mes turime streikuodami reikalauti? (What Must We Demand   1906
    When We're on Strike?)

21. Į Amerikos lietuvius (To American-Lithuanians)   1906

22. Į draugus žydus (To Jewish Friends)   1906

Notes

Introduction

1   See Institute of Party History, *Lietuvos komunistų partijos istorijos apybraiža*, I (Vilnius, 1971), 30.
2   See *Encyclopedia Lituanica* (Boston, 1970–78), II, 523. Cf. ibid., IV, 322.
3   See Kazys Grinius, *Atsiminimai ir mintys* (Tübingen and Chicago, 1947–62), I, 124; Ezra Mendelsohn, *The Jews of East Central Europe between the World Wars* (Bloomington, Ind., 1983), pp. 225–38; *Encyclopaedia Judaica* (Jerusalem, 1971), XI, 362 and 374.
4   Ibid., p. 362; Mendelsohn, pp. 215–16 and 227.
5   On the practical considerations moderating Lithuanian attitude toward the Jews, see Grinius, I, 124–26 and 176.
6   For totals of Old Believers, see Pranas Čepėnas, *Naujųjų laikų Lietuvos istorija* (Chicago, 1977–86), I, 110; *Encyclopedia Lituanica*, IV, 134; *Lietuvių enciklopedija* (Boston, 1953–69), XXVII, 273.
7   See Institute of Party History, *Lietuvos komunistų partijos istorijos apybraiža*, I, 26.
8   For statistics on urban population, see *Lietuviškoji tarybinė enciklopedija* (Vilnius, 1976–85), V, 387; ibid., X, 564; *Lietuvių enciklopedija*, XII, 20; V. Merkys, "Lietuvos miestų gyventojų tautybės XIX a. pabaigoje—XX a. pradžioje klausimu," in *Lietuvos TSR Mokslų Akademijos Darbai*, ser. A, no. 2 (1958), p. 87.
9   See V. Merkys, "Proletariato formavimasis Vilniuje XIX amžiaus pabaigoje," in *Lietuvos TSR Mokslų Akademijos Darbai*, ser. A, no. 1 (1957), p. 12.
10 The discussion of education and the role of the Catholic church is based on research reported in A. Šapoka (ed.), *Lietuvos istorija* (Kaunas, 1936); *Encyclopedia Lituanica*, II, 129–32; Čepėnas, *Naujųjų laikų Lietuvos istorija*, I, especially 59–220; *Lietuvių enciklopedija*, XV, 131–46.
11 Ibid., pp. 166–79; Šapoka (ed.), pp. 342–43.
12 For accounts of Jewish learning, see Israel Cohen, *Vilna* (Philadelphia, 1943); *Encyclopaedia Judaica*, XI, 361–75; *Lietuvių enciklopedija*, XXXV, 283–95; Mendelsohn, pp. 213–39.
13 See Šapoka (ed.), p. 496; *Encyclopedia Lituanica*, I, 46 and 290–93; ibid., II, 34–36 and 486; ibid., V, 375; ibid., VI, 38–43 and 108–9.
14 This section on the cultural effort borrows generally from Čepėnas, *Naujųjų laikų Lietuvos istorija*, I. See also Šapoka (ed.), pp. 507–12 and 526–30.

Chapter 1: The Jewish and Polish Precursors

1   See A. Lietuvis [Alfonsas Moravskis], "Lietuvos darbininkų judėjimo istorija
    sąryšy su Lietuvos valstybės atgimimo judėjimu," *Kultūra*, no. 1 (1933), pp.
    13–14 (hereinafter cited as Moravskis in *Kultūra*); A. Lietuvis [Alfonsas
    Moravskis], "Die lithauische Arbeiterbewegung," *Die Neue Zeit*, no. 49 (1899),
    p. 710.

2   See [Alfonsas Moravskis], "Lietuvos Socialdemokratų Partijos įsikūrimas," *Social-
    demokratas*, May 6, 1926, p. 2.

3   See Moravskis in *Kultūra*, no. 2 (1933), p. 70.

4   See Institute of Party History, "Lietuvos komunistų partijos istorijos apybraiža,"
    Komunistas, no. 1 (1967), p. 89 (hereinafter cited as Apybraiža in *Komunistas*).

5   See Iu. Martov, *Zapiski sotsialdemokrata* (Berlin, 1922), pp. 196–98; see also
    Moravskis in *Kultūra*, no. 2 (1933), pp. 70–71.

6   See Martov, pp. 224–26 and 230–32; Leopold H. Haimson, *The Russian Marxists
    and the Origins of Bolshevism* (Cambridge, Mass., 1955), pp. 71–72 and 82; Richard
    Pipes, *Social Democracy and the St. Petersburg Labor Movement, 1885–1897*
    (Cambridge, Mass., 1963), pp. 60–62; Adam B. Ulam, *The Bolsheviks* (New York,
    1965), pp. 118–20; Leonard Schapiro, *The Communist Party of the Soviet Union*
    (New York, 1964), pp. 23–24 and 28.

7   Ulam, p. 119. See also [Arkadi Kremer], *Ob agitatsii* (Geneva, 1896); A. Kremer,
    "Osnovanie Bunda," *Proletarskaia revoliutsiia*, no. 11 (1922), p. 51. The suggestion
    that the significance of *Ob agitatsii* has been overrated appears in Peisachas Freid-
    heimas, "V. Leninas, Kovos sąjunga ir Lietuvos socialdemokratai," *Komunistas*,
    no. 10 (1985), pp. 53–58.

8   See N. A. Bukhbinder, "I s"ezd 'Vseobshchego evreiskogo rabochego soiuza'
    'Bunda,'" *Proletarskaia revoliutsiia*, no. 11 (1924), p. 203. See also Martov, pp.
    244–46; Schapiro, p. 23.

9   See Bukhbinder, *Proletarskaia revoliutsiia*, no. 11 (1924), p. 203.

10 Ibid., pp. 205–6; Kremer, *Proletarskaia revoliutsiia*, no. 11 (1922), pp. 50–56; Co-
    hen, p. 341; Juozas Vilčinskas, *Lietuvos socialdemokratija kovoje dėl krašto ne-
    priklausomybės* (London, 1985), p. 22; V. Tsoglin [David Katz], "Pervyi s"ezd
    Bunda," in *Revoliutsionnoe dvizhenie sredi evreev*, ed. S. Dimanshtein (Moscow,
    1930), pp. 131–48. An exhaustive examination of the Bund is Henry J. Tobias, *The
    Jewish Bund in Russia: From Its Origins to 1905* (Stanford, Calif., 1972).

11 See Schapiro, p. 22; Z. Angarietis, *Lietuvos revoliucinio judėjimo ir darbininkų
    kovos istorija*, II (N.p., 1922), 429–30; Vincas Kapsukas, *Raštai* (Vilnius, 1960–78),
    II, 328–29. Cf. Tobias, p. 239.

12 See Angarietis, II, 429–30.

13 See Moravskis in *Kultūra*, no. 2 (1933), p. 71; *Lietuviškoji enciklopedija* (Kaunas,
    1933–44), VI, 1207. Cf. V. Merkys, *Narodnikai ir pirmieji marksistai Lietuvoje*
    (Vilnius, 1967), p. 115.

14 See Andrius Domaševičius, "Mano vaikams," Party Archive of the Institute of
    Party History, f. 77, pp. 33 and 36; Andrius Domaševičius, "LSDP pradžia 1896 m.,"
    Party Archive of the Institute of Party History, f. 3377, p. 3.

15 See Polska Akademia Nauk, *Polski słownik biograficzny*, XX (Wrocław, 1975), 424;
    Moravskis in *Kultūra*, no. 3 (1933), pp. 138–39; [Moravskis], *Socialdemokratas*,
    May 6, 1926, p. 2; Merkys, *Narodnikai . . .*, p. 123; Ulrich Haustein, *Sozialismus
    und nationale Frage in Polen* (Köln, 1969), pp. 137 and 141.

16 V. Merkys, "Lietuvių SDP pirmųjų programų kilmė," in *Lietuvos TSR Mokslų Aka-demijos Darbai*, ser. A, no. 3 (1966), p. 136.

17 See Domaševičius, "Mano vaikams," pp. 33–34; V. Perazich, "Nakanune pervogo s"ezda," *Proletarskaia revoliutsiia*, no. 2 (1928), p. 25; Martov, p. 212; Moravskis in *Kultūra*, no. 5 (1931), p. 278; J. Jurginis, V. Merkys, and J. Žiugžda (eds.), *Lietuvos TSR istorija*, II (Vilnius, 1963), 183; *Mažoji lietuviškoji tarybinė enciklopedija* (Vilnius, 1966–71), II, 324 (hereinafter cited as *MLTE*).

18 See *Iskra*, November 20, 1904, p. 8; *Proletarskaia revoliutsiia*, no. 8–9 (1924), p. 203; Jurginis and others, *Lietuvos TSR istorija*, II, 266 and 268–70; Steponas Kairys, *Tau, Lietuva* (Boston, 1964), p. 62; Apybraiža in *Komunistas*, no. 3 (1967), pp. 83 and 93; Angarietis, II, 422; Stasys Matulaitis, *Atsiminimai ir kiti kūriniai* (Vilnius, 1957), p. 146.

19 See Jurginis and others, *Lietuvos TSR istorija*, II, 271; Kairys, p. 321; *MLTE*, II, 322; Institute of Party History, *Lietuvos komunistų partijos istorijos apybraiža*, I (Vilnius, 1971), 205. For a recent account of the SDKPIL, see Robert Blobaum, *Feliks Dzierżyński and the SDKPIL: A Study of the Origins of Polish Communism* (Boulder, Colo., 1984).

Chapter 2: The Inception of Lithuanian Social Democracy

1 On the formation, role, and liquidation of a group guided by Mateusz Błażejewski, see K. Zalewski [Stanisław Trusiewicz], "Isz socializmo istorijos Lietuvoj," *Social-demokratas*, no. 6–8 (May 1916), p. 45; Merkys, *Narodnikai. . .*, pp. 121–23; Institute of Party History, *Lietuvos komunistų partijos istorijos apybraiža*, I, 50–51 and 53.

2 J. Biliūnas, *Raštai*, II (Vilnius, 1955), 255.

3 On the activities of the two circles, see Moravskis in *Kultūra*, no. 3 (1933), p. 139; [Moravskis], *Socialdemokratas*, May 6, 1926, p. 2; Mikas [Mykolas Biržiška], "Lietuvos socijaldemokratų partija," *Kova*, May 17, 1907, p. 277; V. Kapsukas, "Pirmieji L.S.D. žingsniai," *Naujoji gadynė*, no. 3 (August 1916), p. 138; Apybraiža in *Komunistas*, no. 1 (1967), pp. 89–90; Biliūnas, II, 255–56 and 263; *Darbininkų balsas*, no. 5 (September 1904), p. 157; Institute of Party History, *Lietuvos komunis-tų partijos istorijos apybraiža*, I, 50; Merkys, *Narodnikai . . .*, pp. 119–23.

4 See [Moravskis], *Socialdemokratas*, May 6, 1926, p. 2; Moravskis in *Kultūra*, no. 3 (1933), pp. 139–40; [Biržiška], *Kova*, May 17, 1907, p. 277; Kapsukas, *Naujoji gadynė*, no. 3 (August 1916), p. 138; E. Sponti, "Kratkaia avtobiografiia," in *Na zare rabochego dvizheniia v Moskve*, ed. S. I. Mitskevich (Moscow, 1932), p. 97; Merkys, *Narodnikai . . .*, pp. 114–16; Institute of Party History, *Lietuvos komunis-tų partijos istorijos apybraiža*, I, 50; Šešėlis [Mykolas Biržiška], "A. Lietuvio-Moravskio atsiminimai," *Priekalas*, no. 5 (October–November 1931), pp. 210–11; *Darbininkų balsas*, no. 5 (September 1904), pp. 157–58.

5 Merkys, *Narodnikai . . .*, p. 130. See also Biliūnas, II, 257–58; Moravskis in *Kultūra*, no. 3 (1933), p. 140; Jurginis and others, *Lietuvos TSR istorija*, II, 174.

6 See Biliūnas, II, 257.

7 For accounts of May Day demonstrations, see "Święto majowe w Wilnie," *Przedś-wit*, no. 10 (October 1894), pp. 22–23; *Aidas Lietuvos darbininkų gyvenimo*, June 1, 1899, pp. 11–12; *Lietuvos darbininkas*, no. 3 (1899), pp. 19–22; Tsentral'nyi Komitet Litovskoi Sotsial'demokrat. Partii, "Litovskoe rabochee dvizhenie," *Rab-otnik*, no. 5–6 (1899), Pt. 2, p. 4; *Darbininkų balsas*, no. 4 (May 1902), pp. 58–59; ibid., no. 4 (August 1903), pp. 132–40; V. Kapsukas, "Iš Lietuvos S.-D. istorijos,"

Naujoji gadynė, no. 2 (July 1916), p. 77; Kapsukas, *Naujoji gadynė*, no. 3 (August 1916), pp. 140–41; Z. Angarietis, "Pirmosios gegužės šventė Lietuvoj 1897 metais," *Komunaras*, no. 5 (April 1922), pp. 140–42; Merkys, *Narodnikai . . .*, pp. 130–31; J. Komodaitė and C. Fradkina, "Gegužės pirmosios demonstracijos Vilniuje ir Kaune 1902 metais," *Revoliucinis judėjimas Lietuvoje*, ed. R. Šarmaitis (Vilnius, 1957), pp. 47–56; J. Jurginis, *1905 metų revoliucijos įvykiai Vilniuje* (Vilnius, 1958), pp. 14–15 and 43–44; E. Griškūnaitė, V. Merkys, and J. Žiugžda (eds.), *Lietuvos TSR istorijos šaltiniai*, II (Vilnius, 1965), 275–76, 278–79, 296–97, 301–6, 341–42, 368, 436–37, 465–66,and 523.

8   See Moravskis in *Kultūra*, no. 3 (1933), p. 141; Jurginis and others, *Lietuvos TSR istorija*, II, 172; Biliūnas, II, 258–64; *Darbininkų balsas*, no. 5 (September 1904), p. 158.

9   See Domaševičius, "Mano vaikams," pp. 6–7, 22–23, and 25; Domaševičius, "LSDP pradžia 1896 m.," p. 2; Andrius Domaševičius, "Apie Lietuvos socialdemokratų partijos įkūrimą 1896 m. ir jos pirmųjų metų veiklą," Party Archive of the Institute of Party History, f. 3377, p. 7; Merkys, *Narodnikai . . .*, p. 115; *Lietuviškoji enciklopedija*, VI, 1207; Moravskis in *Kultūra*, no. 2 (1933), p. 71.

10 See Steponas Kairys, *Lietuva budo* (New York, 1957), pp. 265–66; *MLTE*, II, 633; Grinius, I, 141; *Encyclopedia Lituanica*, III, 553; Merkys, *Narodnikai . . .*, p. 116; [Alfonsas Moravskis], *W kwestyi taktyki i organizacyi* (N.p., 1899), pp. i–ii; [Moravskis], *Socialdemokratas*, June 3, 1926, p. 2.

11 See Mykolas Biržiška, *Lietuvių tautos kelias*, II (Los Angeles, 1953), 55–57; *MLTE*, I, 414; Martov, p. 211; Kairys, *Lietuva budo*, p. 266; Kipras Bielinis, *Penktieji metai* (New York, 1959), p. 147; Grinius, I, 141; *Lietuviškoji enciklopedija*, VI, 1207; [Biržiška], *Priekalas*, no. 5 (October–November 1931), pp. 210–11; Merkys, *Narodnikai . . .*, p. 118; [Moravskis], *Socialdemokratas*, May 13, 1926, p. 2.

12 See Domaševičius, "Mano vaikams."

13 See [Biržiška], *Priekalas*, no. 5 (October–November 1931), p. 210; Moravskis in *Kultūra*, no. 5 (1931), p. 275; Grinius, I, 143; V. Mitskevich-Kapsukas, "Iz vospominanii F. E. Dzerzhinskogo," *Proletarskaia revoliutsiia*, no. 9 (1926), p. 59.

14 See M. K. Dziewanowski, *The Communist Party of Poland* (Cambridge, Mass., 1959), p. 26; Martov, p. 212; [Trusiewicz], *Socialdemokratas*, no. 6–8 (May 1916), pp. 45–47; [Biržiška], *Priekalas*, no. 5 (October–November 1931), p. 210; Moravskis in *Kultūra*, no. 6–7 (1931), p. 326; [Moravskis], *Socialdemokratas*, May 20, 1926, p. 3.

15 See Jurginis and others, *Lietuvos TSR istorija*, II, 176–77 and 179; *MLTE*, I, 453. A useful analysis of Dzierżyński's early political activity is Jerzy Ochmański, *Rewolucyjna działalność Feliksa Dzierżyńskiego na Litwie w końcu XIX wieku* (Poznán, 1969).

16 See *MLTE*, II, 814–15; [Biržiška], *Priekalas*, no. 5 (October–November 1931),p. 210; [Moravskis], *Socialdemokratas*, May 20, 1926, p. 2.

17 See Bielinis, p. 156; Kairys, *Lietuva budo*, p. 336.

18 See [Biržiška], *Priekalas*, no. 5 (October–November 1931), p. 210; [Moravskis], *Socialdemokratas*, May 20, 1926, p. 3; Domaševičius, "Apie Lietuvos socialdemokratų partijos įkūrimą . . .," p. 5; Domaševičius, "LSDP pradžia 1896 m.," p. 6.

19 See Merkys, *Narodnikai . . .*, p. 116; Kapsukas, *Naujoji gadynė*, no. 3 (August 1916), pp. 138–39; Kairys, *Lietuva budo*, p. 271; Jurginis and others, *Lietuvos TSR istorija*, II, 172. Cf. Sponti, p. 98.

20 See Domaševičius, "Mano vaikams," p. 34; Domaševičius, "LSDP pradžia 1896 m.," p. 2.

21 See Apybraiža in *Komunistas*, no. 1 (1967), p. 90; J. Komodaitė, "Komunistų bendražygis," *Komunistas*, no. 11 (1965), p. 62 [Moravskis], *Socialdemokratas*, May 13,
1926, p. 2; Merkys, *Narodnikai* . . ., pp. 118–19.

22 See Domaševičius, "Mano vaikams," pp. 34–35.

23 See Blobaum, p. 33.

24 See Domaševičius, "Mano vaikams," p. 36; Domaševičius, "LSDP pradžia 1896 m.,"
p. 3.

25 See Griškūnaitė and others (eds.), *Lietuvos TSR istorijos šaltiniai*, II, 243–44.

26 See *Przyczynek do programu Litewskiej socijal-demokracji* reviewed in *Varpas*,
no. 4 (1897), p. 55; Moravskis in *Kultūra*, no. 4 (1931), p. 200; V. Kapsukas, *Trumpa
Lietuvos Social-Demokratų Partijos istorija*, I (St. Petersburg, 1918), 15 (hereinafter
Trumpa partijos istorija); Kapsukas, *Naujoji gadynė*, no. 3 (August 1916), pp. 139–
40; [Moravskis], *Socialdemokratas*, May 6, 1926, p. 2, and May 13, 1926, p. 2;
[Moravskis], *Die Neue Zeit*, no. 49 (1899), p. 711; Apybraiža in *Komunistas*, no. 1
(1967), pp. 92–93; [Alfonsas Moravskis], "Szkic do historji ruchu robotniczego na
Litwie w ostatnich pięciu latach," *Robotnik litewski*, no. 2 (1898), pp. 121–22;
Programas Lietuviškos Social-demokratiškos Partijos (N.p., 1896); Kapsukas, *Raštai*, VII, 555; [Alfonsas Moravskis], "W kwestyi taktyki ruchu robotniczego," *Przedświt*, no. 6 (June 1896), pp. 2–10; A. Janulaitis, "Domaševičius ir Pilsudskis," *Mūsų
senovė*, no. 1 (1940), pp. 57–59; *Rabotnik*, no. 5–6 (1899), Pt. 2, pp. 1 and 7. Cf. V.
Akimov [Makhnovets], *Ocherk razvitiia sotsialdemokratii v Rossii* (St. Petersburg,
1906), p. 17; Schapiro, pp. 24, 28, and 31; A. Lietuvis and N. N. [Alfonsas Moravskis
and Jonas Vileišis], *Augis darbininkų judėjimo Lietuvoje* (Plymouth, Pa., 1900),
pp. 25–31 and 56–57.

27 See Domaševičius, "LSDP pradžia 1896 m.," p. 3; [Trusiewicz], *Socialdemokratas*,
no. 6–8 (May 1916), p. 46; Martov, p. 210; Moravskis in *Kultūra*, no. 5 (1931), p.
276.

28 See [Moravskis], *W kwestyi taktyki i organizacyi*, pp. 8–9; Domaševičius, "Apie
Lietuvos socialdemokratų partijos įkūrimą . . .," p. 6.

29 See [Moravskis], *W kwestyi taktyki i organizacyi*, p. 10.

30 See [Trusiewicz], *Socialdemokratas*, no. 6–8 (May 1916), p. 47; Georg W. Strobel,
Quellen zur Geschichte des Kommunismus in Polen, 1878–1918 (Köln, 1968), p.
38; L. Martov and others (eds.), *Obshchestvennoe dvizhenie v Rossii v nachale
XX-go veka* (St. Petersburg, 1909–14), III, 286; Apybraiža in *Komunistas*, no. 1
(1967), pp. 101–2; Norbert Michta and Jan Sobczak, "Stanisław Trusiewicz (Kazimierz Zalewski)," *Z pola walki*, no. 1 (1975), p. 111.

31 See Kapsukas, *Trumpa partijos istorija*, I, 12; M. Beržas [Zigmas Angarietis], *Antrosios Lietuvos Socialdemokratų Partijos darbai ir mokslas* (Kaunas, 1925), p. 10;
V. Mitskevich-Kapsukas, "Istoki i zarozhdenie kommunisticheskoi partii
Litvy,"*Proletarskaia revoliutsiia*, no. 1 (1929), p. 156; Z. Patirgas [Zenonas Ivins-
kis], "Keli bruožai iš Lietuvos socialdemokratų praeities," *Žiburiai*, May 18, 1946,
p. 3; Grinius, I, p. 172; Strobel, pp. 38–39; Jurginis and others, *Lietuvos TSR istorija*,
II, 180–81; Michał Römer, *Litwa* (Lwów, 1908), pp. 272–73. Cf. F. E. Dzerzhinskii,
Izbrannye proizvedeniia, I (Moscow, 1957), 2; Dziewanowski, p. 51.

32 See Grinius, I, 207; Domaševičius, "Apie Lietuvos socialdemokratų partijos įkūrimą . . .," p. 3.

33 Ibid., p. 4; Domaševičius, "LSDP pradžia 1896 m.," p. 6.

34 Ibid., p. 5; Grinius, I. 142–43; Institute of Party History, *Lietuvos Komunistų
partijos istorijos apybraiža*, I, 67; Griškūnaitė and others (eds.), *Lietuvos TSR istorijos šaltiniai*, II, 244; Ochmański, pp. 23 and 32.

35 See *Programas Lietuviškos Social-demokratiškos Partijos*, pp. 8–9; Jurginis and others, *Lietuvos TSR istorija*, II, 175; [Moravskis], *Socialdemokratas*, May 20, 1926, p. 2; Apybraiža in *Komunistas*, no. 1 (1967), pp. 99 and 102; Grinius, I, 143; Domaševičius, "Apie Lietuvos socialdemokratų partijos įkūrimą . . .," p. 3.

36 See *Programas Lietuviškos Social-demokratiškos Partijos.*

37 See Moravskis in *Kultūra*, no. 4 (1931), p. 199.

38 Ibid., and Moravskis in *Kultūra*, no. 5 (1931), p. 275; Merkys, *Lietuvos TSR Mokslų Akademijos Darbai*, ser. A, no. 3 (1966), pp. 135–36 and 145; Kapsukas, *Trumpa partijos istorija*, I, 9; Kapsukas, *Naujoji gadynė*, no. 3 (August 1916), p. 141.

39 See Merkys, *Lietuvos TSR Mokslų Akademijos Darbai*, ser. A, no. 3 (1966), pp. 136–38 and 148; [Biržiška], *Kova*, May 24, 1907, p. 295; [Moravskis], *Robotnik litewski*, no. 2 (1898), p. 122; Domaševičius, "LSDP pradžia 1896 m.," p. 4.

40 See [Biržiška], *Priekalas*, no. 5 (October–November 1931), p. 211; *Rabotnik*, no. 5–6 (1899), Pt. 2, p. 3; [Trusiewicz], *Socialdemokratas*, no. 6–8 (May 1916), p. 47; Pranas Čepėnas (ed.), *Vladas Požela: Jaunystės atsiminimai* (London, 1971), p. 307; [Moravskis and Vileišis], *Augis darbininkų . . .*, p. 37; [Moravskis], *Socialdemokratas*, May 20, 1926, p. 2.

41 See Jurginis and others, *Lietuvos TSR istorija*, II, 177.

42 See Moravskis in *Kultūra*, no. 5 (1931), p. 275. Cf. Martov, *Zapiski sotsialdemokrata*, pp. 200–1.

43 See [Biržiška], *Priekalas*, no. 5 (October–November 1931), pp. 210–11; [Moravskis], *Socialdemokratas*, May 13, 1926, p. 2; ibid., May 20, 1926, pp. 2–3; ibid., June 3, 1926, p. 2.

44 See Apybraiža in *Komunistas*, no. 1 (1967), pp. 104–5.

45 See [Moravskis], *Socialdemokratas*, June 3, 1926, p. 2; [Moravskis], *W kwestyi taktyki i organizacyi*, p. 5.

46 See [Moravskis and Vileišis], *Augis darbininkų . . .*, p. 54; [Moravskis], *Robotnik litewski*, no. 2 (1898), p. 120; V. Merkys, "Valstiečių judėjimas Lietuvoje XIX a. pabaigoje," in *Lietuvos valstiečiai XIX amžiuje*, ed. K. Jablonskis and others (Vilnius, 1957), pp. 268–69.

47 Angarietis, *Lietuvos revoliucinio judėjimo . . .*, II, 73–74.

48 See Matulaitis, p. 95.

49 See A. Petrika, *Lietuvių tautinio atbudimo pionieriai* (Brooklyn, N.Y., 1939), p. 181; [Moravskis], *W kwestyi taktyki i organizacyi*, p. 8; [Moravskis], *Robotnik litewski*, no. 2 (1898), p. 120; *Przedświt*, no. 6 (1895) quoted in Beržaitis [Jonas Vileišis] "Lietuvių darbininkų judėjimas," *Varpas*, no. 2 (1904), p. 23; Kapsukas, *Raštai*, VII, 554. Cf. [Moravskis], *Socialdemokratas*, May 27, 1926, p. 2; ibid., June 3, 1926, p. 2.

50 See Apybraiža in *Komunistas*, no. 2 (1967), p. 83.

51 See Kairys, *Lietuva budo*, p. 286; Kapsukas, *Trumpa partijos istorija*, I, 15; Apybraiža in *Komunistas*, no. 2 (1967), p. 84; [Trusiewicz], *Socialdemokratas*, no. 6–8 (May 1916), p. 48; Institute of Party History, *Lietuvos komunistų partijos istorijos apybraiža*, I, 74–75; Bielinis, p. 29; *Lietuviškoji enciklopedija*, VI, 1209; Kapsukas, *Raštai*, VII, 556; Matulaitis, p. 136.

52 See Moravskis in *Kultūra*, no. 6–7 (1931), p. 333; Kairys, *Lietuva budo*, pp. 26 and 38; Kapsukas, *Trumpa partijos istorija*, I, 16; Kapsukas, *Raštai*, VII, 556.

53 See Biržiška, *Lietuvių tautos kelias*, II, 48 and 151; Bielinis, p. 156; Kairys, *Lietuva budo*, pp. 322–23; *Lietuvių enciklopedija* (Boston, 1953–69), XXVII, 505–6.

54 Ibid., X, 253; Bielinis, p. 118.

55 See Kairys, *Lietuva budo*, pp. 118 and 340; *MLTE*, I, 672; Biržiška, *Lietuvių tautos kelias*, II, 57–59.

56 See Čepėnas (ed.), pp. 289–94; Kairys, *Tau, Lietuva*, p. 54. For a Kapsukas account of the group's accomplishments, see *Kova*, December 1, 1905, pp. 226–27.

57 See Kapsukas, *Raštai*, I, 93–94; ibid., IV, 274; Apybraiža in *Komunistas*, no. 3 (1967), p. 90; *MLTE*, II, 395. For a contrary Communist view that the rift between Kapsukas and the LSDP was due mainly to personality conflicts, see Angarietis, *Lietuvos revoliucinio judėjimo . . .*, II, 297–309.

58 On the efforts of the Kapsukas group to find support among agricultural workers, see Kairys, *Tau, Lietuva*, pp. 54, 59, and 62–63; Kapsukas, *Raštai*, IV, 274–75; Biržiška, *Lietuvių tautos kelias*, II, 119. On other differences between the two groups, see Kapsukas, *Raštai*, IV, 274.

59 See Kapsukas, *Raštai*, I, 262–63; ibid., IV, 274; ibid., V, 414; Angarietis, *Lietuvos revoliucinio judėjimo . . .*, II, 300.

60 On the divergence between Kapsukas and the LSDP, see Kapsukas, *Raštai*, I, 263–67; ibid., II, 97–101; ibid., V, 402–6; ibid., X., 102–3; *Darbininkų balsas*, no. 11–12 (November–December 1905), pp. 396–99; letter of Vincas Kapsukas to Jurgis Šaulys, April 13, 1904, University of Pennsylvania, Šaulys Archives, f. 58; letter of Vincas Kapsukas to Jurgis Šaulys, December 7, 1904, Šaulys Archives, f. 58; "Vincas Mickevičius-Kapsukas," *Darbo visuomenė*, no. 2 (1935), pp. 46–47; Petrika, pp. 194–95; Kairys, *Lietuva budo*, p. 164; J. L. [Augustinas Janulaitis], "Dėlei Draugo organizacijos," *Vienybė lietuvninkų*, no. 22 (1905), pp. 262–64; Angarietis, *Lietuvos revoliucinio judėjimo . . .*, II, 292–309; E. Griškūnaitė, *Darbininkų judėjimas Lietuvoje, 1895–1914 m.* (Vilnius, 1971), pp. 151–52. See also statement by the central committee of the LSDP quoted in *Kova*, August 18, 1905, pp. 106–8.

61 See Kapsukas, *Raštai*, IV, 263, 349–50, and 367–68; Čepėnas (ed.), p. 265.

62 Kairys, *Lietuva budo*, pp. 323–24. See also Kapsukas, *Raštai*, VII, 557.

63 See *Lietuvių enciklopedija*, V, 329; Kairys, *Lietuva budo*, pp. 329–30 and 326–27.

64 See [Trusiewicz], *Socialdemokratas*, no. 6–8 (May 1916), p. 48; [Moravskis and Vileišis], *Augis darbininkų . . .*, pp. 32–33 and 52; *Vienybė lietuvninkų*, no. 11 (1901), p. 132; Grinius, I, 144; Moravskis in *Kultūra*, no. 6–7 (1931), p. 333; Kairys, *Lietuva budo*, pp. 324–25; Bielinis, pp. 19 and 21; Biržiška, *Lietuvių tautos kelias*, II, 118; Römer, p. 280; [Moravskis], *W kwestyi taktyki i organizacyi*, pp. 2 and 8–9. However, it required a long time for the Lithuanian language to penetrate the worker community. See Grinius, II, 98.

65 See resolutions of the 1903 party conference in *Vienybė lietuvninkų*, no. 20 (1903), p. 234; Kairys, *Lietuva budo*, pp. 287 and 324; Merkys, *Narodnikai . . .*, pp. 131 and 144; Apybraiža in *Komunistas*, no. 1 (1967), pp. 95 and 110; Kapsukas, *Trumpa partijos istorija*, I, 13; Jurginis and others, *Lietuvos TSR istorija*, II, 175; [Moravskis], *Die Neue Zeit*, no. 49 (1899), p. 710; [Biržiška], *Kova*, May 24, 1907, pp. 295–96; Sponti, p. 97; Römer, pp. 282–84.

66 See [Vileišis], *Varpas*, no. 2 (1904), p. 24.

67 See Kapsukas, *Trumpa partijos istorija*, I, 18; Kairys, *Lietuva budo*, pp. 283 and 324–25; *Vienybė lietuvninkų*, no. 20 (1903), p. 234; *Kova*, November 3, 1905, p. 194; [Angarietis], *Antrosios Lietuvos Socialdemokratų Partijos . . .*, p. 13; Z. Angarietis, "Lietuvos Komunistų Partijos įsikūrimas," *Komunistas*, no. 5 (1928), p. 3; P. Ruseckas, *Į laisvę* (Kaunas, 1919), p. 26; Mitskevich-Kapsukas, *Proletarskaia revoliutsiia*, no. 1 (1929), p. 156; Kairys, *Tau, Lietuva*, p. 53; Bielinis, pp. 21 and 28; Biržiška, *Lietuvių tautos kelias*, II, 118–19; V. Mickevičius-Kapsukas, *Pirmoji*

Lietuvos proletarinė revoliucija ir sovietų valdžia (Chicago, 1934), p. 66; Römer, p. 284; Grinius, II, 55.

68 See D. Alseika, *Lietuvių tautinė ideja istorijos šviesoje* (Vilnius, 1924), p. 112; Kapsukas, *Raštai*, VI, 237; Kapsukas, *Trumpa partijos istorija*, I, 19; Manfred Hellmann, "Die litauische Nationalbewegung im 19. und 20. Jahrhundert," *Zeitschrift für Ostforschung*, II (1953), 91; Bielinis, p. 28; Kipras Bielinis, *1905 metai* (Kaunas, 1931), p. 24; Biržiška, *Lietuvių tautos kelias*, II, 119. Cf. Kairys, *Lietuva budo*, p. 325.

69 See Petrika, pp. 110–11 and 184; [Trusiewicz], *Socialdemokratas*, no. 6–8 (May 1916), p. 46; *Lietuviškoji enciklopedija*, VI, 1207–8; Grinius, I, 142–43, 179, and 209; [Vileišis], *Varpas*, no. 2 (1904), p. 25; Kapsukas, *Raštai*, I, 264; [Ivinskis], *Žiburiai*, May 11, 1946, p. 3; V. Perazich, "Iz vospominanii (1896–1897 g.)," *Krasnaia letopis'*, no. 2–3 (1922), p. 115; Kapsukas, *Trumpa partijos istorija*, I, 14; Kairys, *Lietuva budo*, p. 234; Biržiška, *Lietuvių tautos kelias*, II, 55–56; Pranas Klimaitis, "Didysis Vilniaus Seimas," *Židinys*, no. 1 (1931), pp. 50–51; *Varpas*, no. 7–8 (1905), p. 79.

70 See letter of Vincas Kapsukas to Jurgis Šaulys, November 3, 1905, Šaulys Archives, f. 58; Kairys, *Lietuva budo*, pp. 234, 244, 338, and 340; *Vienybė lietuvninkų* (1904), p. 595; Römer, p. 285; Grinius, II, 13.

Chapter 3: National Objectives

1 See Kapsukas, *Raštai*, I, 117; ibid., VII, 549; Kapsukas, *Trumpa partijos istorija*, I, 7; Kairys, *Lietuva budo*, p. 279; Mykolas Biržiška, "Pranas Eidukevičius," *Keleivis*, September 27, 1950, p. 5; *Lietuvos darbininkas*, no. 3 (1899) quoted in Vilčinskas, pp. 29–30; *Darbininkų balsas*, no. 5 (July 1902), p. 5; ibid., no. 6 (September 1902), pp. 25 and 39; *Kas reikia žinoti ir atminti kiekvienam darbininkui* (Paris, 1902), p. 51. Cf. resolutions of the 1903 party conference in *Vienybė lietuvninkų*, no. 20 (1903), p. 234; *Darbininkų balsas*, no. 1 (January–February 1903), pp. 8–9; Grinius, I, 139–40.

2 See Biržiška, *Keleivis*, September 27, 1950, p. 5; *Darbininkų balsas*, no. 2 (February 1905), pp. 46–47; Kapsukas, *Raštai*, VII, 549–50; Kapsukas, *Naujoji gadynė*, no. 3 (August 1916), pp. 140–41; Kapsukas, *Trumpa partijos istorija*, I, 9; Kairys, *Lietuva budo*, pp. 278–79. See also resolutions of the 1903 party conference in *Vienybė lietuvninkų*, no. 20 (1903), p. 234; *Darbininkų balsas*, no. 1 (January–February 1903), pp. 8–9.

3 See resolutions of the 1902 party congress reproduced in *Darbininkų balsas*, no. 3 (March 1902), p. 2. See also resolutions of the 1903 party conference in *Darbininkų balsas*, no. 1 (January–February 1903), p. 5.

4 LSDP statement quoted in [Moravskis], *W kwestyi taktyki i organizacyi*, p. 4. See also [Moravskis], *Robotnik litewski*, no. 2 (1898), p. 123.

5 See resolutions of the 1903 party conference in *Darbininkų balsas*, no. 1 (January–February 1903), pp. 7–8; *Vienybė lietuvninkų*, no. 20 (1903), 234. See also [Moravskis and Vileišis], *Augis darbininkų . . .* , pp. 48–49; [Moravskis], *W kwestyi taktyki i organizacyi*, p. 9; *Lietuvos darbininkas*, no. 3 (1899) quoted in Vilčinskas, p. 30; *Kas reikia žinoti . . .*, p. 51; Matulaitis, p. 130.

6 For similar Jewish arguments about their "dual yoke," see Tobias, especially chapters 7 and 13.

7 See V. Kapsukas, "Dėl A. Lietuvio-Moravskio atsiminimų," *Priekalas*, no. 5 (October–November 1931), p. 207; Kapsukas, *Raštai*, VII, 550; Vilčinskas, p. 19; Perazich,

Krasnaia letopis', no. 2–3 (1922), p. 108; Mitskevich-Kapsukas, *Proletarskaia revoliutsiia*, no. 1 (1929), p. 154; Kairys, *Lietuva budo*, pp. 279–80; Kairys, *Tau, Lietuva*, p. 97; [Moravskis], *W kwestyi taktyki i organizacyi*, pp. 12–13; Merkys, *Lietuvos TSR Mokslų Akademijos Darbai*, ser. A, no. 3 (1966), pp. 145 and 149; Kapsukas, *Naujoji gadynė*, no. 3 (August 1916), p. 141; Martov and others (eds.), III, 285–86. Cf. resolutions of the 1905 party congress in *Darbininkų balsas*, no. 10 (October 1905), p. 326.

8   See Matulaitis, pp. 135–36. For signs of "provincial patriotism" and the desire for some sort of independence displayed by Lithuania's upper class in the early part of the nineteenth century, see comments by Vytautas Merkys reproduced in *Akiračiai*, no. 10 (November 1986), pp. 6–7. See also Domaševičius, "Mano vaikams," p. 3.

9   See Merkys, *Lietuvos TSR Mokslų Akademijos Darbai*, ser. A, no. 3 (1966), p. 134; Kairys, *Lietuva budo*, pp. 274–75; Griškūnaitė and others (eds.), *Lietuvos TSR istorijos šaltiniai*, II, 244.

10 *Programas Lietuviškos Social-demokratiškos Partijos*, pp. 8–9.

11 Ibid., pp. 16–17. See also A. Lietuvis [Alfonsas Moravskis], "Kas gali mums darbininkams lietuviams suteikti geresnę ateitį?" *Aidas Lietuvos darbininkų gyvenimo*, June 1, 1899, p. 3; [Moravskis], *Socialdemokratas*, May 27, 1926, p. 2; Kairys, *Lietuva budo*, p. 394; Matulaitis, pp. 131 and 134; Domaševičius, "LSDP pradžia 1896 m.," p. 4.

12 Griškūnaitė and others (eds.), *Lietuvos TSR istorijos šaltiniai*, II, 244. See also Matulaitis, pp. 134–36; Apybraiža in *Komunistas*, no. 1 (1967), p. 102.

13 Cf. Blobaum, p. 38.

14 See Griškūnaitė and others (eds.), *Lietuvos TSR istorijos šaltiniai*, II, 244; Merkys, *Lietuvos TSR Mokslų Akademijos Darbai*, ser. A, no. 3 (1966), p. 134.

15 See Griškūnaitė and others (eds.), *Lietuvos TSR istorijos šaltiniai*, II, 245; *Rabotnik*, no. 5–6 (1899), Pt. 2, p. 5.

16 See [Moravskis], *Aidas Lietuvos darbininkų gyvenimo*, June 1, 1899, pp. 2–3; Zagranichnyi soiuz litovskikh sotsial'demokratov, "O litovskom rabochem dvizhenii," *Rabochee delo*, no. 2–3 (1899), p. 109; Moravskis in *Kultūra*, no. 4 (1931), p. 199; ibid., no. 5 (1931), p. 276.

17 See [Moravskis], *Aidas Lietuvos darbininkų gyvenimo*, June 1, 1899, p. 3; Domaševičius, "Apie Lietuvos socialdemokratų partijos įkūrimą . . . ," pp. 3–4. Domaševičius later maintained that no changes were made in 1897, and that the formulation approved in 1896 left the door open for Russia's inclusion in the contemplated federation. Ibid., p. 5.

18 See Angarietis, *Komunistas*, no. 5 (1928), p. 2; [Angarietis], *Antrosios Lietuvos Socialdemokratų Partijos . . .*, p. 10; Merkys, *Lietuvos TSR Mokslų Akademijos Darbai*, ser. A, no. 3 (1966), p. 149; Kapsukas, *Naujoji gadynė*, no. 3 (August 1916), p. 141; Kapsukas, *Trumpa partijos istorija*, I, 9–10; [Biržiška], *Priekalas*, no. 5 (October–November 1931), pp. 209–10.

19 See Kapsukas, *Raštai*, VII, 564; Kapsukas, *Trumpa partijos istorija*, I, 24; *Darbininkų balsas*, no. 6 (December 1903), p. 200.

20 See Kapsukas, *Naujoji gadynė*, no. 3 (August 1916), p. 141; Kapsukas, *Trumpa partijos istorija*, I, 10; Kapsukas, *Raštai*, VII, 551; Kairys, *Lietuva budo*, pp. 277–78; Moravskis quoted in Alseika, p. 112; *MLTE*, II, 395; Apybraiža in *Komunistas*, no. 2 (1967), p. 101; [Angarietis], *Antrosios Lietuvos Socialdemokratų Partijos . . .*, pp. 9–10 and 13; *Darbininkų balsas*, no. 5 (July 1902), p. 5.

21 See Kapsukas, *Raštai*, VII, 562 and 571; Kapsukas, *Trumpa partijos istorija*, I, 22;

Kapsukas, *Naujoji gadynė*, no. 3 (August 1916), p. 143; Moravskis in *Kultūra*, no. 4 (1931), p.199; Kairys, *Lietuva budo*, pp. 277–78. Cf. LSDP appeal of April 1904 included in Kipras Bielinis, *Dienojant* (New York, 1958), pp. 447–48; LSDP Manifesto of September 1905 included in Kairys, *Tau, Lietuva*, pp. 333–38; LSDP appeals of 1905, entitled "What the Lithuanian Social Democrats Want" and "To War for the Vilnius Diet," reproduced in Bielinis, *Penktieji metai*, pp. 524–29; LSDP appeal of November 1905 reproduced in Kapsukas, *Raštai*, II, 206–8.

22   See [Biržiška], *Priekalas*, no. 5 (October–November 1931), p. 209; Grinius, I, 220; [Moravskis], *Aidas Lietuvos darbininkų gyvenimo*, June 1, 1899, p. 3; Moravskis in *Kultūra*, no. 4 (1931), p. 199; Moravskis quoted in Alseika, p. 111; Lietuvis [Moravskis] quoted in Hellmann, *Zeitschrift für Ostforschung*, II (1953), 90; Kapsukas, *Naujoji gadynė*, no. 3 (August 1916), pp. 140–41. Cf. Blobaum, p. 38.

23   See Kairys, *Lietuva budo*, p. 279.

24   See [Moravskis], *Socialdemokratas*, May 27, 1926, p. 2; Kairys, *Lietuva budo*, p. 278; Kairys, *Tau, Lietuva*, p. 61. For a contrary view see Moravskis in *Kultūra*, no. 5 (1931), p. 276. Cf. Martov and others (eds.), I, 356–57; Grinius, I, 221; Tobias, p. 166.

25   See Moravskis in *Kultūra*, no. 5 (1931), p. 279; ibid., no. 3 (1933), p. 138; Moravskis quoted in Alseika, p. 112; Kairys, *Lietuva budo*, p. 278; Kapsukas, *Naujoji gadynė*, no. 3 (August 1916), pp. 139–41; Kapsukas, *Trumpa partijos istorija*, I, 6; Mitskevich-Kapsukas, *Proletarskaia revoliutsiia*, no. 1 (1929), pp. 154–55; Haustein, pp. 255–56.

26   See [Moravskis], *Socialdemokratas*, May 20, 1926, p. 3; Kapsukas, *Trumpa partijos istorija*, I, 10–12; Apybraiža in *Komunistas*, no. 1 (1967), pp. 101–2. On other reasons for the estrangement of the Trusiewicz group, see Moravskis in *Kultūra*, no. 6–7 (1931), p. 326; [Moravskis], *Socialdemokratas*, May 20, 1926, p. 3.

Chapter 4: New Vistas

1   See Kairys, *Lietuva budo*, p. 337; Kapsukas, *Raštai*, VI, 99; *Darbininkų balsas*, no. 3 (June 1903), p. 112; ibid., no. 4 (August 1903), p. 141; ibid., no. 1 (January 1904), pp. 2 and 22.

2   See Kairys, *Lietuva budo*, pp. 337–39 and 403–5; [Biržiška], *Kova*, June 7, 1907, p. 328; K. Bielinis, "Žemaičiuose," *Socialdemokratas*, July 21, 1927, p. 3; Bielinis, *Penktieji metai*, p. 22; Biržiška, *Lietuvių tautos kelias*, II, 120. For conference resolutions, see Kapsukas, *Raštai*, VI, 243–44.

3   See *Darbininkų balsas*, no. 1 (January–February 1903), p. 47; ibid., no. 2 (February 1904), p. 63.

4   Ibid., no. 1 (January 1904), p. 16; Čepėnas, *Naujųjų laikų Lietuvos istorija*, I, 386.

5   See *Darbininkų balsas*, no. 3 (May 1904), p. 72; ibid., no. 6 (June 1905), p. 195; LSDP appeal quoted in Kairys, *Tau, Lietuva*, p. 382; A. Tyla, *1905 metų revoliucija Lietuvos kaime* (Vilnius, 1968), pp. 53–54; V. Kondratas, "Žemės ūkio darbininkų ir valstiečių revoliucinis judėjimas Lietuvoje 1905–1907 metais," in *Revoliucinis judėjimas Lietuvoje*, ed. R. Šarmaitis (Vilnius, 1957), p. 88.

6   See *Darbininkų balsas*, no. 1 (January 1905), p. 36.

7   Ibid., p. 14; ibid., no. 2 (February 1905), pp. 66–67.

8   Ibid., no. 2 (February 1904), p. 38. See also *Darbininkų balsas*, no. 3 (May 1904), p. 84; ibid., no. 5 (September 1904), p. 129.

9   Ibid., no. 4 (July 1904), p. 99.

10 Ibid., no. 3 (May 1904), pp. 68–70; ibid., no. 4 (July, 1904), p. 99; ibid., no. 5 (September 1904), pp. 129–30.

11 Ibid., no. 4 (July 1904), pp. 103–4.

12 Ibid., pp. 101–5. See also A. Sadomis, "1905 m. Vilniaus Seimas ir socialdemokratai," *Socialdemokratas*, December 20–27, 1930, p. 1.

13 See *Darbininkų balsas*, no. 3 (May 1904), pp. 74–78; ibid., no. 7 (December 1904), p. 196; ibid., no. 1 (January 1905), pp. 7–10.

14 Ibid., pp. 6–7; ibid., no. 3 (March 1906), p. 87. See also LSDP manifestos reproduced in Kairys, *Tau Lietuva*, p. 373; Griškūnaitė and others (eds.), *Lietuvos TSR istorijos šaltiniai*, II, 377–78.

15 See *Darbininkų balsas*, no. 3 (May 1904), p. 78.

16 See Michael T. Florinsky, *Russia: A History and an Interpretation* (New York, 1947), II, 1171–72; Adam B. Ulam, *Russia's Failed Revolutions: From the Decembrists to the Dissidents* (New York, 1981), pp. 161–62.

17 See Kairys, *Tau, Lietuva*, pp. 38–40; Jurginis and others, *Lietuvos TSR istorija*, II, 303; Jurginis, *1905 metų revoliucijos įvykiai Vilniuje*, pp. 27 and 63.

18 On the January strikes, see *Darbininkų balsas*, no. 2 (February 1905), p. 59; ibid., no. 3 (March 1905), pp. 73 and 88–96; [Biržiška], *Kova*, June 7, 1907, p. 329; J. Kaminskas [Steponas Kairys], "LSDP 1905 metų įvykiuose," *Darbas*, no. 2 (1955), p. 2; J. Komodaitė, "Lietuvos darbo žmonių revoliucinė kova 1905 metais," in *Revoliucinis judėjimas Lietuvoje*, ed. R. Šarmaitis (Vilnius, 1957), pp. 61–62; V. Kondratas, "1905–1907 metų revoliucijos pradžia Lietuvoje," in *Revoliucinis judėjimas Lietuvoje*, ed. R. Šarmaitis (Vilnius, 1957), pp. 78–79; Apybraiža in *Komunistas*, no. 3 (1967), pp. 98–99; Griškūnaitė and others (eds.), *Lietuvos TSR istorijos šaltiniai*, II, 346–51; Kapsukas, *Raštai*, II, 21–24 and 325; ibid., IX, 430–31; Kairys, *Tau, Lietuva*, pp. 38–41; Bielinis, *Penktieji metai*, pp. 45–47; Jurginis and others, *Lietuvos TSR istorija*, II, 300–303; Čepėnas, *Naujųjų laikų Lietuvos istorija*, I, 335–36; Angarietis, *Lietuvos revoliucinio judėjimo . . .* , II, 238–39; Institute of Party History, *Lietuvos komunistų partijos istorijos apybraiža*, I, 128–29; Griškūnaitė, *Darbininkų judėjimas Lietuvoje . . .* , pp. 140–47; Jurginis, *1905 metų revoliucijos įvykiai Vilniuje*, pp. 22–31. For a contrary view depreciating the role of the LSDP, see Angarietis, *Lietuvos revoliucinio judėjimo . . .* , II, 239 and 330–31; [Angarietis], *Antrosios Lietuvos Socialdemokratų Partijos . . .* , p. 12.

19 See *Darbininkų balsas*, no. 3 (March 1905), p. 89.

20 Ibid., pp. 73–74 and 93.

21 Ibid., no. 2 (February 1905), pp. 41–42.

22 Ibid., pp. 43–44. See also Kairys, *Tau, Lietuva*, p. 46.

23 For decisions of the conference, see *Darbininkų balsas*, no. 7 (July 1905), pp. 230–31.

24 Kairys, *Tau, Lietuva*, p. 53.

25 Ibid., pp. 53–54 and 59.

26 Ibid., p. 53.

27 Ibid.; *Darbininkų balsas*, no. 7 (July 1905), pp. 230–31.

28 See resolutions of the congress in *Darbininkų balsas*, no. 10 (October 1905), pp. 325–27. See also [Biržiška], *Kova*, June 7, 1907, p. 329.

29 See *Darbininkų balsas*, no. 10 (October 1905), p. 325; Tyla, pp. 176–77; Matulaitis, pp. 126–28; Kapsukas, *Raštai*, III, 31 and 42–47.

30 See *Darbininkų balsas*, no. 11–12 (November–December 1905), pp. 329–30.

31 Ibid., no. 3 (March 1906), pp. 86–88.

32 See Klimaitis, *Židinys*, no. 2 (1931), p. 154; Kairys, *Tau, Lietuva*, p. 89; P. Višinskis,

"Pirmutinis didysis lietuvių susivažiavimas Vilniuje," *Lietuvos ūkininkas*, December 1 / 14, 1905, p. 4; Jonas Basanavičius, *Rinktiniai raštai* (Vilnius, 1970), p. 237.

33 For LSDP efforts to restrain anti-Jewish sentiment and agitation, see *Darbininkų balsas*, no. 7 (December 1904), pp. 202–5; ibid., no. 1 (January 1905), pp. 26–28; ibid., no. 2 (February 1905), p. 67; ibid., no. 3 (March 1905), p. 89; ibid., no. 5 (May 1905), p. 143; ibid., no. 7 (July 1905), pp. 216 and 221; ibid., no. 9 (September 1905), p. 285; ibid., no. 10 (October 1905), pp. 303 and 314; ibid., no. 11–12 (November–December 1905), pp. 336, 378, and 380–81; LSDP appeals quoted in Kairys, *Tau, Lietuva*, pp. 339–40, 343, and 345; Griškūnaitė, *Darbininkų judėjimas Lietuvoje* . . . , p. 154; Čepėnas, *Naujųjų laikų Lietuvos istorija*, I, 357; *Kova*, September 8, 1905, p. 130; P. Girdzijauskienė, *1905–1907 metų revoliucija Lietuvoje* (Vilnius, 1955), p. 11; Angarietis, *Lietuvos revoliucinio judėjimo* . . . , II, 415; Jurginis, *1905 metų revoliucijos įvykiai Vilniuje*, pp. 49 and 96; Jurgita Smalstytė, *Mano tėvas*, trans. V. Kauneckas (Vilnius, 1967), pp. 65–71.

34 See Čepėnas (ed.), *Vladas Požela* . . . , pp. 229–34.

35 See Biržiška, *Keleivis*, September 13, 1950, p. 5.

Chapter 5: Strikes and Demonstrations

1 On the October unrest in the Lithuanian cities, see Jurginis and others, *Lietuvos TSR istorija*, II, 320–27; K. Jablonskis and others (eds.), *Lietuvos TSR istorija* (Vilnius, 1958), pp. 238–39; Institute of Party History, *Lietuvos komunistų partijos istorijos apybraiža*, I, 160–65; Kapsukas, *Raštai*, II, 374–76 and 378–80; ibid., IX, 434–36; Bielinis, *Penktieji metai*, pp. 146–49; Griškūnaitė, *Darbininkų judėjimas Lietuvoje* . . . , pp. 161–68; B. Glikas, "Visuotinis 1905 metų spalio politinis streikas Lietuvoje," in *Revoliucinis judėjimas Lietuvoje*, ed. R. Šarmaitis (Vilnius, 1957), pp. 95–105; Kairys, *Tau, Lietuva*, pp. 75–78.

2 The casualty total for 1905 has been derived from fragmentary accounts, including Griškūnaitė and others (eds.), *Lietuvos TSR istorijos šaltiniai*, II, 366, 370, 373, and 384–85; Kairys, *Tau, Lietuva*, pp. 47, 76, and 78; Kapsukas, *Raštai*, II, 376; ibid., IX, 434–35; ibid., X, 220–21; Institute of Party History, *Lietuvos komunistų partijos istorijos apybraiža*, I, 148 and 162–64; Glikas, pp. 95–96, 98, and 101; Griškūnaitė, *Darbininkų judėjimas Lietuvoje* . . . , pp. 164 and 166; Jurginis and others, *Lietuvos TSR istorija*, II, 323; Čepėnas, *Naujųjų laikų Lietuvos istorija*, I, 371; K. A. Matulaitis, "Sukilimas Sūduvoje," *Tautos praeitis*, II, Bks. 3–4 (1967), 267; Jurginis, *1905 metų revoliucijos įvykiai Vilniuje*, pp. 44, 76, 91, 95–96.

3 On the December actions, see Jurginis and others, *Lietuvos TSR istorija*, II, 338–39; Griškūnaitė and others (eds.), *Lietuvos TSR istorijos šaltiniai*, II, 402–3; J. Komodaitė, "1905 metų gruodžio politinis streikas Lietuvoje," in *Revoliucinis judėjimas Lietuvoje*, ed. R. Šarmaitis (Vilnius, 1957), pp. 124–29; Iu. I. Zhiugzhda and others (eds.), *Revoliutsiia 1905–1907 gg. v Litve: Dokumenty i materialy* (Vilnius, 1961), pp. 217–19; Institute of Party History, *Lietuvos komunistų partijos istorijos apybraiža*, I, 185–88; Griškūnaitė, *Darbininkų judėjimas Lietuvoje* . . . , pp. 172–76.

4 See Kairys, *Tau, Lietuva*, pp. 76–77; Griškūnaitė, *Darbininkų judėjimas Lietuvoje* . . . , pp. 161 and 173; Institute of Party History, *Lietuvos komunistų partijos istorijos apybraiža*, I, 161 and 186; Jurginis and others, *Lietuvos TSR istorija*, II, 321, 327, and 338; Komodaitė, "1905 metų . . . ," p. 124.

5 See Griškūnaitė, *Darbininkų judėjimas Lietuvoje* . . . , p. 188.

6   See Jurginis and others, *Lietuvos TSR istorija*, II, 342.
7   See Griškūnaitė, *Darbininkų judėjimas Lietuvoje* . . . , p. 292.
8   Ibid., pp. 187–88.
9   The data on strikes are reported in Tyla, pp. 208–10 and 213. Cf. Jurginis and others, *Lietuvos TSR istorija*, II, 319 and 349; R. Šarmaitis, "Vincas Kapsukas," in Kapsukas, *Raštai*, I, 11–12; Kondratas, "Žemės ūkio darbininkų . . . ," pp. 87 and 92.
10 See S. Matulaitis, p. 154; *Lietuvos ūkininkas*, no. 30 (1906), p. 412; ibid., no. 31 (1906), p. 421; ibid., no. 45 (1906), pp. 532–33; Jurginis and others, *Lietuvos TSR istorija*, II, 319; Kondratas, "Žemės ūkio darbininkų . . . ," p. 85; Tyla, p. 203.
11 Angarietis, *Lietuvos revoliucinio judėjimo* . . . , II, 254, 271–72, and 356.
12 See Kairys, *Tau, Lietuva*, pp. 54 and 59; Jurginis and others, *Lietuvos TSR istorija*, II, 318–19 and 349; Bielinis, *Penktieji metai*, p. 301; Kondratas, "Žemės ūkio darbininkų . . . ," pp. 83 and 93; Tyla, pp. 8, 198, and 200; S. Matulaitis, p. 153; [Angarietis], *Antrosios Lietuvos Socialdemokratų Partijos* . . . , p. 12; J. Stankūnas, "Šiaulių darbininkų tarpe," in *Revoliucinis judėjimas Lietuvoje*, ed. R. Šarmaitis (Vilnius, 1957), p. 114; *Kova*, May 17, 1907, p. 283. Cf. Tyla, 199–200.
13 See *Lietuvos ūkininkas*, no. 31 (1906), p. 421; ibid., no. 34 (1906), p. 443; ibid., no. 38 (1906), p. 475; Tyla, pp. 164 and 204; Čepėnas, *Naujųjų laikų Lietuvos istorija*, I, 383; Biržiška, *Lietuvių tautos kelias*, II, 126. For statistics on the destruction of the landed estates in Estonia and Latvia, see Toivo U. Raun, "The Revolution of 1905 in the Baltic Provinces and Finland," *Slavic Review*, no. 3 (1984), pp. 460–62.
14 See Kondratas, "Žemės ūkio darbininkų . . . ," pp. 87–88.
15 See Tyla, p. 212; Grinius, II, 103.
16 See Kairys, *Tau, Lietuva*, pp. 380–82. See also *Lietuvos ūkininkas*, no. 34 (1906), p. 443; *Vienybė lietuvninkų*, no. 37 (1906), p. 439; [Angarietis], *Antrosios Lietuvos Socialdemokratų Partijos* . . . , p. 11; Kapsukas, *Raštai*, X, 210.
17 This section is based on research reported in Tyla, pp. 57–91 and 222–25. Since the totals cited in this work appear to be somewhat discrepant, the count of 240 which is used in the present survey derives from meetings and demonstrations identified in Tyla by place and date.
18 See Griškūnaitė and others (eds.), *Lietuvos TSR istorijos šaltiniai*, II, 390–91.
19 See Tyla, pp. 74 and 81.
20 For decisions of the November 23 / December 6 meeting, see Griškūnaitė and others (eds.), *Lietuvos TSR istorijos šaltiniai*, II, 392–96. An LSDP manifesto issued in September 1905 also recommended the formation of local revolutionary committees. Ibid., p. 379. See also Čepėnas (ed.), *Vladas Požela* . . . , pp. 186–87.
21 For an analysis of changes in local government, school reorganization, and the nonpayment of taxes, see Tyla, pp. 91–152.
22 Ibid., pp. 85–86; Stanisław Kalabiński and Feliks Tych (eds.), *Walki chłopów Królestwa Polskiego w rewolucji 1905–1907* (Warsaw, 1958–61), II, 750, 758, 761–68, 782–85; Čepėnas, *Naujųjų laikų Lietuvos istorija*, I, 352, 373, and 365–66; Kondratas, "Žemės ūkio darbininkų . . . ," pp. 89–90; Griškūnaitė and others (eds.), *Lietuvos TSR istorijos šaltiniai*, II, 398–99; *Materialy do dziejów ziemi Sejnenskiej* (Białystok, 1963) quoted in K. A. Matulaitis, pp. 268–69; Jurginis, *1905 metų revoliucijos įvykiai Vilniuje*, p. 74.
23 For the *Darbininkas* reports, see Kapsukas, *Raštai*, II, 335–422.
24 See Tyla, pp. 8, 10, and 89; Klimaitis, p. 159; Z. Angarietis, "Leninizmas ir mūsų partija," *Komunistas*, no. 1 (1932), pp. 4 and 6; Kapsukas, *Raštai*, IX, 441 and 443; Kairys, *Tau, Lietuva*, p. 50; Institute of Party History, *Lietuvos komunistų partijos istorijos apybraiža*, I, 176.

25 See Tyla, pp. 67 and 87–88; Angarietis, *Lietuvos revoliucinio judėjimo . . .* , II, 280.
26 For an unusually strong clerical denunciation of the revolutionaries circulated in July 1905, see statement by the Rev. Juozapas Antanavičius, the administrator of the diocese of Sejny, reproduced in Griškūnaitė and others (eds.), *Lietuvos TSR istorijos šaltiniai*, II, 361–64.

Chapter 7: Image and Control

1 See *Darbininkų balsas*, no. 3 (March 1905), p. 97; ibid., no. 5 (September 1904), pp. 132–34 and 138; ibid., no. 9 (September 1905), pp. 282–83; Kapsukas, *Raštai*, II, 337–38 and 341; *Kova*, August 11, 1905, p. 98.
2 For LSDP position on religious freedom, see Griškūnaitė and others (eds.), *Lietuvos TSR istorijos šaltiniai*, II, 377–78. On sentiment critical of the socialists, see *Darbininkų balsas*, no. 5 (September 1904), pp. 133 and 137; ibid., no. 3 (March 1905), p. 98; ibid., no. 4 (April 1905), pp. 124–25 and 127–30; ibid., no. 6 (June 1905), p. 187; ibid., no. 8 (August 1905), p. 253; ibid., no. 9 (September 1905), pp. 282–85 and 289–90; ibid., no. 10 (October 1905), pp. 297, 313, and 316; ibid., no. 11–12 (November–December 1905), pp. 371 and 386–89; ibid., no. 1 (January 1906), pp. 6 and 26–27; ibid., no. 2 (February 1906), p. 40; ibid., no. 3 (March 1906), p. 84; Tyla, pp. 69–70; Kapsukas, *Raštai*, II, 337 and 347; Bielinis, *Socialdemokratas*, July 21, 1927, p. 2.
3 Kairys, *Tau, Lietuva*, p. 178.
4 See *Darbininkų balsas*, no. 5 (September 1904), p. 132; ibid., no. 4 (April 1905), p. 128; ibid., no. 10 (October 1905), p. 318.
5 Ibid., no. 7 (July 1905), p. 228.
6 Ibid., no. 1 (January 1906), p. 6; ibid., no. 11–12 (November–December 1905), p. 386.
7 Ibid., no. 3 (March 1905), p. 98; ibid., no. 4 (April 1905), p. 127; ibid., no. 11–12 (November–December 1905), p. 386; ibid., no. 1 (January 1906), p. 29; Bielinis, *Penktieji metai*, p. 434.
8 See *Darbininkų balsas*, no. 5 (September 1904), p. 133.
9 Ibid., p. 134. See also *Darbininkų balsas*, no. 4 (April 1905), p. 126; ibid., no. 6 (June 1905), pp. 186–87; ibid., no. 11–12 (November–December 1905), p. 389; ibid., no. 3 (March 1906), p. 92; Klimaitis, *Židinys*, no. 4 (1931), p. 374; Čepėnas, *Naujųjų laikų Lietuvos istorija*, I, 367; Grinius, II, 103.
10 For a suggestion that this Russian fear of physical mistreatment was inspired by the government to justify the ruthlessness of its repressive measures, see A. Šapoka (ed.), p. 518.
11 See *Lietuvos ūkininkas*, no. 47 (1906), p. 548; *Darbininkų balsas*, no. 5 (September 1904), p. 137; ibid., no. 11–12 (November–December 1905), p. 389; ibid., no. 1 (January 1906), p. 29; ibid., no. 3 (March 1906), pp. 93–94; Čepėnas, *Naujųjų laikų Lietuvos istorija*, I, 385; K. Grinius, "1905-tieji metai," *Lietuvos ūkininkas*, January 5/18, 1906, p. 39; M. Baltasis [Mykolas Biržiška], "Dveji metai atgal," *Žarija*, November 27 / December 10, 1907, p. 331; [Biržiška], *Kova*, June 14, 1907, p. 343; Petrika, p. 129; Kapsukas, *Raštai*, IX, 442; Bielinis, *Penktieji metai*, p. 52.
12 See D. [Steponas Kairys], "Kurio darbo imties," *Žarija*, February 5/18, 1908, pp. 82–83; [Biržiška], *Žarija*, November 27/December 10, 1907, p. 331.
13 *Darbininkų balsas*, no. 6 (June 1905), p. 186. See also Kapsukas, *Raštai*, II, 338.
14 See *Darbininkų balsas*, no. 6 (June 1905), p. 186; ibid., no. 7 (July 1905), pp. 213 and 222; ibid., no. 11–12 (November–December 1905), p. 386; Bielinis, *Penktieji*

metai, pp. 165, 379, 426–27 and 437; Tyla, p. 83 and 202; Kapsukas, *Raštai*, II, 363; *Partijos žinios*, no. 1 (1906), p. 4; [Kairys], *Žarija*, February 5/18, 1908, p. 82; Grinius, *Atsiminimai ir mintys*, II, 90.

15 See Kairys, *Tau, Lietuva*, p. 80.

16 See Angarietis, *Lietuvos revoliucinio judėjimo* . . . , II, 340–41.

17 See Tyla, p. 178.

18 See *Partijos žinios*, no. 1 (1906), p. 4; Jurginis, *1905 metų revoliucijos įvykiai Vilniuje*, p. 92; Angarietis, *Lietuvos revoliucinio judėjimo* . . . , II, 287.

19 See Tyla, p. 159; Bielinis, *Penktieji metai*, p. 427. See also *Vienybė lietuvninkų*, no. 37 (1906), p. 440.

20 See Tyla, p. 145; *Darbininkų balsas*, no. 10 (October 1905), p. 317; ibid., no. 11–12 (November–December 1905), pp. 374–76.

21 See Tyla, p. 136.

22 Ibid., p. 141; Čepėnas, *Naujųjų laikų Lietuvos istorija*, I, 365–66.

23 Cf. *Darbininkų balsas*, no. 5 (September 1904), p. 131.

24 See Tyla, pp. 178–79.

25 *Darbininkų balsas*, no. 5 (September 1904), p. 133.

26 Kairys, *Tau, Lietuva*, p. 61.

27 *Darbininkų balsas*, no. 5 (September 1904), p. 130.

28 Ibid., pp. 129–32.

29 See [Kairys], *Žarija*, February 5/18, 1908, pp. 82–83. See also Kapsukas, *Raštai*, II, 279–81 and 284. On LSDP unpreparedness, see also *Partijos žinios*, no. 1 (1906), p. 1; letter of Vincas Kapsukas to Jurgis Šaulys, October 22, 1905, Šaulys Archives, f. 58.

30 See Klimaitis, *Židinys*, no. 1 (1931), pp. 43–56; ibid., no. 2 (1931), pp. 146–60; ibid., no. 4 (1931), pp. 365–76. See also Kairys, *Tau, Lietuva*, p. 84; Sadomis, p. 2. For decisions made at the convention, see Griškūnaitė and others (eds.), *Lietuvos TSR istorijos šaltiniai*, II, 390–91. On the Grand Diet in general, see P. J. Gabrys, "Didysis Vilniaus Seimas ir jo reikšmė Lietuvai," *Naujoji Romuva*, December 6, 1936, to February 14, 1937 (serialized in a weekly journal); Pranas Klimaitis, "Didysis Vilniaus Seimas," *Židinys*, no. 1 (1931) to no. 4 (1931) (serialized in a monthly journal); J. S-lius [Jonas Basanavičius], *Iš didžiojo Vilniaus seimo istorijos* (Vilnius, 1925); P. Ruseckas, *Didysis Vilniaus Seimas* (Kaunas, 1930); *Lietuviškoji enciklopedija*, VI, 690–705; Kairys, *Tau, Lietuva*, pp. 82–104; J. Kaminskas [Steponas Kairys], "Didysis Vilniaus Seimas," *Darbas*, no. 4 (1955), pp. 19–24; Kapsukas, *Raštai*, IX, 442–47; ibid., X, 203–14; P. Višinskis, "Pirmutinis Didysis Lietuvių Susivažiavimas Vilniuje," *Lietuvos ūkininkas*, December 1/14, 1905, pp. 3–7; L. Gerulis [Liūdas Gira], "Atmintinos sukaktuvės," *Lietuvos ūkininkas*, November 23 / December 6, 1906, pp. 681–84; St [eponas] Kairys, "Vilniaus Seimas," *Kultūra*, no. 12 (1930), pp. 619–24; Petrika, pp. 123–28; Jurginis, *1905 metų revoliucijos įvykiai Vilniuje*, pp. 101–15; Alfred Erich Senn, *Jonas Basanavičius: The Patriarch of the Lithuanian National Renaissance* (Newtonville, Mass., 1980), pp. 25–28; Čepėnas, *Naujųjų laikų Lietuvos istorija*, I, 339–49; Römer, pp. 382–436.

31 Klimaitis, *Židinys*, no. 1 (1931), pp. 50–52.

32 See *Darbininkų balsas*, no. 2 (February 1904), p. 61; ibid., no. 5 (September 1904), p. 159; Grinius, I, 172, 208, and 220; Kairys, *Lietuva budo*, pp. 284 and 294–95; Kairys, *Tau, Lietuva*, p. 321; [Ivinskis], *Žiburiai*, May 18, 1946, p. 3.

33 Ibid.; Klimaitis, *Židinys*, no. 1 (1931), p. 51; *Darbininkų balsas*, no. 2 (February 1904), p. 60.

34 Klimaitis, *Židinys*, no. 1 (1931), p. 52.

35   Ibid. See also Kairys, *Tau, Lietuva*, p. 83.
36   Ibid. See also Sadomis, p. 2.
37   See LSDP Manifesto reproduced in Griškūnaitė and others (eds.), *Lietuvos TSR istorijos šaltiniai*, II, 379. See also Kairys, *Tau, Lietuva*, p. 101.
38   See Klimaitis, *Židinys*, no. 1 (1931), p. 52.
39   See *Partijos žinios*, no. 1 (1906), p. 4; *Vienybė lietuvninkų*, no. 37 (1906), p. 439; *Žarija*, August 29 / September 11, 1907, pp. 137–38; ibid., September 20 / October 3, 1907, pp. 177–78; ibid., November 21 / December 4, 1907, p. 326; ibid., April 23 / May 6, 1908, p. 250; ibid., May 29 / June 11, 1908, p. 301; *Darbininkų balsas*, no. 1 (January 1906), p. 6; Bielinis, *Penktieji metai*, pp. 425–28, 438, and 430–32.
40   Kapsukas, *Raštai*, IV, 37. See also *Lietuvos ūkininkas*, no. 49 (1906), p. 567.
41   See Bielinis, *Penktieji metai*, pp. 379, 425–29, and 436; Kairys, *Tau, Lietuva*, pp. 48 and 178; *Žarija*, January 4/17, 1908, p. 3; [Kairys], *Žarija*, February 5/18, 1908, p. 82; Kapsukas, *Raštai*, II, 278–81, 320, 408, and 364; ibid., IV, 37 and 58; Čepėnas, *Naujųjų laikų Lietuvos istorija*, I, 376–77; K. Matulaitis, pp. 369–70; *Vienybė lietuvninkų*, no. 37 (1906), p. 439; Grinius, II, 90–95.
42   See Kapsukas, *Raštai*, II, 365 and 377; Kapsukas, *Naujoji gadynė*, no. 2 (July 1916), p. 79.
43   See *Darbininkų balsas*, no. 10 (October 1905), p. 326.
44   See Klimaitis, *Židinys*, no. 1 (1931), p. 52; *Lietuvos ūkininkas*, no. 49 (1906), p. 567.
45   See Bielinis, *Penktieji metai*, p. 427; Kapsukas, *Raštai*, II, 281–82 and 320–21.
46   Ibid., p. 281.
47   See *Darbininkų balsas*, no. 2 (February 1906), p. 52; *Lietuvos ūkininkas*, no. 8 (1906), p. 108; ibid., no. 10 (1906), p. 139; Čepėnas, *Naujųjų laikų Lietuvos istorija*, I, 375; Kairys, *Tau, Lietuva*, p. 108.
48   See Bielinis, *Penktieji metai*, pp. 425, 427, and 440; *Vienybė lietuvninkų*, no. 37 (1906), p. 439; *Priekalas*, no. 1–2 (March–May 1931), p. 53.
49   See Bielinis, *Penktieji metai*, p. 435.
50   See *Priekalas*, no. 1–2 (March–May 1931), p. 53; ibid, no.3–4 (June–September 1931), p. 124.
51   See Griškūnaitė and others (eds.), *Lietuvos TSR istorijos šaltiniai*, II, 449; Kapsukas, *Naujoji gadynė*, no. 2 (July 1916), p. 78.
52   See Bielinis, *Penktieji metai*, p. 379.
53   Ibid., pp. 428 and 436; Kairys, *Tau, Lietuva*, p. 48.
54   Ibid., p. 172; Biclinis, *Penktieji metai*, pp. 426 and 429; *Darbininkų balsas*, no. 1 (January 1906), p. 6; *Vienybė lietuvninkų*, no. 37 (1906), pp. 439–40.
55   See Bielinis, *Penktieji metai*, p. 436.
56   See Kapsukas, *Raštai*, VII, 586 and 591; *Vienybė lietuvninkų* no. 37 (1906), p. 439; *Naujoji gadynė*, November 30/December 13, 1906, p. 440.

Chapter 8: Changing Prospects

1   The troop total is adapted from Griškūnaitė, *Darbininkų judėjimas Lietuvoje . . .*, pp. 177–78.
2   *Darbininkų balsas*, no. 1 (January 1906), p. 3; ibid., pp. 8–14; ibid., no. 3 (March 1906), p. 66; ibid., no. 4 (April 1906), p. 114.
3   Ibid., no. 1 (January 1906), p. 8.
4   Ibid., no. 3 (March 1906), p. 66.

5   Ibid., p. 67; ibid., no. 1 (January 1906), pp. 2–3. See also letter of Vincas Kapsukas to Jurgis Šaulys, April 7, 1906, Šaulys Archives, f. 58.

6   *Darbininkų balsas*, no. 1 (January 1906), pp. 10–11.

7   Ibid., no. 3 (March 1906), p. 70. See also *Priekalas*, no. 3–4 (June–September 1931), p. 129; *Darbininkų balsas*, no. 1 (January 1906), p. 14; ibid., no. 3 (March 1906), pp. 68–70.

8   See *Priekalas*, no. 3–4 (June–September 1931), p. 126; *Darbininkų balsas*, no. 4 (April 1906), p. 113; letter of Vincas Kapsukas to Jurgis Šaulys, June 15, 1906, Šaulys Archives, f. 58; Kapsukas, *Raštai*, IV, 77.

9   For a preliminary agenda of the planned congress, see letter of Vincas Kapsukas to Jurgis Šaulys, June 15, 1906, Šaulys Archives, f. 58; letter of Vladas Požela to Jurgis Šaulys, May 20, 1906, Šaulys Archives, f. 63; *Naujoji gadynė*, July 5/18, 1906, p. 112.

10   See *Darbininkų balsas*, no. 3 (March 1906), pp. 65–70; ibid., no. 4 (April 1906), p. 114.

11   See Kairys, *Tau, Lietuva*, p. 176; S. Matulaitis, p. 152.

12   See Kairys, *Tau, Lietuva*, pp. 176–77.

13   *Partijos žinios*, no. 1 (1906), p. 2.

14   Cf. Šešėlis [Mykolas Biržiška], "'Pirmeivių' darbas ir visuomenės demokratai," *Visuomenė*, no. 4 (1910), p. 113.

15   See *Partijos žinios*, no. 1 (1906), p. 3.

16   See *Žarija*, December 12/25, 1907, p. 366; ibid., January 4/17, 1908, p. 2.

17   [Kairys], *Žarija*, February 5/18, 1908, p. 82.

18   See V. Kapsukas, "Kas gi toliau bus?" *Žarija*, December 12/25, 1907, pp. 366–67.

19   *Žarija*, January 4/17, 1908, p. 3; [Kairys], ibid., February 5/18, 1908, p. 82.

20   The overview of the twenty-two conferences held by the Kaunas, Panevėžys, Šiauliai, Suwałki, and Vilnius organizations, including the statistics on party membership, is based largely on the following sources: *Žarija*, July 24/August 6, 1907, p. 58; ibid., August 1/14, 1907, pp. 74–75; ibid., August 8/21, 1907, pp. 89–90; ibid., August 29/September 11, 1907, pp. 137–38; ibid., September 20/October 3, 1907, pp. 177–78; ibid., September 26/October 9, 1907, p. 197; ibid., November 21/December 4, 1907, p. 326; ibid., January 15/28, 1908, p. 48; ibid., February 5/18, 1908, pp. 93–94; ibid., March 12/25, 1908, pp. 171–72; ibid., March 27/April 9, 1908, p. 203; ibid., April 3/16, 1908, p. 220; ibid., April 23/May 6, 1908, p. 250; ibid., May 29/June 11, 1908, pp. 299 and 301; ibid., June 13/26, 1908, pp. 332–33; Bielinis, *Penktieji metai*, pp. 235, 413–14, 416, 428, 430–32, 436–38, and 441–42; Kapsukas, *Raštai*, VII, 586–91, 597, 601, 612–15, and 618; Kapsukas, *Naujoji gadynė*, no. 2 (July 1916), pp. 78–79; V. Kapsukas, "Juodosios reakcijos metais," *Naujoji gadynė*, no. 4 (September 1916), pp. 208–13 and no. 5 (October 1916), pp. 267–72; *Kova*, June 28, 1907, pp. 378–79; ibid., September 6, 1907, pp. 538–39.

21   See, for example, Kapsukas, *Naujoji gadynė*, no. 2 (July 1916), pp. 79–80; Angarietis, *Lietuvos revoliucinio judėjimo . . .*, II, 349–50.

22   Čepėnas (ed.), *Vladas Požela . . .*, p. 255.

23   Cf. Bielinis, *Penktieji metai*, p. 432.

24   For evidence suggesting the possibility of an undisclosed LSDP activity, see police report quoted in *Komunistas*, May 9, 1918, pp. 48–49; Čepėnas (ed.), *Vladas Požela . . .*, p. 255; *Kova*, no. 6 (1909) quoted in Kapsukas, *Raštai*, VII, 619; Griškūnaitė, *Darbininkų judėjimas Lietuvoje . . .*, p. 224; letter of Vladas Požela to Jurgis Šaulys, February 15, 1909, Šaulys Archives, f. 63; Kapsukas, *Naujoji gadynė*, no. 2 (July 1916), pp. 82–83, and no. 4 (September 1916), p. 212.

25   *Partijos žinios*, no. 1 (1912), pp. 3–9.

26   See Bielinis, *Penktieji metai*, pp. 494 and 514; *MLTE*, I, 225–26; *Lietuviškoji enciklopedija*, III, 923.
27   See *MLTE*, I, 60.
28   See *Lietuvių enciklopedija*, IX, 260–61.
29   See *MLTE*, II, 50–51; R. Šarmaitis, "V. Kapsukas kovoje dėl Lietuvos komunistų partijos sukūrimo," *Komunistas*, no. 4 (1965), p. 38.
30   See Čepėnas (ed.), *Vladas Požela* . . . , pp. 201, 209–10, 226–27, and 254; Kapsukas, *Raštai*, VII, 647; *MLTE*, II, 895; ibid., p. 893; ibid., III, 239; Smalstytė, pp. 146–59 and 165–72.
31   *Lietuvių enciklopedija*, XXI, 377; III, 379; letter of Mykolas Biržiška to the Foreign Bureau of the LSDP, June 11, 1913, quoted in Kapsukas, *Raštai*, VII, 650; Živilė Kriaučiūnienė, "Revoliucionierius literatas," *Komunistas*, no. 8 (1985), p. 77.
32   See *MLTE*, I, 678; ibid., II, 539; Bielinis, *Penktieji metai*, p. 434.
33   See *MLTE*, I, 459; Biržiška, *Keleivis*, September 20, 1950, p. 5.
34   Letter of Mykolas Biržiška to the foreign bureau of the LSDP, June 11, 1913, quoted in Kapsukas, *Raštai*, VII, 649. See also *MLTE*, II, 18.
35   Ibid., p. 633; Biržiška, *Lietuvių tautos kelias*, II, 161; S. Matulaitis, p. 162.
36   Ibid., pp. 161–62; *Lietuviškoji enciklopedija*, VI, 1210; *MLTE*, I, 414; Biržiška, *Lietuvių tautos kelias*, II, 161.
37   See S. Matulaitis, pp. 157, 161–62, and 164; *MLTE*, II, 531.
38   Postcard of Mykolas Biržiška to Jurgis Šaulys, April 9, 1910, Šaulys Archives, f. 53; Biržiška, *Lietuvių tautos kelias*, II, 161; letter of Mykolas Biržiška to the Foreign Bureau of the LSDP, June 11, 1913, quoted in Kapsukas, *Raštai*, VII, 649.
39   See *Žarija*, November 21/December 4, 1907, p. 326; ibid., April 3/16, 1908, p. 220; ibid., April 23/May 6, 1908, p. 250; Bielinis, *Penktieji metai*, pp. 442 and 438; Kapsukas, *Raštai*, VII, 618; Kapsukas, *Naujoji gadynė*, no. 2 (July 1916), p. 83.
40   For figures on the number of strikes, see Florinsky, II, 1229 and 1376.
41   See *Partijos žinios*, no. 1 (1912), pp. 1–2; Kapsukas, *Raštai*, IV, 283.
42   See *Partijos žinios*, no. 1 (1912), pp. 4–5.
43   See Čepėnas (ed.), *Vladas Požela* . . . , pp. 256–57; Jurginis and others, *Lietuvos TSR istorija*, II, 380.
44   See Kapsukas, *Raštai*, VII, 648; Vilčinskas, p. 96; [Angarietis], *Antrosios Lietuvos Socialdemokratų Partijos* . . . , p. 19; *MLTE*, II, 51 and 396; Kapsukas, *Raštai*, VI, 7.
45   See Čepėnas (ed.), *Vladas Požela* . . . , pp. 261–63; Kapsukas, *Raštai*, VII, 648–52.
46   Cf. Čepėnas (ed.), *Vladas Požela* . . . , pp. 258–60.

Chapter 9: Unity Efforts

1   See *Lietuviškoji tarybinė enciklopedija*, V, 48.
2   See *Darbininkų balsas*, nos. 11–12 (November–December 1905), pp. 396–98; ibid., pp. 329–30 and 399; Kairys, *Tau, Lietuva*, p. 169.
3   See Kairys, *Lietuva budo*, p. 346.
4   See Kairys, *Tau, Lietuva*, pp. 53–54, 168–69.
5   Ibid., pp. 169 and 186–89. Cf. Kapsukas, *Raštai*, IV, 77; Angarietis, *Lietuvos revoliucinio judėjimo* . . . , II, 418.
6   Ibid., p. 421; Biržiška, *Keleivis*, September 13, 1950, p. 5; Biržiška, *Lietuvių tautos kelias*, II, 119; Menachim Wajner, "Do historii P.P.S. na Litwie," *Niepodległość*, XV (1937), 337–38.

7 See *Darbininkų balsas*, no. 1 (January 1906), p. 7; Kairys, *Tau, Lietuva*, pp. 169 and 186. See also Wajner, p. 342.

8 See Kairys, *Tau, Lietuva*, p. 169; *Darbininkų balsas*, no. 1 (January 1906), p. 7.

9 See *Partijos žinios*, no. 1 (1906), p. 5; Kairys, *Tau, Lietuva*, pp. 186–87.

10 See letter of Vincas Kapsukas to Jurgis Šaulys, June 15, 1906, Šaulys Archives, f. 58; Kapsukas, *Raštai*, VII, 578.

11 See Kairys, *Tau, Lietuva*, pp. 187–89.

12 See resolutions of the congress quoted in Kairys, *Tau Lietuva*, p. 388.

13 Ibid., p. 189.

14 Ibid., p. 188; *Naujoji gadynė*, November 16/29, 1906, p. 411; ibid., November 30/December 13, 1906, p. 441; *Kova*, January 4, 1907, p. 6; Kapsukas, *Raštai*, IV, 390; Bielinis, *Penktieji metai*, pp. 421–22; Angarietis, *Lietuvos revoliucinio judėjimo* . . . , II, 422.

15 See Kairys, *Lietuva budo*, p. 303; Kairys, *Tau, Lietuva*, p. 188; Kapsukas, *Raštai*, IV, 77; ibid., VII, 594–95.

16 Ibid., p. 594; Kairys, *Tau, Lietuva*, p. 188; Wajner, pp. 34 and 346.

17 See Angarietis, *Lietuvos revoliucinio judėjimo* . . . , II, 376 and 380.

18 For a rare clash of the Bund and the LSDP during the elections to the second Duma, see Kairys, *Tau, Lietuva*, pp. 196 and 327; Bielinis, *Penktieji metai*, p. 238; [Angarietis], *Antrosios Lietuvos Socialdemokratų Partijos* . . . , p. 11.

19 See *Darbininkų balsas*, no. 10 (October 1905), p. 327; ibid., no. 3 (March 1906), pp. 86–88.

20 [Trusiewicz], *Socialdemokratas*, no. 6–8 (May 1916), p. 46.

21 See Kapsukas, *Naujoji gadynė*, no. 2 (July 1916), p. 80; Kapsukas, *Raštai*, VII, 601.

22 See Bielinis, *Penktieji metai*, p. 413.

23 See Kairys, *Tau, Lietuva*, p. 326. Cf. Griškūnaitė and others (eds.), *Lietuvos TSR istorijos šaltiniai*, II, 448.

24 See party by-laws reproduced in Kairys, *Tau, Lietuva*, pp. 397–400.

25 Ibid., pp. 326–27; *Partijos žinios*, no. 1 (1906), p. 8.

26 See Kairys, *Tau, Lietuva*, p. 395.

27 Ibid., p. 191.

28 See *Partijos žinios*, no. 1 (1906), p. 4; Kapsukas, *Raštai*, VII, 582.

29 See *Darbininkų balsas*, no. 4 (April 1906), p. 115.

30 See *Kova*, June 7, 1907, p. 332; *Partijos žinios*, no. 1 (1906), p. 8; cf. Bielinis, *Penktieji metai*, p. 447.

31 See *Žarija*, January 29/February 11, 1908, p. 78; Kapsukas, *Naujoji gadynė*, no. 5 (October 1916), p. 271; Kapsukas, *Raštai*, IV, 205–6; letter of Vanda Didžiulytė-Mickienė to Jurgis Šaulys, [June, 1908], Šaulys Archives, f. 58.

32 See Bielinis, *Dienojant*, pp. 344–45; *Lietuviškoji tarybinė enciklopedija*, IX, 432.

33 See *Žarija*, August 1/14, 1907, p. 75; ibid., August 8/21, 1907, p. 90; ibid., August 16/29, 1907, p. 106; ibid., October 10/23, 1907, p. 230; ibid., October 31/November 13, 1907, p. 280; *Kova*, September 6, 1907, pp. 538–39; Bielinis, *Penktieji metai*, pp. 491–92.

34 On Lithuanian social democracy in Riga, see Bielinis, *Dienojant*, pp. 331–64; Bielinis, *Penktieji metai*, pp. 480–514; [Moravskis], *Socialdemokratas*, May 27, 1926, p. 2; V. Kapsukas, "Rusijos lietuvių komunistai," *Komunaras*, no. 4 (March 1922), p. 10. On the history of the Lithuanian labor movement in Riga, see Bielinis, *Dienojant*, pp. 331–39; K. Bielinis, "Iš darbininkų judėjimo istorijos," *Socialdemokratas*, May 12 to June 30, 1927 (serialized in a weekly newspaper).

35   See *Partijos žinios*, no. 1 (1906), p. 8; *Naujoji gadynė*, December 7/20, 1906, p. 461; *Žarija*, July 4/17, 1907, p. 30; Bielinis, *Penktieji metai*, pp. 447–48.

36   On the Lithuanian social democrats in Scotland, see *Žarija*, September 20/October 3, 1907, p. 178; ibid., January 29/February 11, 1908, p. 77; Kapsukas, *Raštai*, VI, 99–102.

37   See *Lietuvių enciklopedija*, XXVIII, 224–25; *MLTE*, II, 368; *Žarija*, June 13/26, 1908, p. 338; *Darbininkų balsas*, no. 7 (July 1905), p. 228.

38   See Kremer, *Proletarskaia revoliutsiia*, no. 11 (1922), p. 55; Institut Marksizma-leninizma pri TSK KPSS, *Pervyi s"ezd RSDRP: Dokumety i materialy* (Moscow, 1958), pp. 197–98; Tobias, p. 79. Domaševičius denies there was an invitation to attend the congress. See Domaševičius, "Apie Lietuvos socialdemokratų partijos įkūrimą . . . ," p. 6.

39   *Darbininkų balsas*, no. 10 (October 1905), p. 327. Cf. *Darbininkų balsas*, no. 1 (January 1905), p. 14.

40   See Kairys, *Tau, Lietuva*, pp. 191 and 193.

41   *Partijos žinios*, no. 1 (1906), p. 1.

42   Ibid., p. 5. See also Kapsukas, *Raštai*, VII, 582.

43   For the merger conditions adopted in 1907, see Griškūnaitė and others (eds.), *Lietuvos TSR istorijos šaltiniai*, II, 452; Kairys, *Tau Lietuva*, pp. 390–91.

44   See *Partijos žinios*, no. 1 (1906), p. 8; P. Grigaitis, "Kodėl LSDP nesusivienijo su Rusijos SDDP?" *Kova*, August 16, 1907, p. 489; Kapsukas, *Raštai*, VII, 582; Kairys, *Tau, Lietuva*, p. 218.

45   For the text of the central committee reply, see *Partijos žinios*, no. 1 (1906), p. 8.

46   See Institut Marksizma-leninizma pri TSK KPSS, *Piatyi (londonskii) s"ezd RSDRP: Protokoly* (Moscow, 1963), pp. 5–8; Kairys, *Tau, Lietuva*, pp. 217–20 and 384–86; Angarietis, *Lietuvos revoliucinio judėjimo . . .* , II, 424.

47   Kairys, *Tau, Lietuva*, pp. 220–21 and 192; Kapsukas quoted in Bielinis, *Penktieji metai*, p. 441; Grigaitis, p. 489.

48   See the text of their protest in *Partijos žinios*, no. 1 (1906), p. 7.

49   See Griškūnaitė and others (eds.), *Lietuvos TSR istorijos šaltiniai*, II, 452; Kairys, *Tau, Lietuva*, p. 391.

50   See *Žarija*, March 12/25, 1908, p. 174; Kapsukas, *Raštai*, VII, 627 and 631–32; *Partijos žinios*, no. 1 (1912), p. 11.

51   Cf. Kapsukas, *Raštai*, VII, 632.

52   See *Partijos žinios*, no. 1 (1912), p. 7.

53   See Kapsukas, *Raštai*, VII, 646.

Chapter 10: Structural Contours

1   See party by-laws reproduced in Kairys, *Tau, Lietuva*, pp. 397–401. See also *Žarija*, March 12/25, 1908, pp. 174–75; Kapsukas, *Raštai*, VII, 597–601.

2   See *Priekalas*, no. 3–4 (June–September 1931), p. 129; *Partijos žinios*, no. 1 (1906), p. 1.

3   See Kapsukas, *Raštai*, VII, 601; Bielinis, *Penktieji metai*, p. 450.

4   See letter of Vincas Kapsukas to Jurgis Šaulys, November 3, 1905, Šaulys Archives, f. 58.

5   See Angarietis, *Lietuvos revoliucinio judėjimo . . .* , II, 342.

6   See letter of Vincas Kapsukas to Jurgis Šaulys, November 3, 1905, Šaulys Archives, f. 58.

7 For an account ascribing to the LSDP a clearly proletarian character, see Bielinis, *Penktieji metai*, p. 450.
8 See Kapsukas, *Raštai*, VII, 599–600; Kapsukas, *Naujoji gadynė*, no. 2 (July 1916), p. 79.
9 See Kapsukas, *Raštai*, VII, 612; Kapsukas, *Naujoji gadynė*, no. 4 (September 1916), p. 209; Bielinis, *Penktieji metai*, p. 416.
10 See Čepėnas, *Naujųjų laikų Lietuvos istorija*, II, 679; Šapoka (ed.), p. 569.
11 See [Biržiška], *Priekalas*, no. 5 (October–November 1931), p. 211.
12 See V. Daugirdaitė Sruogienė, *Lietuvos istorija* (6th ed.; Chicago, n.d.), p. 339.
13 See Kairys, *Lietuva budo*, pp. 346–47.
14 See *Darbininkų balsas*, no. 1 (January–February 1903), p. 47; ibid., no. 2 (February 1904), p. 63; ibid., no. 1 (January 1905), p. 38; *Kova*, May 3, 1907, pp. 263–66; ibid., May 17, 1907, pp. 282–85; *Žarija*, March 12/25, 1908, p. 174.
15 See *Kova*, May 17, 1907, p. 284.
16 Ibid., pp. 284–85.

Chapter 11: Images of the Lithuanian Future

1 For a concise analysis of Rosa Luxemburg's treatment of the national question, see J. P. Nettl, *Rosa Luxemburg* (Abridged edition; London, 1969), pp. 500–519. On the dilemmas which the national question brought to the Jews, see Tobias. See also Biržiška, *Lietuvių tautos kelias*, II, 112; Kairys, *Tau, Lietuva*, pp. 61, 191, 193, and 226; Kapsukas, *Raštai*, VII, 578. On attitudes in Latvia and Estonia, see Raun, pp. 453–67.
2 Biržiška, *Keleivis*, September 27, 1950, p. 5.
3 Filius Vitae [Jonas Šepetys], "Artimesnysis Liet. Soc. Dem. Partijos uždavinys," *Darbininkų balsas*, no. 4 (April 1906), pp. 99–103.
4 Ibid., p. 101.
5 Ibid.
6 *Partijos žinios*, no. 1 (1906), p. 1.
7 Cf. S. [Stasys Matulaitis], "Lietuvos autonomija," *Žarija*, May 30 / June 12, 1907, p. 2; Kairys, *Tau, Lietuva*, p. 226.
8 See Kairys, *Tau, Lietuva*, p. 192; *Partijos žinios*, no. 1 (1906), p. 7; *Priekalas*, no. 3–4 (June–September 1931), p. 128; Institute of Party History, *Lietuvos komunistų partijos istorijos apybraiža*, I, 219.
9 See Kapsukas, *Raštai*, VII, 575; Kairys, *Tau, Lietuva*, p. 192; *Priekalas*, no. 3–4 (June–September 1931), p. 128; Institute of Party History, *Lietuvos komunistų partijos istorijos apybraiža*, I, 217.
10 See letter of Vincas Kapsukas to Jurgis Šaulys, June 15, 1906, Šaulys Archives, f. 58; Kapsukas, *Raštai*, VII, 577; Bielinis, *Penktieji metai*, pp. 440–41; Institute of Party History, *Lietuvos komunistų partijos istorijos apybraiža*, I, 217.
11 See *Naujoji gadynė*, July 13/26, 1906, p. 124; Angarietis, *Lietuvos revoliucinio judėjimo . . .* , II, 372–75 and 379–80; *Naujoji gadynė*, August 2/15, 1906, pp. 172–73.
12 See *Partijos žinios*, no. 1 (1906), p. 2.
13 For the Autonomist project, see *Partijos žinios*, no. 1 (1906), pp. 6–7; Kapsukas, *Raštai*, VII, 575.
14 See *Partijos žinios*, no. 1 (1906), p. 6.
15 For an exposition of Federalist views, see Kapsukas quoted in Bielinis, *Penktieji metai*, p. 441; *Darbininkų balsas*, no. 7 (December 1904), p. 196; ibid., no. 3 (March

1906), pp. 86–88; *Partijos žinios*, no. 1 (1906), p. 6; [S. Matulaitis], *Žarija*, May 30/ June 12, 1907, pp. 2–4; Kapsukas, *Raštai*, VII, 576. Cf. *Darbininkų balsas*, no. 2 (February 1905), p. 45; *Priekalas*, no. 3–4 (June–September 1931), p. 128. For the favorable impression that the Czech social democrats made on their Lithuanian counterparts when they suggested in 1907 that Austria should become a federal state, see V. Kapsukas, "Čechų socijaldemokratai," *Žarija*, May 30 / June 12, 1907, pp. 6–7; Sébraitis [Stasys Matulaitis], "Autonomija ir federacija," *Žarija*, July 4/17, 1907, p. 24.

16 For discussions of the Federalist and Autonomist drafts by the local organizations, see Kapsukas, *Raštai*, VII, 596; Kairys, *Tau, Lietuva*, p. 226; Biržiška, *Keleivis*, October 4, 1950, p. 5; *Kova*, June 28, 1907, p. 379; Institute of Party History, *Lietuvos komunistų partijos istorijos apybraiža*, I, 220.

17 See *Žarija*, May 30 / June 12, 1907, pp. 2–4; ibid., July 4/17, 1907, pp. 22–24. See also *Partijos žinios*, no. 1 (1906), pp. 5–6; Kapsukas, *Žarija*, May 30/June 12, 1907, p. 7.

18 See *Partijos žinios*, no. 1 (1906), p. 3; *Kova*, July 27, 1906, p. 234; ibid., June 28, 1907, p. 379; Kapsukas, *Raštai*, VII, 578–79.

19 See *Kova*, December 27, 1907, p. 795.

20 See Angarietis, *Lietuvos revoliucinio judėjimo* . . . , II, 385 and 388; Kapsukas, *Raštai*, VII, 579; Kairys, *Tau, Lietuva*, pp. 388–89; *Kova*, December 27, 1907, p. 795.

21 See Bielinis, *Penktieji metai*, p. 441; Kairys, *Tau, Lietuva*, pp. 190–91.

22 See Angarietis, *Lietuvos revoliucinio judėjimo* . . . , II, 372; [S. Matulaitis], *Žarija*, July 4/17, 1907, p. 24; Kairys, *Tau, Lietuva*, pp. 185, 190–93, and 229–30. Cf. Kapsukas, *Raštai*, VII, 582; [Angarietis], *Antrosios Lietuvos Socialdemokratų Partijos* . . . , p. 14; *Priekalas*, no. 3–4 (June–September 1931), p. 128.

23 See Kapsukas, *Raštai*, VII, 580 and 582; [Šepetys], *Darbininkų balsas*, no. 4 (April 1906), p. 99.

24 See Kairys, *Tau, Lietuva*, p. 193.

25 Ibid., p. 191; Kapsukas, *Raštai*, VII, 577 and 581–82; Angarietis, *Komunistas*, no. 5 (1928), pp. 3–4; *Partijos žinios*, no. 1 (1906), pp. 1–2, 4, and 8; [Angarietis], *Antrosios Lietuvos Socialdemokratų Partijos* . . . , pp. 12–14; [Šepetys], *Darbininkų balsas*, no. 4 (April 1906), pp. 99–100 and 102–3; Griškūnaitė, *Darbininkų judėjimas Lietuvoje* . . . , pp. 208–9; Angarietis, *Lietuvos revoliucinio judėjimo* . . . , II, 379.

26 Griškūnaitė, *Darbininkų judėjimas Lietuvoje* . . . , p. 210. See also Kapsukas, *Raštai*, VII, 579, and XI, 387; Jurginis and others (eds.), *Lietuvos TSR istorija*, II, 355; *MLTE*, I, 60; ibid., II, 396; Angarietis, *Komunistas*, no. 5 (1928), p. 5; Z. A. [Zigmas Angarietis], "Iš mūsų praeities," *Komunaras*, no. 3 (February 1922), p. 77; [Angarietis], *Antrosios Lietuvos Socialdemokratų Partijos* . . . , p. 15; Komodaitė, "Lietuvos darbo žmonių revoliucinė kova 1905 metais," p. 77; Šarmaitis, *Komunistas*, no. 4 (1965), p. 37. The Institute of Party History cautiously states that at the congress the Autonomists had the upper hand. See its *Lietuvos komunistų partijos istorijos apybraiža*, I, 223.

27 Kairys, *Tau, Lietuva*, pp. 227, 229–30, and 232. See also [Angarietis], *Antrosios Lietuvos Socialdemokratų Partijos* . . . , pp. 16–19.

28 Angarietis, *Lietuvos revoliucinio judėjimo* . . . , II, 385.

Chapter 12: Realignment on the Land

1 See Kairys, *Tau, Lietuva*, p. 53.

2 See Angarietis, *Lietuvos revoliucino judėjimo* . . . , II, 179–80, 259, 270, 272, and

278; Angarietis quoted in Kapsukas, *Raštai,* VII, 593 and 624; Angarietis, *Komunistas,* no. 5 (1928), p. 3; [Angarietis], *Komunaras,* no. 3 (February 1922), p. 77; Petrika, p. 57; S. Matulaitis, *Atsiminimai ir kiti kūriniai,* pp. 95 and 146; Bielinis, *Penktieji metai,* pp. 21 and 443; Tyla, p. 196; Kairys, *Tau Lietuva,* pp. 53 and 81; "Andrius Baltrušaitis," *Žarija,* October 17/30, 1907, p. 237; *Kova,* November 3, 1905, p. 194; Ruseckas, p. 26; Kapsukas, *Raštai,* X, 226; ibid., XI, 386; Kapsukas, *Naujoji gadynė,* no. 5 (October 1916), p. 269. Cf. Kapsukas, *Raštai,* IX, 443.

3 See Kapsukas, *Raštai,* IV, 42; ibid., V, 301–2; Kapsukas, *Trumpa partijos istorija,* I, 18; Kapsukas, *Naujoji gadynė,* no. 5 (October 1916), p. 269; *Vienybė lietuvninkų,* no. 37 (1906), p. 439; Z. Angarietis, "Mūsų organizacijos pamatas Lietuvoj," *Komunistas,* June 27, 1918, p. 109; [Vileišis], *Varpas,* no. 2 (1904), p. 24; Kairys, *Tau, Lietuva,* pp. 53 and 81. On the numerical proportions of the rural population, see Tyla, pp. 14–46; Apybraiža in *Komunistas,* no. 1 (1967), p. 73; Komodaitė, "Lietuvos darbo žmonių revoliucinė kova 1905 metais," p. 67.

4 See Kairys, *Tau, Lietuva,* p. 81; Kapsukas, *Raštai,* VII, 557 and 593; Kapsukas, *Naujoji gadynė,* no. 5 (October 1916), p. 269.

5 Cf. Kapsukas, *Raštai,* VII, 593.

6 Ibid., IX, 443; Bielinis, *Penktieji metai,* p. 28; Kairys, *Tau, Lietuva,* pp. 81 and 111; Biržiška, *Lietuvių tautos kelias,* II, 119; *Žarija,* October 17/30, 1907, p. 237. Cf. Tyla, pp. 50–52; Kapsukas, *Raštai,* VII, 604.

7 Ruseckas, p. 26.

8 See letter of Vincas Kapsukas to Jurgis Šaulys, April 7, 1906, Šaulys Archives, f. 58; Kairys, *Tau, Lietuva,* p. 81.

9 See *Vienybė lietuvninkų,* no. 37 (1906), p. 439; [Biržiška], *Kova,* June 14, 1907, p. 343; ibid., June 28, 1907, pp. 378–79; letter by Pranas Mažylis quoted in Kapsukas, *Raštai,* IV, 57–59; ibid., IX, 444; Kairys, *Tau, Lietuva,* pp. 82 and 168; Bielinis, *Penktieji metai,* p. 425; *Darbininkų balsas,* no. 11–12 (November–December 1905), p. 388; *Komunistas,* May 1, 1918, p. 41; Biržiška, *Lietuvių tautos kelias,* II, 160; Ruseckas, p. 26; *Priekalas,* no. 3–4 (June–September 1931), p. 129.

10 *Darbininkų balsas,* no. 1 (January 1906), p. 2. See also Kapsukas, *Raštai,* II, 260–61; Kairys, *Tau, Lietuva,* p. 179.

11 See *Priekalas,* no. 1–2 (March–May 1931), p. 52.

12 See *Darbininkų balsas,* no. 1 (January 1906), p. 4.

13 See *Priekalas,* no. 1–2 (March–May 1931), p. 49.

14 *Žarija,* January 4/17, 1908, p. 3. See also Kairys, *Tau, Lietuva,* p. 179; [Kairys], *Žarija,* February 5/18, 1908, p. 83; *Darbininkų balsas,* no. 1 (January 1906), pp. 2–3; Kapsukas, *Raštai,* II, 261; ibid., IX, 444.

15 Ibid., VII, 585. See also *Vienybė lietuvninkų,* no. 37 (1906), p. 439.

16 See Kapsukas, *Raštai,* II, 279 and 260; ibid., VII, 584.

17 Ibid., II, 260; K. Matulaitis, pp. 269–70; *Lietuvos ūkininkas,* no. 30 (1906), p. 412; ibid., no. 49 (1906), pp. 567–68; ibid., no. 57 (1906), p. 668; Kairys, *Tau, Lietuva,* p. 178; Čepėnas, *Naujųjų laikų Lietuvos istorija,* I, 366–77.

18 See Kapsukas, *Raštai,* II, 260; ibid., X, 221; [Angarietis], *Antrosios Lietuvos Social-demokratų Partijos . . . ,* p. 12.

19 See *Darbininkų balsas,* no. 1 (January 1906), pp. 3–4; Kapsukas, *Raštai,* II, 260–61; *Žarija,* September 20 / October 3, 1907, p. 178.

20 [Kairys], *Žarija,* February 5/18, 1908, pp. 82–83.

21 See *Darbininkų balsas,* no. 10 (October 1905), p. 325; Kairys, *Tau, Lietuva,* p. 394; *Partijos žinios,* no. 1 (1912), p. 10; *Darbininkų balsas,* no. 1 (January 1906), p. 4. Cf. *Partijos žinios,* no. 1 (1912), pp. 5 and 7.

22 Cf. Zigmas Angarietis quoted in Kapsukas, *Raštai*, VII, 630.
23 See Kairys, *Tau, Lietuva*, p. 181; Kapsukas, *Raštai*, VII, 586, 591, and 593; Tyla, p. 197; Angarietis, *Komunistas*, June 27, 1918, p. 109.
24 See Kairys, *Tau, Lietuva*, p. 394; Tyla, p. 197–98. Cf. Kapsukas, *Raštai*, VII, 602.
25 Ibid., pp. 594–95.
26 Ibid., pp. 586, 588, and 591–93; Angarietis, *Komunistas*, June 27, 1918, p. 109; Angarietis, *Lietuvos revoliucino judėjimo* . . . , II, 352 and 357; Tyla, p. 197.
27 Angarietis, *Lietuvos revoliucinio judėjimo* . . . , II, 270–71.

Chapter 13: Divided They Stood

1 Griškūnaitė and others (eds.), *Lietuvos TSR istorijos šaltiniai*, II, 404.
2 See *Partijos žinios*, no. 1 (1906), p. 3; *Naujoji gadynė*, October 19 / November 1, 1906, p. 337; *Žarija*, July 24 / August 6, 1907, p. 50. See also Bielinis, *Penktieji metai*, pp. 221 and 245.
3 *Naujoji gadynė*, May 24 / June 6, 1906, p. 50. See also *Partijos žinios*, no. 1 (1906), p. 3; *Naujoji gadynė*, May 5/18, 1906, pp. 2–4.
4 See *Partijos žinios*, no. 1 (1906), p. 3; *Naujoji gadynė*, September 27 / October 10, 1906, p. 299; ibid., October 26 / November 8, 1906, pp. 354–56; ibid., November 2/15, 1906, pp. 369–70.
5 On the campaign effort, see *Naujoji gadynė*, September 27 / October 10, 1906, p. 290; ibid., November 30 / December 13, 1906, pp. 440–41; ibid., December 28, 1906 / January 10, 1907, p. 506; Kairys, *Tau, Lietuva*, pp. 195–202; Bielinis, *Penktieji metai*, p. 239.
6 See Čepėnas, *Naujųjų laikų Lietuvos istorija*, I, 379; Kairys, *Tau, Lietuva*, pp. 200, 209, and 465–66; *Encyclopedia Lituanica*, II, 400; ibid., IV, 333; ibid., V, 294; *Lietuvių enciklopedija*, VIII, 26–27; ibid., XXIII, 378; ibid., XXVIII, 461–62.
7 See Kairys, *Tau, Lietuva*, pp. 207 and 209.
8 See *Žarija*, December 20, 1907 / January 2, 1908, pp. 378–79.
9 Ibid., May 30/June 12, 1907, p. 15; Kairys, *Tau, Lietuva*, p. 209.
10 Ibid., p. 212; Bielinis, *Penktieji metai*, p. 241; Griškūnaitė and others (eds.), *Lietuvos TSR istorijos šaltiniai*, II, 428–32.
11 See Bielinis, *Penktieji metai*, p. 250.
12 See *Žarija*, July 10/23, 1907, p. 34; ibid., July 24/August 6, 1907, pp. 49–50 and 58–59; ibid., August 1/14, 1907, p. 75; ibid., August 8/21, 1907, p. 89; ibid., August 16/29, 1907, pp. 98–101; ibid., August 29/September 11, 1907, p. 138.
13 See Griškūnaitė and others (eds.), *Lietuvos TSR istorijos šaltiniai*, II, 452–53.
14 See *Žarija*, October 24/November 6, 1907, p. 253; ibid., December 20, 1907/January 2, 1908, p. 379; *Lietuvių enciklopedija*, XIII, 450; *MLTE*, II, 270.
15 See *Žarija*, October 24/November 6, 1907, pp. 249–50.
16 See *Naujoji gadynė*, August 2/15, 1906, p. 172; Institute of Party History, *Lietuvos komunistų partijos istorijos apybraiža*, I, 205; Kairys, *Lietuva budo*, p. 345.
17 See Kapsukas, *Raštai*, VII, 597–98.
18 Ibid., pp. 577 and 595–97; ibid., XI, 386–87; Kapsukas, *Pirmoji Lietuvos proletarinė revoliucija ir sovietų valdžia*, pp. 68–69; [Angarietis], *Antrosios Lietuvos Socialdemokratų Partijos* . . . , pp. 13–14; Angarietis, *Komunistas*, June 27, 1918, p. 109; Angarietis, *Komunistas*, no. 5 (1928), pp. 3–6; [Angarietis], *Komunaras*, no. 3 (February 1922), p. 76; *MLTE*, I, 60 and 673; ibid., II, 689.
19 See Biržiška, *Keleivis*, September 13, 1950, p. 5; ibid., October 4, 1950, p. 5; ibid.,

October 18, 1950, p. 5; Biržiška, *Lietuvių tautos kelias*, II, 119 and 160–61; Kairys, *Tau, Lietuva*, p. 288.

20 See Biržiška, *Keleivis*, September 20, 1950, p. 5; Biržiška, *Lietuvių tautos kelias*, II, 163.

21 See Biržiška, *Keleivis*, September 20, 1950, p. 5; ibid., October 11, 1950, p. 5; Kairys, *Tau, Lietuva*, p. 288.

22 See Biržiška, *Keleivis*, September 13, 1950, p. 5; ibid., October 4, 1950, p. 5; Biržiška, *Lietuvių tautos kelias*, II, 161.

23 Ibid., pp. 116 and 161; Biržiška, *Keleivis*, September 20, 1950, p. 5; ibid., October 11, 1950, p. 5; ibid., October 18, 1950, p. 5; Kairys, *Tau, Lietuva*, pp. 289 and 291.

24 See Biržiška, *Lietuvių tautos kelias*, II, 161–63.

25 See Kairys, *Tau, Lietuva*, p. 393.

26 [Kairys], *Žarija*, February 13/26, 1908, pp. 98–101.

27 Biržiška, *Keleivis*, October 4, 1950, p. 5.

28 See *Visuomenė*, no. 11–12 (1910), pp. 354–57; Biržiška, *Lietuvių tautos kelias*, II, 165–67.

29 Cf. Biržiška, *Keleivis*, September 20, 1950, p. 5; ibid., October 4, 1950, p. 5; Biržiška, *Lietuvių tautos kelias*, II, 160–61.

30 Ibid., pp. 160–62.

31 Ibid., pp. 142–43; [Biržiška], *Visuomenė*, no. 4 (1910), pp. 115–16.

32 Ibid., p. 116. See also Biržiška, *Keleivis*, October 4, 1950, p. 5.

33 See Petrika, p. 57; Biržiška, *Lietuvių tautos kelias*, II, 160 and 165–66; Kapsukas, *Raštai*, VII, 636.

34 See [Biržiška], *Visuomenė*, no. 4 (1910), pp. 116–17; ibid., no. 11–12 (1910), pp. 354–55 and 357; Biržiška, *Lietuvių tautos kelias*, II, 162 and 164–66.

35 See Angarietis, *Proletarskaia revoliutsiia*, no. 11 (1922), pp. 75–77.

36 See Biržiška, *Lietuvių tautos kelias*, II, 162; *Lietuviškoji enciklopedija*, VI, 1210.

37 See letter of Mykolas Biržiška to Jurgis Šaulys, April 9, 1910, Šaulys Archives, f. 53; Biržiška, *Lietuvių tautos kelias*, II, 165.

38 Ibid., pp. 162–63; Biržiška, *Keleivis*, October 4, 1950, p. 5; Griškūnaitė, *Darbininkų judėjimas Lietuvoje* . . . , p. 227; M. M., "Dvi srovės lietuvių socialistų tarpe," *Komunistas*, January 10, 1919, p. 2.

39 *Partijos žinios*, no. 1 (1912), p. 1.

40 See Biržiška, *Keleivis*, October 4, 1950, p. 5; Biržiška, *Lietuvių tautos kelias*, II, 164.

41 Ibid., p. 165; Kapsukas, VII, 640–41; Biržiška, *Keleivis*, October 4, 1950, p. 5; [Angarietis], *Antrosios Lietuvos Socialdemokratų Partijos* . . . , p. 18; Kapsukas, *Komunaras*, no. 4 (March 1922), p. 106; ibid., no. 6 (May 1922), p. 172.

42 Ibid., no. 4 (March 1922), p. 106; Kapsukas, *Raštai*, IV, 296; Kapsukas, *Naujoji gadynė*, no. 4 (September 1916), p. 213; Kairys, *Tau, Lietuva*, pp. 62–63; letter of Vladas Požela to Jurgis Šaulys, February 15, 1909, Šaulys Archives, f. 63.

43 See Kapsukas, *Žarija*, December 12/25, 1907, p. 367. See also M. M., *Komunistas*, January 10, 1919, pp. 1–2; Angarietis, *Komunistas*, no. 5 (1928), p. 6.

44 J. Adomavičius [Jonas Šepetys], "Švietimo draugijos," *Žarija*, March 18/31, 1908, pp. 180–82; Kapsukas, *Raštai*, VII, 640 and 634; Biržiška, *Lietuvių tautos kelias*, II, 163; [Angarietis], *Antrosios Lietuvos Socialdemokratų Partijos* . . . , p. 17; Kapsukas, *Naujoji gadynė*, no. 4 (September 1916), p. 213; Angarietis, *Komunistas*, no. 5 (1928), p. 7.

45 For the conference and congress resolutions, see *Žarija*, March 12/25, 1908, pp. 174–75; *Partijos žinios*, no. 1 (1912), pp. 8–12. See also [Angarietis], *Antrosios*

Lietuvos Socialdemokratų Partijos . . . , p. 16; M. M., *Komunistas*, January 10, 1919, p. 1.

46   Ibid., p. 2; Angarietis, *Komunistas*, no. 5 (1928), pp. 5–7; Angarietis, *Komunistas*, June 27, 1918, p. 109; [Angarietis], *Antrosios Lietuvos Socialdemokratų Partijos* . . . , pp. 15–17; [Angarietis], *Komunaras*, no. 3 (February 1922), pp. 76–77; Biržiška, *Lietuvių tautos kelias*, II, 164 and 166–67; Kapsukas, *Raštai*, IV, 283; ibid., VI, 230; ibid., VII, 631–43; Kapsukas, *Naujoji gadynė*, no. 4 (September 1916), p. 213; ibid., no. 5 (October 1916), pp. 267–70; V. Kapsukas, "Trumpa L. K. P. istorija," *Komunaras*, no. 3 (February 1922), pp. 79–80; Mickevičius-Kapsukas, *Pirmoji Lietuvos proletarinė revoliucija ir sovietų valdžia*, pp. 70–71.

47   See Biržiška, *Keleivis*, October 11, 1950, p. 5.

48   See *MLTE*, I, 60–61; ibid., II, 50–52; [Romas Šarmaitis], "Aukos, kurių neturėjo būti," *Tiesa*, April 5, 1988, p. 2.

49   Kapsukas, *Raštai*, IV, 137–38, 205, and 354–55.

Bibliography

General Sources

Abramavičius, V., ed. *Rankraščių rinkiniai*. Vilnius, 1963.

Adomonienė, O., and others, eds. *Lietuvos TSR istorijos bibliografija, 1940–1965*. Vilnius, 1969.

American Lithuanian Cultural Archives. Putnam, Connecticut. [Established by the Very Rev. Francis M. Juras, this collection preserves some valuable material about Lithuania, including books, magazines, newspapers, items of folk art, archival holdings, and personal papers of noted Lithuanians.]

Balys, John P. "Lithuanian Materials Available in the Library of Congress," *Lituanus*, no. 4 (1974), pp. 32–41.

———. "The American Lithuanian Press," *Lituanus*, no. 1 (1976), pp. 42–53.

Balys, Jonas, comp. *Lithuania and Lithuanians: A Selected Bibliography*. New York, 1961.

———. *Lithuanian Periodicals in American Libraries*. Washington, D.C., 1982.

Cadzow, John F. "The Lithuanian Collection in the Kent State University Library," *Lituanus*, no. 1 (1975), pp. 40–44.

Čepėnas, Pranas. *Naujųjų laikų Lietuvos istorija*. 2 vols. Chicago, 1977–86.

Dainauskas, J. "Lituanistika 'Tarptaut. santykių bibliotekoje' Chicagoj," *Draugas*, July 3, 1970, p. 5.

Daugirdaitė Sruogienė, V. *Lietuvos istorija*. 6th ed. Chicago, n.d.

Encyclopaedia Judaica. 16 vols. Jerusalem, 1971.

Encyclopedia Lituanica. 6 vols. Boston, 1970–78.

Florinsky, Michael T. *Russia: A History and an Interpretation*. 2 vols. New York, 1947.

Grimsted, Patricia Kennedy. *Archives and Manuscript Repositories in the USSR: Estonia, Latvia, Lithuania, and Belorussia*. Princeton, N.J., 1981.

Griškūnaitė, E., and others, eds. *Lietuvos TSR istorijos šaltiniai*. Vol. II. Vilnius, 1965.

Hundert, Gershon David, and Bacon, Gershon C. *The Jews in Poland and Russia: Bibliographical Essays*. Bloomington, Ind., 1984.

Institut Marksizma-leninizma pri TSK KPSS. *Pervyi s"ezd RSDRP: Dokumenty i materialy*. Moscow, 1958.

———. *Vtoroi s"ezd RSDRP: Protokoly*. Moscow, 1959.

———. *Piatyi (londonskii) s"ezd RSDRP: Protokoly*. Moscow, 1963.

Institute of Lithuanian Studies. *Lietuvių išeivijos spaudos bibliografija, 1970–1974*. Compiled for the Institute of Lithuanian Studies by Povilas Gaučys. Chicago, 1977.

————. *Lietuvių išeivijos spaudos bibliografija, 1975–1979*. Compiled for the Institute of Lithuanian Studies by Povilas Gaučys. Chicago, 1984.

Institute of Party History, Party archive of. Vilnius, Lithuania. [This collection preserves the following typewritten memoirs of Andrius Domaševičius: "Apie Lietuvos socialdemokratų partijos įkūrimą 1896 m.," "LSDP pradžia 1896 m.," and "Mano vaikams."]

Ivanov, L. M., ed. *Rabochee dvizhenie v Rossii v XIX veke: Sbornik dokumentov i materialov*. Vol. IV, Pts. 1–2. Moscow, 1961–63.

Jablonskis, K., and others, eds. *Lietuvos TSR istorija*. Vilnius, 1958.

Jurginis, J., Merkys, V., and Žiugžda, J., eds. *Lietuvos TSR istorija*. Vol. II. Vilnius, 1963.

Kalabiński, Stanisław, and Tych, Feliks, eds. *Walki chłopów królestwa polskiego w rewolucji 1905–1907*. 3 vols. Warsaw, 1958–61.

Kantautas, Adam and Filomena. *A Lithuanian Bibliography*. Edmonton, Alberta, 1975.

————. *Supplement to a Lithuanian Bibliography*. Edmonton, Alberta, 1979.

Kent State University. Lithuanian Collection: Periodicals as of November, 1971. (Mimeographed.)

Kisinas, Izidorius, comp. *Lietuviškų knygų sistematinis katalogas*. Kaunas, 1938.

Kriaučiūnas, Juozas, "ALKA Preserves Material of Lithuanian Culture," *Lituanus*, no. 1 (1986), pp. 67–74.

Kukk, Hilja. "The Monograph and Serial Holdings at the Hoover Institution Pertaining to Baltic Area Studies," *Lituanus*, no. 4 (1976), pp. 60–64.

Lassner, Franz G. "Baltic Archival Materials at the Hoover Institution on War, Revolution, and Peace," *Lituanus*, no. 4 (1974), pp. 42–47.

Laučka, Isabelle T. "The Monsignor and His Archives," *Lituanus*, no. 4 (1982), pp. 48–54.

Lietuviškoji enciklopedija. 9 vols. Kaunas, 1933–44.

Lietuviškoji tarybinė enciklopedija. 13 vols. Vilnius, 1976–85.

Lietuvių enciklopedija. 36 vols. Boston, 1953–69.

Lietuvos TSR bibliografija (series A). Vols. I–II: *Knygos lietuvių kalba*. Vilnius, 1969–85.

Lithuanian World Archives. Chicago, Illinois. [This collection of Lithuanian materials consists of unpublished correspondence, manuscripts, books, magazines, and newspapers, including the 1906 issues of *Naujoji gadynė*.]

Maciūnas, Vincas. "Dr. Jurgio Šaulio archyvas," in *Proceedings of the Institute of Lithuanian Studies, 1973* (Chicago, 1975), pp. 39–63.

Maciūnas, Vincas, and Ostrauskas, Kostas. "The Šaulys Collection," *Library Chronicle* (University of Pennsylvania Library), XX (1954), 35–46.

Materialy do dziejów ziemi Sejneńskiej. Białystok, 1963.

Mažoji lietuviškoji tarybinė enciklopedija. 3 vols. Vilnius, 1966–71.

Ochmański, Jerzy. *Historia Litwy*. 2d ed. Wrocław, 1982.

"Paremkime lituanistikos statybą," *Draugas*, August 25 to August 30, 1965 (serialized in a daily newspaper).

Petrauskienė, Z., and Valentėlienė, P. *Lietuvos TSR mokslininkų disertacijos, 1945–1968: Bibliografija*. Vilnius, 1971.

Polska Akademia Nauk. *Polski słownik biograficzny*. 28 vols. Kraków, 1935–85.

Private Archives of the Social Democratic Party of Lithuania. In the possession of Mykolas Pranevičius, Chicago, Illinois. [This collection includes unpublished correspondence of some of the leading Lithuanian socialists.]

"Rare Baltica in the Bonaparte Collections," *Lituanus*, no. 3–4 (1964), pp. 103–11.

Reklaitis, Povilas. "Rytinei Europai tirti dokumentacijos ir informacijos centrai Vokietijos Feder [alinėje] Respublikoje. Jų reikšmė Lituanistikai," in *Lituanistikos darbai*, II (1969), 35–65.

Šapoka, A., ed. *Lietuvos istorija*. Kaunas, 1936.

Šaulys, Jurgis, Archives of. University of Pennsylvania Library, Philadelphia. [This collection includes personal correspondence between Šaulys and some of the leading Lithuanian socialists.]

Šešplaukis, Alf. "Lituanika Europos bibliotekose," in *Proceedings of the Institute of Lithuanian Studies, 1971* (Chicago, 1971), pp. 236–44.

Sukiennicki, W. "The Origin of the Communist Party of Lithuania and Belorussia." Paper read before the meeting of the Association for the Advancement of Baltic Studies, San Jose, California, November 26–29, 1970.

Urniežiūtė, E., and others, comps. *Lietuvos TSR spauda, 1940–1955*. Vol. I, Bks. 1–2. Vilnius, 1962–64.

Vaitkevičius, Bronius, and others, eds. *Lietuvos TSR istorija*. Vol. I. Vilnius, 1985.

Vilčinskas, Juozas. Personal letter. July 13, 1987.

Zhiugzhda, Iu. I., and others, eds. *Revoliutsiia 1905–1907 gg. v Litve: Dokumenty i materialy*. Vilnius, 1961.

Books

Akimov, V. [Makhnovets]. *Ocherk razvitiia sotsialdemokratii v Rossii*. St. Petersburg, 1906.

Alseika, D. *Lietuvių tautinė ideja istorijos šviesoje*. Vilnius, 1924.

Angarietis, Z. *Agrarinis klausimas Lietuvoje*. Vilnius, 1972.

———. *Lietuvos revoliucinio judėjimo ir darbininkų kovos istorija*. 2 vols. N.p., 1921–22.

———. *LKP įsikūrimas ir proletarinė revoliucija Lietuvoje (1918–1919 m.)*. Vilnius, 1962.

———. *Nepriklausomybė ir Lietuvos darbininkai*. St. Petersburg, 1918.

Angarietis, Z., and others. *Tautų klausimas ir lietuviai bolševikai*. Voronezh, 1918.

Barzdaitis, J. *Ateizmo tradicijos Lietuvoje*. Vilnius, 1980.

Basanavičius, Jonas. *Rinktiniai raštai*. Vilnius, 1970.

Beržas, M. [Zigmas Angarietis]. *Antrosios Lietuvos Social-Demokratų Partijos darbai ir mokslas*. Kaunas, 1925.

Bielinis, Kipras. *Dienojant*. New York, 1958.

———. *Gana to jungo*. New York, 1971.

———. "Iš susirašinėjimo su Vladu Požela," in Pranas Čepėnas, ed. *Vladas Požela: Jaunystės atsiminimai*. London, 1971.

———. *1905 metai: Atsiminimai ir dokumentai*. Kaunas, 1931.

———. *Penktieji metai*. New York, 1959.

Biliūnas, J. *Raštai*. Vol. II. Vilnius, 1955.

Biržiška, M. *Lietuvių tautos kelias*. 2 vols. Los Angeles, 1952–53.

Blobaum, Robert. *Feliks Dzierżyński and the SDKPIL: A Study of the Origins of Polish Communism*. Boulder, Colo., 1984.

Burokevičius, M., ed. *Už socializmo sukūrimą Lietuvoje*. Vilnius, 1969.

Čepėnas, Pranas, ed. *Vladas Požela: Jaunystės atsiminimai*. London, 1971.

Cohen, Israel. *Vilna*. Philadelphia, 1943.

Dimanshtein, S., ed. *Revoliutsionnoe dvizhenie sredi evreev*. Moscow, 1930.

Dzerzhinsky, F. E. *Izbrannye proizvedeniia*. 2 vols. Moscow, 1957.

Dziewanowski, M. K. *The Communist Party of Poland*. Cambridge, Mass., 1959.

Fradkina, C. "Darbininkų judėjimas Lietuvoje naujo revoliucinio pakilimo metais (1910–1914 m.) ir bolševikinė 'Pravda'," in R. Šarmaitis, ed., *Revoliucinis judėjimas Lietuvoje*. Vilnius, 1957.

Gaigalaitė, A. *Klerikalizmas Lietuvoje, 1917–1940*. Vilnius, 1970.

[Gira, Liūdas, ed.] *Lietuvos albumas*. Kaunas, [1921].

Girdzijauskienė, P. *1905–1907 metų revoliucija Lietuvoje*. Vilnius, 1955.

Glikas, B. "Visuotinis 1905 metų spalio politinis streikas Lietuvoje," in R. Šarmaitis, ed., *Revoliucinis judėjimas Lietuvoje*. Vilnius, 1957.

Gozhanskii, S. N. "Evreiskoe rabochee dvizhenie nachala 90-kh godov," in S. Dimanshtein, ed., *Revoliutsionnoe dvizhenie sredi evreev*. Moscow, 1930.

Grinius, Kazys. *Atsiminimai ir mintys*. 2 vols. Tübingen and Chicago, 1947–62.

Griškūnaitė, E. *Darbininkų judėjimas Lietuvoje 1908–1914 metais*. Vilnius, 1959.

———. *Darbininkų judėjimas Lietuvoje, 1895–1914 m.* Vilnius, 1971.

———. "Laikraščio 'Vilnis' reikšmė Lietuvos darbo žmonių revoliuciniame judėjime," in R. Šarmaitis, ed., *Revoliucinis judėjimas Lietuvoje*. Vilnius, 1957.

———. "Revoliucinis judėjimas Lietuvoje 1908–1911 metais," in R. Šarmaitis, ed. *Revoliucinis judėjimas Lietuvoje*. Vilnius, 1957.

Haimson, Leopold H. *The Russian Marxists und the Origins of Bolshevism*. Cambridge, Mass., 1955.

Haustein, Ulrich. *Sozialismus and nationale Frage in Polen*. Köln, 1969.

Institute of Party History. *Lietuvos komunistų partijos istorijos apybraiža*. 2 vols. Vilnius, 1971–78.

Jablonskis, K., and others, ed. *Lietuvos valstiečiai XIX amžiuje*. Vilnius, 1957.

Jurginis, J. *1905 metų revoliucijos įvykiai Vilniuje*. Vilnius, 1958.

Jurginis, J., Merkys, V., and Tautavičius, A. *Vilniaus miesto istorija*. Vilnius, 1968.

Kairys, A. "Zigmas Angarietis—marksistinės filosofijos ir mokslinio socializmo propaguotojas Stolypino reakcijos metais (1907–1910 m.)," in M. Burokevičius, ed., *Už socializmo sukūrimą Lietuvoje*. Vilnius, 1969.

Kairys, Steponas. *Lietuvo budo*. New York, 1957.

———. *Tau, Lietuva*. Boston, 1964.

Kapsukas, Vincas. *Raštai*. 12 vols. Vilnius, 1960–78.

———. *Trumpa Lietuvos Social-Demokratų Partijos istorija, 1896–1905 m.* Pt. 1. St. Petersburg, 1918.

Komodaitė, J. "Lietuvos darbo žmonių revoliucinė kova 1905 metais," in R. Šarmaitis, ed., *Revoliucinis judėjimas Lietuvoje*. Vilnius, 1957.

———. "1905 metų gruodžio politinis streikas Lietuvoje," in R. Šarmaitis, ed., *Revoliucinis judėjimas Lietuvoje*. Vilnius, 1957.

Komodaitė, J., and Fradkina, C. "Gegužės pirmosios demonstracijos Vilniuje ir Kaune 1902 metais," in R. Šarmaitis, ed., *Revoliucinis judėjimas Lietuvoje*. Vilnius, 1957.

Kondratas, V. "1905–1907 metų revoliucijos pradžia Lietuvoje," in R. Šarmaitis, ed., *Revoliucinis judėjimas Lietuvoje*. Vilnius, 1957.

———. "Žemės ūkio darbininkų ir valstiečių revoliucinis judėjimas Lietuvoje 1905–1907 metais," in R. Šarmaitis, ed., *Revoliucinis judėjimas Lietuvoje*. Vilnius, 1957.

Kopel'zon, T. M. "Evreiskoe rabochee dvizhenie kontsa 80-kh i nachala 90-kh godov," in S. Dimanshtein, ed., *Revoliutsionnoe dvizhenie sredi evreev*. Moscow, 1930.

[Kremer, Arkadi]. *Ob agitatsii*. Geneva, 1896.

Lietuvis, A., and N. N. [Alfonsas Moravskis and Jonas Vileišis]. *Augis darbininkų judėjimo Lietuvoje*. Plymouth, Pa., 1900.

Lietuviškoji Social-Demokratų Partija. *Darbo diena*. Paris, 1902.

———. *Kas reikia žinoti ir atminti kiekvienam darbininkui*. Paris, 1902.

Lietuvos Demokratų Partija. *Lietuvos Demokratų Partijos Programa*. Tilsit, 1906.
Lietuvos TSR Mokslų Akademija, Istorijos Institutas. *Klasės ir politinės partijos Lietuvoje 1919–1926 metais*. Vilnius, 1978.
Łossowski, Piotr. *Po tej i tamtej stronie Niemna*. Warsaw, 1985.
Martov, Iu. *Zapiski sotsialdemokrata*. Berlin, 1922.
Martov, L., and others, eds. *Obshchestvennoe dvizhenie v Rossii v nachale XX-go veka*. 4 vols. St. Petersburg, 1909–14.
Matulaitis, Stasys. *Atsiminimai ir kiti kūriniai*. Vilnius, 1957.
Mendelsohn, Ezra. *Class Struggle in the Pale: The Formative Years of the Jewish Workers' Movement in Tsarist Russia*. Cambridge, 1970.
———. *The Jews of East Central Europe between the World Wars*. Bloomington, Ind., 1983.
Merkelis, Aleksandras. *Antanas Smetona: Jo visuomeninė, kultūrinė ir politinė veikla*. New York, 1964.
Merkys, V. *Narodnikai ir pirmieji marksistai Lietuvoje*. Vilnius, 1967.
———. "Valstiečių judėjimas Lietuvoje XIX a. pabaigoje," in K. Jablonskis and others, eds., *Lietuvos valstiečiai XIX amžiuje*. Vilnius, 1957.
Merkys, V., and others. *Lietuvių nacionalinio išsivadavimo judėjimas, ligi 1904 metų*. Vilnius, 1987.
Mickevičius-Kapsukas, V. [Vincas Kapsukas]. *Pirmoji Lietuvos proletarinė revoliucija ir sovietų valdžia*. Chicago, 1934.
Mitskevich, S. I., ed. *Na zare rabochego dvizheniia v Moskve*. Moscow, 1932.
[Moravskis, Alfonsas]. *W kwestyi taktyki i organizacyi*. N.p., 1899.
Nettl, J. P. *Rosa Luxemburg*. Abridged ed. London, 1969.
Ochmański, Jerzy. *Feliks Dzierżyński, 1877–1926*. Poznań, 1975.
———. *Litewski ruch narodowo-kulturalny w XIX wieku (do 1890 r.)*. Białystok, 1965.
———. *Rewolucyjna działalność Feliksa Dzierżyńskiego na Litwie w końcu XIX wieku*. Poznań, 1969.
Palčikas, A. "Bolševikai Vilniuje 1905 metais," in R. Šarmaitis, ed., *Revoliucinis judėjimas Lietuvoje*. Vilnius, 1957.
Petrika, A. *Lietuvių tautinio atbudimo pionieriai*. [Brooklyn, N.Y.], 1939.
Pipes, Richard. *Social Democracy and the St. Petersburg Labor Movement, 1885–1897*. Cambridge, Mass., 1963.
Programas Lietuviškos Social-demokratiškos Partijos. N.p., 1896.
Raudeliūnienė, G. "Lietuvos socialdemokratų partija," in Lietuvos TSR Mokslų Akademija, Istorijos Institutas, *Klasės ir politinės partijos Lietuvoje 1919–1926 metais*. Vilnius, 1978.
Rimka, Albinas. *Lietuvos ūkis: Statistikos tyrinėjimai*. Kaunas and Vilnius, 1922.
Römer, Michał. *Litwa: Studyum o odrodzeniu narodu litewskiego*. Lwów, 1908.
Ruseckas, P. *Didysis Vilniaus Seimas*. Kaunas, 1930.
———. *Į laisvę*. Kaunas, 1919.
Šalčius, M. *Dešimt metų tautiniai-kultūrinio darbo Lietuvoje, 1905–1915*. Chicago, 1917.
Šapoka, Adolfas. *Vilnius in the Life of Lithuania*. Translated by E. J. Harrison. Toronto, 1962.
Šarmaitis, R. "Lietuvos darbininkų judėjimas XIX a. pabaigoje," in R. Šarmaitis, ed., *Revoliucinis judėjimas Lietuvoje*. Vilnius, 1957.
———. "Pranas Eidukevičius," in R. Šarmaitis, ed., *Revoliucinis judėjimas Lietuvoje*. Vilnius, 1957.
———. "Vincas Kapsukas," in Vincas Kapsukas, *Raštai*. Vol. I. Vilnius, 1960.

————. "Zigmas Aleksa-Angarietis," in R. Šarmaitis, ed., *Revoliucinis judėjimas Lietuvoje*. Vilnius, 1957.

Šarmaitis, R., ed. *Revoliucinis judėjimas Lietuvoje*. Vilnius, 1957.

Schapiro, Leonard. *The Communist Party of the Soviet Union*. New York, 1964.

Senn, Alfred Erich. *Jonas Basanavičius: The Patriarch of the Lithuanian National Renaissance*. Newtonville, Mass., 1980.

S-lius, J. [Jonas Basanavičius]. *Iš didžiojo Vilniaus seimo istorijos*. Vilnius, 1925.

Smalstytė, Jurgita. *Mano tėvas*. Translated by V. Kauneckas. Vilnius, 1967.

Sniečkus, A. "F. Dzeržinskis—proletarinio internacionalizmo idėjų propagandistas Lietuvoje," in R. Šarmaitis, ed., *Revoliucinis judėjimas Lietuvoje*. Vilnius, 1957.

————. *Vincas Mickevičius-Kapsukas*. Vilnius, 1957.

————. "Vincas Mickevičius-Kapsukas," in R. Šarmaitis, ed., *Revoliucinis judėjimas Lietuvoje*. Vilnius, 1957.

Sponti, E. "Kratkaia avtobiografiia," in S. I. Mitskevich, ed., *Na zare rabochego dvizheniia v Moskve*. Moscow, 1932.

Stankūnas, J. "Šiaulių darbininkų tarpe," in R. Šarmaitis, ed., *Revoliucinis judėjimas Lietuvoje*. Vilnius, 1957.

Strobel, Georg W. *Quellen zur Geschichte des Kommunismus in Polen, 1878–1918: Programme und Statuten*. Köln, 1968.

Sverdlov, Ia. M. *Izbrannye Proizvedeniia*. 3 vols. Moscow, 1957–60.

Tobias, Henry J. *The Jewish Bund in Russia: From Its Origins to 1905*. Stanford, Calif., 1972.

Trumpa, Vincas. *Lietuva XIX-tame amžiuje*. Chicago, 1989.

Tsoglin, V. [David Katz]. "Pervyi s"ezd Bunda," in S. Dimanshtein, ed., *Revoliutsionnoe dvizhenie sredi evreev*. Moscow, 1930.

Tyla, A. *1905 metų revoliucija Lietuvos kaime*. Vilnius, 1968.

Ulam, Adam B. *Russia's Failed Revolutions: From the Decembrists to the Dissidents*. New York, 1981.

————. *The Bolsheviks*. New York, 1965.

Vilčinskas, Juozas. *Lietuvos socialdemokratija kovoje dėl krašto nepriklausomybės*. London, 1985.

Zalevskii, K. [Stanisław Trusiewicz]. "Natsional'nyia partii v Rossii," in L. Martov and others, eds., *Obshchestvennoe dvizhenie v Rossii v nachale XX-go veka*. Vol. III. St. Petersburg, 1914.

Articles

A., Z. [Zigmas Angarietis]. "Iš mūsų praeities," *Komunaras*, no. 3 (February 1922), pp. 75–78.

Adomavičius, J. [Jonas Šepetys]. "Švietimo draugijos," *Žarija*, March 18/31, 1908, pp. 180–82.

————. "Darganos metu," *Rankpelnis*, November 12, 1909, pp. 129–30.

"Andrius Baltrušaitis," *Žarija*, October 17/30, 1907, pp. 237–38.

Andriušaitytė, J. "Kai kurie Lietuvos revoliucinio judėjimo klausimai V. Lenino raštuose," in *Vilniaus Valstybinio V. Kapsuko Vardo Universiteto Mokslo Darbai: Istorija*, II (1960), 5–21.

Angaretis (Aleksa), Z. [Zigmas Angarietis]. "Iz deiatel'nosti s.-d.p. Litvy v gody reaktsii," *Proletarskaia revoliutsiia*, no. 11 (1922), pp. 73–90.

Angarietis, Z. "Leninizmas ir mūsų partija," *Komunistas*, no. 1 (1932), pp. 3–15.

————. "Lietuvos Komunistų Partijos įsikūrimas," *Komunistas*, no. 5 (1928), pp. 1–13.

————. "LKP įsikūrimas," *Balsas*, November 25, 1928, pp. 671–73.
————. "Mūsų organizacijos pamatas Lietuvoj," *Komunistas*, June 27, 1918, pp. 109–10.
————. "Pirmosios gegužės šventė Lietuvoj 1897 metais," *Komunaras*, no. 5 (April 1922), pp. 140–42.
B. C. "Dėlei programo Lietuvos Demokratų Partijos," *Vienybė lietuvninkų*, no. 11 (1903), pp. 127–28, and no. 12 (1903), pp. 144–45.
B. M. [Zigmas Angarietis]. "Iš Lietuvos social-demokratų partijos praeities," *Komunistas*, May 1, 1918, pp. 41–42, and May 9, 1918, pp. 48–49.
Baltasis, M. [Mykolas Biržiška]. "Dveji metai atgal," *Žarija*, November 27/December 10, 1907, pp. 330–33.
————. "'Naujoji Gadynė'," *Žarija*, May 7/20, 1908, pp. 278–81, and May 29/June 11, 1908, pp. 294–96.
————. "Socialdemokratų laikraščiai lietuvių kalboje 1896–1906 metu," *Žarija*, May 1/14, 1908, pp. 265–66.
Beržaitis. [Jonas Vileišis]. "Lietuvių darbininkų judėjimas," *Varpas*, no. 2 (1904), pp. 20–25.
Bielinis, Kipras. "Kas ugdė Lietuvos Steigiamojo Seimo šūkį," *Darbas*, no. 3 (1955), pp. 6–9.
————. "Karolis Kautskis," *Darbas*, no. 1 (1955), pp. 22–25.
————. "Iš darbininkų judėjimo istorijos," *Socialdemokratas*, May 12 to June 30, 1927 (serialized in a weekly newspaper).
————. "1905 metai," *Kultūra*, no. 12 (1930), pp. 624–30.
————. "Socialistinė spauda spaudos draudimo metu," *Kultūra*, no. 5 (1929), pp. 254–56.
————. "50 metų kovos lauke (LSDP 1896–1946)," *Varpas*, no. 5 (1946), pp. 2–6.
————. "Žemaičiuose," *Socialdemokratas*, July 7 to August 11, 1927 (serialized in a weekly newspaper).
Bikulčius, V. "Konspiraciniais adresais," *Tiesa*, September 19, 1971, p. 2.
————. "Neužmirštamas Lenino apsilankymas," *Tiesa*, June 29, 1973, p. 2.
Biržiška, Mykolas. "Pranas Eidukevičius," *Keleivis*, September 13 to October 18, 1950 (serialized in a weekly newspaper).
Biržiška, V. "Lapelis iš Lietuvos S. D. Partijos istorijos," *Darbas*, no. 1 (1950), pp. 4–9, and no. 2 (1952), pp. 6–10.
Bukhbinder, N. A. "I s"ezd 'Vseobshchego evreiskogo rabochego soiuza' 'Bunda'," *Proletarskaia revoliutsiia*, no. 11 (1924), pp. 203–8.
D. [Steponas Kairys]. "Kurio darbo imties," *Žarija*, February 5/18, 1908, pp. 82–84, and February 13/26, 1908, pp. 98–101.
Danilevičius, Eugenijus. "Revoliucijos riterio kova už gyvenimą," *Tiesa*, September 11, 1987, p. 2.
"Dar apie skeliaudras nuo LSDP," *Kova*, August 18, 1905, pp. 106–8.
Darginavičienė, A. "Marksistinio ateizmo revidavimas lietuviškosios socialdemokratijos ideologų darbuose ir jo kritika Z. Angariečio raštuose," in *Lietuvos TSR Aukštųjų Mokyklų Mokslo Darbai: Filosofija*, VII (1966), 151–65.
Demokratas. "Dėlei dolerių," *Lietuvos ūkininkas*, November 16/29, 1906, pp. 668–69, and November 23/December 6, 1906, pp. 686–87.
Exesdek. "Ekonomiškos sąlygos Vilniaus gub.," *Vienybė lietuvninkų*, no. 11 (1901), p. 132.
Filius Vitae. [Jonas Šepetys]. "Artimesnysis Liet. Soc. Dem. Partijos uždavinys," *Darbininkų balsas*, no. 4 (April 1906), pp. 99–103.

Gabrys, P. J. "Didysis Vilniaus Seimas ir jo reikšmė Lietuvai," *Naujoji Romuva*, December 6, 1936, to February 14, 1937 (serialized in a weekly journal).
——. "Didžiojo Vilniaus Seimo rytojus," *Naujoji Romuva*, March 21, 1937, pp. 270–72.
——. "Lietuvos Valstiečių Sąjunga," *Naujoji Romuva*, March 28, 1937, pp. 306–7.
Gerulis, L. [Liūdas Gira]. "Atmintinos sukaktuvės," *Lietuvos ūkininkas*, November 23/December 6, 1906, pp. 681–84.
Glik, B. "Pod"em revoliutsionnogo dvizheniia v Litve osen'iu 1905 g.," in *Lietuvos TSR Aukštųjų Mokyklų Mokslo Darbai: Istorija*, III (1962), 115–44.
——. "Sotsial'no-ekonomicheskie i politicheskie predposylki revoliutsii 1905–1907 godov v Litve," in *Lietuvos TSR Aukštųjų Mokyklų Mokslo Darbai: Istorija*, IV (1963) 35–60.
Grigaitis, P. "Kodėl LSDP nesusivienijo su Rusijos SDDP?" *Kova*, August 16, 1907, pp. 488–89.
Grinius, K. "1905-tieji metai," *Lietuvos ūkininkas*, January 5/18, 1906, pp. 37–40.
Griškevičius, P. "Vincas Kapsukas—Lenino mokinys ir bendražygis, ištikimas Lietuvos liaudies sūnus," *Tiesa*, April 8, 1980, pp. 1–2.
Griškūnaitė, Emilija. "Lietuvos revoliucinių socialdemokratų kova dėl darbininkų klasės vienybės 1905 metais," in *Lietuvos istorijos metraštis, 1975 metai* (Vilnius, 1976), pp. 42–50.
"Gyvenimas, skirtas liaudžiai, partijos reikalui," *Tiesa*, December 2, 1972, p. 2.
Hellmann, Manfred. "Die litauische Nationalbewegung im 19. und 20. Jahrhundert," *Zeitschrift für Ostforschung*, Vol. II (1953), pp. 66–106.
Institute of Party History. "Lietuvos komunistų partijos istorijos apybraiža," *Komunistas*, January 1967, to April 1968 (serialized in a monthly journal).
"Iš literatūros ir gyvenimo," *Varpas*, no. 7–8 (1905), pp. 78–80.
"Iš 1905 m. revoliucijos archyvo," *Priekalas*, no. 1–2 (March–May 1931), pp. 48–53, and no. 3–4 (June–September 1931), pp. 124–30.
"Isz Lietuvių Demokratų Partijos nusprendimų," *Vienybė lietuvninkų*, no. 49 (1903), p. 581.
Janulaitis, A. "Domaševičius ir Pilsudskis," *Mūsų senovė*, III, no. 1 (1940), 53–62.
Jonaitis, L. "Socializmas ir mūsų ekonomiškos užduotys," *Varpas*, no. 4 (1896), pp. 46–53.
"Jonas Zacharevičius," *Naujoji gadynė*, May 31 / June 13, 1906, p. 75.
Juknienė, G. "Lietuvos socialdemokratų partijos pažiūros į religiją ir klerikalizmą 1920–1940 m.," in *LKP istorijos klausimai*, XXXVIII (1986), 32–42.
K., J. [Steponas Kairys]. "Vladas Požela," *Darbas*, no. 3 (1954), pp. 14–17.
Kairys, St[eponas]. "Vilniaus Seimas," *Kultūra*, no. 12 (1930), pp. 619–24.
Kairys, Steponas. "Z maikh uspaminau pra Tsetku," *Konadni*, no. 1 (1954), pp. 68–78.
Kaminskas, J. [Steponas Kairys]. "Didysis Vilniaus Seimas," *Darbas*, no. 4 (1955), pp. 19–24.
——. "LSDP 1905 metų įvykiuose," *Darbas*, no. 2 (1955), pp. 1–5.
Kapsukas, V. "Čechų socialdemokratai," *Žarija*, May 30/June 12, 1907, pp. 6–7.
——. "Dėl A. Lietuvio-Moravskio atsiminimų," *Priekalas*, no. 5 (October–November 1931), pp. 206–8.
——. "Inteligentijos klausimu," *Naujoji gadynė*, no. 1 (June 1916), pp. 8–14.
——. "Iš Lietuvos S.-D. istorijos," *Naujoji gadynė*, no. 2 (July 1916), pp. 76–78 and 81–83.
——. "Juodosios reakcijos metais," *Naujoji gadynė*, no. 4 (September 1916), pp. 208–13, and no. 5 (October 1916), pp. 267–72.

————. "Ką yra atlikusi buvusioji 'Draugo' organizacija," *Kova*, December 1, 1905, pp. 226–27.

————. "Kam mums reikalingas Vilniuje seimas," *Kova*, February 23, 1906, pp. 57–58, and March 2, 1906, pp. 67–68.

————. "Kas gi toliau bus?" *Žarija*, December 12/25, 1907, pp. 366–68.

————. "Lietuvos nepriklausomybės klausimu," *Naujoji gadynė*, no. 6 (November 1916), pp. 342–47.

————. "Nauji diplomatai," *Naujoji gadynė*, no. 3 (August 1916), pp. 172–75.

————. "Pirmieji L. S. D. žingsniai," *Naujoji gadynė*, no. 3 (August 1916), pp. 138–43.

————. "Rusijos lietuvių komunistai," *Komunaras*, no. 4 (March 1922), pp. 105–10, and no. 6 (May 1922), pp. 169–75.

————. "Trumpa L. K. P. istorija," *Komunaras*, no. 3 (February 1922), pp. 78–81.

————. "Trumpa Lietuvos Social-Demokratų Partijos istorija," *Tiesa*, January 18, 1918, pp. 2–3.

Kazlauskas, V. "Marksistinė filosofinė mintis lietuvių legaliojoje socialdemokratinėje spaudoje 1906–1908 metais," in *Lietuvos TSR Aukštųjų Mokyklų Mokslo Darbai: Filosofija*, VII (1966), 167–76.

"Keletas žodžių apie 'Lietuvos Socijaldemokratų Partijos Manifestą'," *Varpas*, no. 9–10 (1905), pp. 93–94.

Kirvelis, Dobilas, and others. "Lietuvos socialdemokratai," *Gimtasis kraštas*, April 27–May 3, 1989, pp. 1 and 5.

Klajūnas, R. [Pranas Mažylis]. "Laiškas iš Suvalkų gubernijos," *Naujoji gadynė*, October 19/November 1, 1906, pp. 346–47.

Klimaitis, Pranas. "Didysis Vilniaus Seimas," *Židinys*, January 1931, to April 1931 (serialized in a monthly journal).

Komodaitė, J. "Komunistų bendražygis," *Komunistas*, no. 11 (1965), pp. 61–64.

Komodaitė, Iu. B. [J. Komodaitė]. "Revoliutsionnaia deiatel'nost' F. E. Dzerzhinskogo v Litve v 1895–1899 gg.," *Istoricheskie zapiski*, no. 45 (1954), pp. 220–34.

Kremer, A. "Osnovanie Bunda," *Proletarskaia revoliutsiia*, no. 11 (1922), pp. 50–56.

Kriaučiūnienė, Živilė. "Revoliucionierius literatas," *Komunistas*, no. 8 (1985), pp. 76–78.

Krivickas, Vladas. "The Programs of the Lithuanian Social Democratic Party, 1896–1931," *Journal of Baltic Studies*, no. 2 (1980), pp. 99–111.

"Kuklios sukakties proga: LSDP, 1896–1956," *Darbas*, no. 2 (1956), pp. 1–5 and 36.

Kvieska, V. "Lietuvių tautinis judėjimas ir varpininkai," *Varpas*, no. 1 (1931), pp. 33–62.

L., J. [Augustinas Janulaitis]. "Dėlei Draugo organizacijos," *Vienybė lietuvninkų*, no. 22 (1905), pp. 262–64.

Lietuvis, A. [Alfonsas Moravskis]. "Die lithauische Arbeiterbewegung," *Die Neue Zeit*, no. 49 (1899), pp. 708–16.

————. "Kas gali mums darbininkams lietuviams suteikti geresnę ateitį?" *Aidas Lietuvos darbininkų gyvenimo*, June 1, 1899, pp. 1–6.

————. "Lietuvos darbininkų judėjimo istorija sąryšy su Lietuvos valstybės atgimimo judėjimu," *Kultūra*, April 1931 to March 1933 (serialized in a monthly journal).

Lietuvis, A., and N. N. [Alfonsas Moravskis and Jonas Vileišis]. "Augis darbininkų judėjimo Lietuvoje," *Vienybė lietuvninkų*, no. 23 (1900) to no. 30 (1900) (serialized in a weekly newspaper).

"Lietuvių Social-Demokratų Partijos konferencija," *Vienybė lietuvninkų*, no. 19 (1903), pp. 222–23, and no. 20 (1903), pp. 234–35.

"Lietuvos komunistų partijos centro komiteto pranešimas," *Priekalas*, no. 3 (March 1935), pp. 129–32.

L-is, A. [Alfonsas Moravskis]. "Iz Litvy," *Rabochee delo*, no. 4–5 (1899), pp. 125–29.

"L.S.D. Partija, 1893–1918," *Darbo balsas*, November 26, 1918, pp. 1–2 and November 29, 1918, pp. 1–2.

"LSDP Suvalkų gub. organizacijų delegatų susivažiavimo atskaita," *Vienybė lietuvninkų*, no. 37 (1906), pp. 439–40.

Lukoševičius, V. "Prano Eidukevičiaus socialinių-ekonominių pažiūrų formavimasis į nuoseklias marksistines-leninines pažiūras," in *Lietuvos TSR Aukštųjų Mokyklų Mokslo Darbai: Ekonomika*, VI, Pt. 1 (1965), 21–38.

M. M. "Dvi srovės lietuvių socialistų tarpe," *Komunistas*, January 10, 1919, pp. 1–2.

Matulaitis, K. A. "Sukilimas Sūduvoje 1905–1906 metais," *Tautos praeitis*, II, Bks. 3–4 (1967), 257–70.

Merkys, V. "Lietuvių SDP pirmųjų programų kilmė," in *Lietuvos TSR Mokslų Akademijos Darbai*, series A, no. 3 (1966), pp. 133–51.

———. "Lietuvos miestų gyventojų tautybės XIX a. pabaigoje—XX a. pradžioje klausimu," in *Lietuvos TSR Mokslų Akademijos Darbai*, series A, no. 2 (1958), pp. 85–97.

———. "Proletariato formavimasis Vilniuje XIX amžiaus pabaigoje," in *Lietuvos TSR Mokslų Akademijos Darbai*, series A, no. 1 (1957), pp. 3–16.

———. "Vilniaus darbininkų streikai 1895–1900 metais," in *Lietuvos TSR Mokslų Akademijos Darbai*, series A, no. 1 (1959), pp. 169–90.

[Merkys, Vytautas]. "V. Merkio pastabos," *Akiračiai*, no. 10 (1986), pp. 6–7.

Michta, Norbert, and Sobczak, Jan. "Stanisław Trusiewicz (Kazimierz Zalewski)," *Z pola walki*, no. 1 (1975), pp. 103–31.

Mikas. [Mykolas Biržiška]. "Lietuvos socialdemokratų partija," *Kova*, May 17 to June 14, 1907 (serialized in a weekly newspaper).

Mitskevich-Kapsukas, V. [Vincas Kapsukas]. "Istoki i zarozhdenie kommunisticheskoi partii Litvy," *Proletarskaia revoliutsiia*, no. 1 (1929), pp. 153–78.

———. "Iz vospominanii F. E. Dzerzhinskogo," *Proletarskaia revoliutsiia*, no. 9 (1926), pp. 55–64.

———. "1905 g. v Litve," *Proletarskaia revoliutsiia*, no. 11 (1922), pp. 57–72.

Moravskis, Alfonsas. Letter to Franciszek Żytkiewicz, January 20, 1898. *Z pola walki*, no. 1 (1985), pp. 112–17.

[Moravskis, Alfonsas]. "Lietuvos Socialdemokratų Partijos įsikūrimas," *Socialdemokratas*, May 6 to June 3, 1926 (serialized in a weekly newspaper).

———. "Szkic do historji ruchu robotniczego na Litwie w ostatnich pięciu latach," *Robotnik litewski*, no. 2 (1898), pp. 118–24.

———. "W kwestyi taktyki ruchu robotniczego," *Przedświt*, no. 6 (June 1896), pp. 2–10.

Motulaitė, Violeta. "Vienybė brendo kovoje," *Komunistas*, no. 6 (1986), pp. 80–84.

Mulevičius, Leonas. "Agrarinis klausimas Lietuvoje 1905–1907 m. revoliucijos metu," in *Lietuvos istorijos metraštis, 1976 metai* (Vilnius, 1977), pp. 17–30.

Naujukas, V. [Danielius Alseika]. "Lietuvos Valstiečių Sąjunga," *Lietuvos ūkininkas*, August 30/September 12, 1906, pp. 522–23.

Patirgas, Z. [Zenonas Ivinskis]. "Keli bruožai iš Lietuvos socialdemokratų praeities," *Žiburiai*, May 11, 1946, p. 3, and May 18, 1946, p. 3.

Pavilonis, V. "Buržuazinių politinių partijų pažiūra į Lietuvos valstybingumą (1905–1918 m.)," in *Lietuvos TSR Aukštųjų Mokyklų Mokslo Darbai: Teisė*, V (1965), 48–62.

Perazich, V. "Iz vospominanii (1896–1897 g.)," *Krasnaia letopis'*, no. 2–3 (1922), pp. 103–15.

———. "Nakanune pervogo s"ezda," *Proletarskaia revoliutsiia*, no. 2 (1928), pp. 23–39.

Pierre, André. "Dzeržinskis, raudonojo teroro organizatorius," translated by P. Povilaitis, *Naujoji Romuva*, June 20, 1937, pp. 520–21.

Pietkiewicz, Kazimierz. "Mojżesz Łurje i 'Raboczeje Znamia'," *Niepodległość*, VI, no. 1 (1932), 26–40.

Ponarski, Zenowiusz. "Socjaldemokracja litewska a PPS w końcu XIX w.," *Z pola walki*, no. 1 (1985), pp. 105–12.

Požela, Vladas. Letters to Vincas Kapsukas, *Priekalas*, no. 1–2 (March–May 1931), pp. 48–53, and no. 3–4 (June–September 1931), pp. 124–30.

"Programas Lietuvių Demokratų Partijos (Projektas)," *Vienybė lietuvninkų*, no. 6 (1903) to no. 8 (1903) (serialized in a weekly newspaper).

P-tis. "Iš Lietuvos inteligentų susivažiavimų nutarimų," *Varpas*, no. 7–8 (1905), pp. 73–76.

Raun, Toivo U. "The Revolution of 1905 in the Baltic Provinces and Finland," *Slavic Review*, no. 3 (1984), pp. 453–67.

Repšys, J. "Zigmas Angarietis—marksizmo propagandistas Lietuvoje 1917–1918 m.," in *Vilniaus Valstybinio V. Kapsuko Vardo Universiteto Mokslo Darbai: Istorija*, I (1958), 63–71.

Rimka, Albinas. "Lietuvių tautos atgimimo socialiniai pagrindai ir 'Auszros'—'Varpo' gadynės (1883–1893) socialekonominiai raštai," in *Vytauto Didžiojo Universiteto Teisių Fakulteto Darbai*, VI (1932), 209–45.

S. [Stasys Matulaitis]. "Lietuvos autonomija," *Žarija*, May 30 / June 12, 1907, pp. 2–4.

Sadomis, A. "1905 m. Vilniaus Seimas ir socialdemokratai," *Socialdemokratas*, December 20–27, 1930, pp. 1–2.

Šalčius, Petras. "'Auszros' ir 'Szwiesos' ekonomika," in *Vytauto Didžiojo Universiteto Teisių Fakulteto Darbai*, VI (1932), 419–49.

[Šarmaitis, Romas]. "Aukos, kurių neturėjo būti," *Tiesa*, April 5, 1988, p. 2.

Šarmaitis, R. "Aistringas revoliucijos karys," *Tiesa*, June 24, 1972, p. 2.

———. "Galingas komunizmo idėjų šaltinis," *Tiesa*, January 20, 1974, p. 2.

———. "Įžvalgus komunistų partijos veikėjas," *Tiesa*, June 24, 1982, p. 2.

———. "Marksizmo-leninizmo idėjos Lietuvoje," *Tiesa*, May 5, 1983, p. 2.

———. "V. Kapsukas kovoje dėl Lietuvos Komunistų partijos sukūrimo," *Komunistas*, no. 4 (1965), pp. 36–41.

———. "Zigmo Angariečio literatūrinis palikimas," *LKP istorijos klausimai*, III (1963), 5–19.

Sėbraitis. [Stasys Matulaitis]. "Autonomija ir federacija," *Žarija*, July 4/17, 1907, pp. 22–24.

Selvanas, A. "Iš Lietuvos komunistų partijos agrarinės programos parengimo istorijos," in *Lietuvos TSR Aukštųjų Mokyklų Mokslo Darbai: Ekonomika*, IV, Pt. 2 (1964), 23–36.

Senn, Alfred Erich. "A Correspondence with Steponas Kairys," *Lituanus*, no. 1 (1975), pp. 63–69.

Šešėlis. [Mykolas Biržiška]. "A. Lietuvio-Moravskio atsiminimai," *Priekalas*, no. 5 (October–November 1931), pp. 209–11.

———. "'Pirmeivių' darbas ir visuomenės demokratai," *Visuomenė*, no. 4 (1910), pp. 113–17.

"Šiometine LSDP konferencija," *Kova*, November 3, 1905, p. 194.

Siulelis, Pranas. "Dveji metai," *Lietuvos ūkininkas*, November 9/22, 1906, pp. 650–52.

Skliarskaitė, F. "Kai kurie dialektinio materializmo klausimai V. Kapsuko raštuose," in *Lietuvos TSR Aukštųjų Mokyklų Mokslo Darbai: Filosofija*, III (1963), 139–51.

Sliesoriūnienė, Elena. "Įžymus visuomenės veikėjas: Stasio Matulaičio gimimo 120-osioms metinėms," *Komunistas*, no. 10 (1986), pp. 84–86.

"Socializmas Prusų Lietuvoje," *Lietuvos darbininkas*, no. 3 (1899), pp. 22–25.

"Socializmas Prusų Lietuvoje," *Vienybė lietuvninkų*, no. 13 (1899), pp. 154–55.

"Susijungimo sąlygos LSDDP su LSDP," *Kova*, December 1, 1905, p. 227.

"Święto majowe w Wilnie," *Przedświt*, no. 10 (October 1894), pp. 22–23.

Tamošiūnas, J. "Procesai Lietuvos kaimo socialiniame gyvenime 1861–1914 metais," in *Lietuvos TSR Aukštųjų Mokyklų Mokslo Darbai: Ekonomika*, V. Pt. 2 (1965), 111–25.

Trumpa, Vincas, "Iš V. Kapsuko revoliucinės ir kultūrinės veiklos 1903–1911 m.," in *Lituanistikos darbai*, IV (1979), 215–46.

Tsentral'nyi Komitet Litovskoi Sotsial'demokrat. Partii. "Litovskoe rabochee dvizhenie," *Rabotnik*, Pt. II, no. 5–6 (1899), pp. 1–8.

Tumas, J. "Lietuvių krikščionių-demokratų veiksmas," *Draugija*, no. 3 (1907), pp. 257–66.

Ugis. [Kazys Grinius]. "Naujas apsireiškimas," *Varpas*, no. 4 (1897), pp. 54–55, and no. 5 (1897), pp. 69–70.

Vanagaitis, J. "Apie Vincą Mickevičių Kapsuką," *Naujoji Romuva*, April 7, 1935, pp. 329–30.

Vasiliauskas, Z. "Jonas Šepetys," *Komunistas*, no. 8 (1975), pp. 74–75.

Vasys, Dalius. "The Lithuanian Social Democratic Party and the Revolution of 1905," *Lituanus*, no. 3 (1977), pp. 14–40.

Vederaitė, D. "Agrariniai klausimai V. Mickevičiaus-Kapsuko raštuose 1905–1907 Rusijos buržuazinės demokratinės revoliucijos metais," in *Lietuvos TSR Aukštųjų Mokyklų Mokslo Darbai: Ekonomika*, IV, Pt. 1 (1963), 5–17.

———. "V. Mickevičius-Kapsukas apie darbininkų klasės ekonominę padėtį Lietuvoje (1905–1907)," in *Lietuvos TSR Aukštųjų Mokyklų Mokslo Darbai: Ekonomika*, IV, Pt. 2 (1964), 5–19.

Vilčinskas, J. "Socializmas Lietuvoje," *Mintis*, no. 1 (1971), pp. 36–52.

"Vincas Mickevičius-Kapsukas," *Darbo visuomenė*, no. 2 (1935), pp. 46–48.

"Vincas Mickevičius-Kapsukas, 1880–1980," *Tiesa*, April 6, 1980, p. 2.

Višinskis, P. "Pirmutinis didysis lietuvių susivažiavimas Vilniuje," *Lietuvos ūkininkas*, December 1/14, 1905, pp. 3–7.

Vyšniauskas, Arūnas, "K. Marksas, F. Engelsas ir Lietuva," *Mokslas ir gyvenimas*, no. 5 (1987), pp. 4–5.

Wajner, Menachim. "Do historji PPS na Litwie," *Niepodległość*, IX (1934), 221–35.

———. "Do historii PPS na Litwie," *Niepodległość*, XV (1937), 329–47.

Wasilewski, Leon. "L.S.D.-Litewska socjalna demokracja," *Niepodległość*, XVI (1937), 3–10.

Wr., A. [W. Jodko-Narkiewicz]. "Ruch robotniczy na Litwie," *Przedświt*, no. 8 (August 1898), pp. 9–14.

Zagranichnyi Soiuz Litovskikh Sotsial'demokratov. "O litovskom rabochem dvizhenii," *Rabochee delo*, no. 2–3 (1899), pp. 109–13.

Zalewski, K. [Stanisław Trusiewicz]. "Isz socializmo istorijos Lietuvoj," *Socialdemokratas*, no. 6–8 (May 1916), pp.45–48.

Žilėnas, A. "Lietuvos valstietijos diferenciacija ir klasinis jos apmokestinimo pobūdis XIX a. pabaigoje ir XX a. pradžioje," in *Lietuvos TSR Aukštųjų Mokyklų Mokslo Darbai: Ekonomika*, II (1962), 125–39.

Zinkevičius, Zigmas, and others. "Teisybė turi nugalėti," *Komjaunimo tiesa*, March 30, 1989, pp. 1–2.

Resolutions

Fifth congress of the LSDP, January 1902. *Darbininkų balsas*, no. 3 (March 1902), pp. 1–3.
Conference of the LSDP, January 1903. *Darbininkų balsas*, no. 1 (January–February 1903), pp. 4–12.
Conference of Socialist Youth, 1904. In Steponas Kairys, *Tau, Lietuva*. Boston, Mass., 1964.
Conference of the LSDP, Fall 1904. *Darbininkų balsas*, no. 6 (October 1904), p. 191.
Central Committee of the LSDP, 1905. *Kova*, August 18, 1905, pp. 106–8.
Conference of the LSDP, May 1905. *Darbininkų balsas*, no. 7 (July 1905), pp. 230–31.
Sixth congress of the LSDP, June 1905. *Darbininkų balsas*, no. 10 (October 1905), pp. 325–27.
The Grand Diet of Vilnius, November/December 1905. In E. Griškūnaitė, and others, eds., *Lietuvos TSR istorijos šaltiniai*. Vol. II. Vilnius, 1965.
Conference of rural workers and peasants, November/December 1905. In E. Griškūnaitė and others, eds., *Lietuvos TSR istorijos šaltiniai*. Vol. II. Vilnius, 1965.
Conference of the LSDP, January 1906. *Darbininkų balsas*, no. 1 (January 1906), pp. 1–8.
Conference of the LSDP, September 1906. *Partijos žinios*, no. 1 (1906), pp. 3–5.
Seventh congress of the LSDP, August 1907. In Steponas Kairys, *Tau, Lietuva*. Boston, 1964.
Conference of the LSDP, February 1908. *Žarija*, March 12/25, 1908, pp. 174–75.
Eighth congress of the LSDP, January 1909. *Partijos žinios*, no. 1 (1912), pp. 9–12.
Conference of the LSDP, May 1912. *Partijos žinios*, no. 1 (1912), pp. 3–8.

Newspapers and Journals

Aidas Lietuvos darbininkų gyvenimo (Bittehnen), 1899.
Balsas (Königsberg, Tilsit, Berlin), 1928–1933.
Darbininkas (Tilsit), 1905–1906.
Darbininkų balsas (Tilsit, Bittehnen), 1901–1906.
Darbo visuomenė (Kaunas), 1935.
Kibirkštis (Smolensk), 1924–1925.
Komunaras (Moscow), 1921–1923.
Komunistas (Voronezh, Vilnius, etc.), 1918–1932, 1967–1987.
Kova (Philadelphia), 1905–1907.
Kultūra (Šiauliai, Kaunas), 1925–1926, 1928–1929, 1931–1934.
Laisvoji mintis (Scranton, Pa.), 1910–1915.
Lietuvos darbininkas (Zürich, Tilsit, Bittehnen), 1896–1899.
Lietuvos ūkininkas (Vilnius), 1905–1906.
Lituanus (Brooklyn, Chicago), 1954–1987.
Mintis (London), 1971–1972.
Nauja gadynė (Shenandoah, Pa., Scranton, Pa.), 1894–1896.
Naujoji gadynė (Vilnius), 1906.
Naujoji gadynė (Philadelphia), 1916–1917.
Naujoji gadynė (Kaunas), 1926.

Partijos žinios (Vilnius), 1906, 1912.
Priekalas (Moscow), 1931–1938.
Rankpelnis (Bellshill), 1909–1910.
Robotnik litewski (Tilsit), 1898.
Skardas (Vilnius), 1907.
Socialdemokratas (Bellshill), 1916.
Socialdemokratas (Kaunas), 1919–1933.
Tiesa (Vilnius, Kaunas, etc.), 1919–1922, 1924–1929, 1934–1940, 1967–1987.
Varpas (Tilsit, Ragnit), 1895–1905.
Vienybė lietuvninkų (Plymouth, Pa.), 1896–1901, 1903–1906.
Visuomenė (Vilnius), 1910.
Žarija (Vilnius), 1907–1908.

Index

About the Author

Leonas Sabaliūnas is Professor of Political Science
at Eastern Michigan University. He is the author
of *Lithuania in Crisis: Nationalism to
Communism, 1939–1940.*

Library of Congress Cataloging-in-Publication Data
Sabaliūnas, Leonas.
Lithuanian social democracy in perspective, 1893–1914/Leonas
Sabaliūnas.
(Duke Press policy studies)
Includes bibliographical references.
ISBN 0-8223-1015-5
1. Socialism—Lithuania—History. 2. Socialists—Lithuania—
History. 3. Lithuania—Politics and government. I. Title.
II. Series.
HX315.L77S22 1990
335.5'0947'5—dc20   89-27306 CIP